Strategies of Deconstruction

Strategies of Deconstruction
Derrida and the Myth
of the Voice

J. Claude Evans

University of Minnesota Press
Minneapolis   Oxford

Published by the University of Minnesota Press
2037 University Avenue Southeast, Minneapolis, MN 55414
Printed in the United States of America on acid-free paper

Library of Congress Cataloging-in-Publication Data

Evans, Joseph Claude.
    Strategies of deconstruction: Derrida and the myth of the voice/
J. Claude Evans.
        p. cm.
    Includes bibliographical references and index.
    ISBN 0–8166–1925–5. — ISBN 0–8166–1926–3 (pbk.)
    1. Derrida, Jacques. 2. Deconstruction. I. Title.
B2430.D484E83 1991
194—dc20   90–40877
                                                                CIP

A CIP catalog record for this book is available from the British Library

The University of Minnesota
is an equal-opportunity
educator and employer

For Jill

Contents

Acknowledgments

I first encountered Jacques Derrida's *Speech and Phenomena* in a seminar led by Professor Bernhard Waldenfels at the Ruhr-Universität Bochum some ten years ago. The argument of the present book began taking shape when I gave a seminar on Derrida at Washington University in 1988. I am indebted to the Department of Philosophy and the College of Arts and Sciences of Washington University for a research leave that allowed me to write the book. Both Lucian Krukowski and Roger Gibson, who have chaired the Philosophy Department during this period, have been very supportive. Terry Cochran and Biodun Iginla of the University of Minnesota Press have been very helpful, and Frank Hunt did a philosophically sophisticated job of copyediting. Jill Petzall, Terry Cochran, J. Claude Evans, Sr., Jim Bohman, Jonathan Lee, Jerome Schiller, Red Watson, Carl Wellman, and an anonymous reader for the Press helped me see aspects of the manuscript that needed improvement. My colleague Herbert Spiegelberg has been a constant resource and inspiration. The late Steven S. Schwarzschild always offered critical encouragement. In the months since his sudden death, his voice has often raised questions, sometimes uncomfortable ones, and it will continue to do so.

The years in which this study was conceived and executed were difficult ones. Jill Petzall's emotional and intellectual support accompanied every step of the way. Without her, it is unlikely that it would have been completed.

Abbreviations

Introduction

The Reception of Derrida's Early Work

It is often said that Jacques Derrida's early critiques of Husserl and Saussure provide the most carefully argued introductions to his "deconstructive" approach to the tradition of Western philosophy. Indeed, it has been said that one virtue of his early texts of the late 1960s is that in them Derrida still *argued*. Many writers on Derrida have found that his texts generally measure up to the highest standards of scholarly rigor. Thus in the preface to the English translation of *La voix et le phénomène*, Newton Garver writes that "Derrida's critique of Husserl is a first-class piece of analytical work in the philosophy of language" (Garver, ix); Richard Rorty has written that "Derrida does a first-class, highly professional, job on Husserl" (Rorty 1989b, 207); David Wood has recently described *Speech and Phenomena* as "a detailed scholarly analysis of Husserl, . . . a careful deconstruction of Husserl's commitment to self-presence" (Wood 1987, 182; see also Wood 1989, 303); and Hans-Georg Gadamer has recently spoken of Derrida's "quite accurate criticism of Husserl's *Logical Investigations* and of his concept of *Kundgabe*—developed in his fine book *Speech and Phenomena*" (Gadamer 1989c, 95). Manfred Frank writes:

> Those works by Derrida devoted to Husserl exhibit, judged within the context of neostructuralist texts in general, an exceptional clarity. One can scarcely reproach them with the claim that they thrust upon their subject matter consequences that are completely foreign to it. On the contrary, in his readings of Husserl Derrida is amplifying a voice

resonant in Husserl's texts themselves, but one which can assert itself against the epistemic framework of his philosophizing only with great effort. (Frank 228/222–23)

Jonathan Culler refers to "Derrida's brilliant and scrupulous reading" of Saussure (Culler, 78), and Robert Strozier calls Derrida's critique of Saussure in *Of Grammatology* "incisive" (Strozier, 160).[1] This list could easily be extended.

But there have been other voices as well. Rorty himself has agreed with John Searle's statement that "a lot of Derrida's arguments . . . are just awful" (Rorty 1984, 22 n. 12; cf. Searle 1983a); Strozier has argued that "Derrida . . . appears to place Saussure within a version of the metaphysical tradition that does more to obscure the workings of the *Cours* than to reveal the theory of that text" (Strozier, 228); and John Ellis has recently argued that Derrida and the general discussion of Saussure inspired by Derrida's work perpetuate fundamental misunderstandings (Ellis, chap. 2). Others, some generally sympathetic to Derrida (such as Llewelyn and Wood), and some generally critical (such as Zaner, Mohanty, Depp, Hopkins, White, Descombes, Edie, and Schwab), have begun to question specific points in Derrida's readings of Husserl.

Searle deplores what he describes as "the low level of philosophical argumentation, the deliberate obscurantism of the prose, the wildly exaggerated claims, and the constant striving to give the appearance of profundity by making claims that seem paradoxical, but under analysis often turn out to be silly or trivial" in Derrida and in deconstructive writing in general (Searle 1984, 48).[2]

Finally, on the basis of a reading similar to Searle's, John Scanlon has argued that "the strange little piece entitled *Speech and Phenomena* can be read, justifiably, as a sophisticated parody of a pompously pedantic exegesis of the first chapter of the first investigation of Husserl's *Logical Investigations*." Scanlon argues that Derrida's argument is "preposterous" in several respects. In the first place, to take distinctions that arise in the course of a reflection on the sense of logic as if they belonged to a general theory of language is to distort them from the very beginning. Second, while Derrida realizes that intuitionism is only one strand in Husserl, he puts it at the center of his analysis, giving it the status of a metaphysical axiom, a status foreign to the thrust of Husserl's phenomenology. In addition, Scanlon accuses Derrida of assimilating texts taken from different contexts, as if the context did not matter, and of reading the texts themselves pedantically, rather than reading them in the light of the phenomena they refer to. "To construct elaborate arguments in order to show conclusively that this strange little piece distorts Husserl's texts would be rather like constructing an elaborate argument to show that it is wrong to eat one-year-old Irish children, even if one pays the fair market price for them." Since Derrida is clearly quite familiar with Husserl, Scanlon concludes that his distortions are deliberate and therefore satirical. On this reading, *Speech and Phenomena* presents the "bumbling" reading of a fictitious exegete whose "reading is dictated throughout by a pedantic fixation upon the conceit that the text being interpreted must, in every respect, be subordinated to a mythic master text known as the metaphysics of presence" (Scanlon).

This range of critical response is quite unusual: beyond the normal debate about the cogency of Derrida's arguments, which ranges from the critical approval we have noted to Searle's scathing rejection, Scanlon finds the purported deconstruction of Husserl so preposterous that it can only be considered a satire that cannot be read "as offering either exegetic or philosophical assertions to be defended or to be disputed" (Scanlon). Scanlon's reading stands in stark contrast to Wood's analysis of the critical situation. Recalling Heraclitus's dictum that "dogs bark at what they do not recognize," Wood writes of Derrida's critics: "Now the dogs have stopped barking, sniffed cautiously, and turned tail. Where they [that is, the Husserlians] have paused to offer reasons, however, those reasons hardly survive scrutiny" (Wood 1987, 175).

But this debate is not the only one that swirls around Derrida's work. As noted earlier, Rorty finds Derrida's deconstruction of Husserl quite convincing if evaluated in traditional, professional terms. But Rorty's position vis-à-vis Derrida's texts is actually much more radical, even among those whom he calls "Derrida's American admirers" (Rorty 1989a, 207). Rorty distinguishes two main groups among these admirers. In the first place, there are those who are taken by the rigor of Derrida's arguments. Here we find such writers as Culler, Christopher Norris, Irene Harvey, and Rodolphe Gasché. On the other side we find Geoffrey Hartman and above all Rorty himself. Rorty denies that deconstruction can provide "*both* 'rigorous argument within philosophy and displacement of philosophical categories and philosophical attempts at mastery' " (Rorty 1989a, 207, quoting Culler, 28). One or the other has to go, Rorty says, and he chooses to give up the demand for rigorous argument, stressing instead Derrida as a "private writer — writing for the delight of us insiders who share his background, who find the same rather esoteric things as funny or beautiful or moving as he does." The demand for rigorous argument rests on an illusion: "I do not think that demonstrations of 'internal incoherence' or of 'presuppositional relationships' ever do much to disabuse us of bad old ideas or institutions. Disabusing gets done, instead, by offering us sparkling new ideas, or utopian visions of glorious new institutions" (Rorty 1989a, 208–9). On this reading, Derrida is inviting his readers to a new form of play, and to look for rigorous arguments in his texts is precisely to misunderstand the new game. It is a bit ironic that Rorty's general position concerning Derrida ends up very close to Scanlon's reading of *Speech and Phenomena*, though Scanlon comes from the opposite direction, finding the book at most professional comedy, and does not join Rorty in the ranks of "Derrida's American admirers." One does not get the impression that Scanlon finds the inside joke all that amusing.

Deconstruction and Critical Reading

Given the extreme variation in responses to Derrida's deconstructions, a sustained close reading of some of Derrida's early, more theoretical texts is called for. Such an enterprise may appear problematic for a variety of reasons.

In the first place, it must be admitted that there may be a very un-Derridean prejudice at work in the very distinction between "theoretical" or "philosophical" texts such as *Speech and Phenomena* and *Of Grammatology* and more "literary" texts such as *Glas* and *Envois*, not to mention the decision to place the former at the center of attention. After all, doesn't Derrida deconstruct this very distinction? But to call this a prejudice is to presuppose the cogency of the earlier, more "philosophical" texts, for the significance claimed for the new kind of writing in the later texts is deeply dependent on the results of the earlier texts. The "literary" texts stand firmly in the tradition of the avant-garde, and one crucial aspect of avant-garde art is that it tends to appear in the space opened up by a manifesto (written or unwritten) that announces a radical break with all preceding art and claims a privileged status for the art that moves within the scope of the manifesto. At issue in *Of Grammatology* is not just a new "science of writing" (*OG*, 43/27), but also a new writing, a writing not constrained by "logocentric" presuppositions and constraints, a writing not oriented toward logicality and the presence of truth (cf. Derrida 1983, 42, 46). In this sense, Derrida's work opens up the postmodern world of unlimited play with a very modernist gesture. The apocalyptic tone with which *Of Grammatology* introduces its themes — the "closure" of an epoch (*OG*, 14/4) and "the crevice through which the yet unnameable glimmer beyond the closure can be glimpsed" (*OG*, 25/14) — is the language of a manifesto. It is also, of course, deeply Heideggerian. Thus one's acceptance of the significance and importance of the art, in this case the more literary or experimental works, will depend on one's critical evaluation of the manifesto. Much discussion of Derrida presupposes such an evaluation: Norris has noted literary critics' "strongly marked preference for those texts where the deconstructive groundwork (so to speak) is very largely taken as read, and where Derrida most thoroughly exploits the *resultant* opportunities for experiments in style" (Norris, 21, emphasis added). In contrast, the Derrida we will interrogate here is "Derrida for the academy, Derrida without *Glas*" (Bernasconi 1988, 223–24), but this enterprise is not for that reason irrelevant to the Derrida of *Glas*.[3] One may regard the more theoretical work as a ladder that one throws away once it has served its contextually necessary purpose, but this again presupposes that *Glas*land is in fact the promised land and not Cloudcuckooland (itself perhaps a distinction to be deconstructed?). In addition, given Derrida's own penchant for putting the marginal at the "center" of his own reading, we might well be suspicious of any attempt to marginalize his own early work. Thus a careful look at the argumentative strategies employed in these early works is of special interest.

But there remain systematic reasons why such an enterprise might be considered ill conceived from the start. Thus Heinz Kimmerle has argued that because Derrida has "radically changed the practice of writing," any attempt to give a general account of what writing means for Derrida is impossible. Such an attempt remains committed to an ideal of general description that is itself deconstructed by Derridean writing (Kimmerle, 15). In the present case, it could be argued that the very idea of a critical reading is committed to ideals of truth and epistemic accountability that are deconstructed by the texts under consideration. We seem to be caught in a dilemma: either we move within the medium of Derridean writing, in which case we cannot raise the traditional questions of justification and legitimation, or we don't move within that medium, in which case our traditional questions will a priori receive a negative answer, while the Derridean will reject or deconstruct the very questions themselves. In either case, a critic may well accuse us of being philosophically naive.

But it is less than clear that the project of a critical reading of Derrida is really this misguided. The point of such a critical reading of Derrida is not to measure his work against some external, traditional standard that is rejected by the texts under consideration. The task is rather to measure his work against a standard that it claims for itself. Derrida has always been emphatic in his claim that deconstruction is not a simple *rejection* of traditional scholarship and rigor: critical, deconstructive reading has to pass *through* traditional rigor even if the ultimate effect is to show that such rigor is never as absolute and well founded as it claims to be:

> This moment of doubling commentary should no doubt have its place in a critical reading. To recognize and respect all its classical exigencies is not easy and requires all the instruments of traditional criticism. Without this recognition and this respect, critical production would risk developing in any direction at all and authorize itself to say almost anything. But this indispensable guardrail has always only *protected*, it has never *opened*, a reading. (*OG*, 227/158)[4]

Derrida is careful to state of his deconstructive readings, "I have had to respect classical norms, or at least I have attempted to respect them," and he explicitly refers to the "argument" of *Of Grammatology* (*OG*, 8/lxxxix). Thus the texts we shall be dealing with themselves contest Rorty's rejection of argumentation, and Derrida still insists on the necessity of this traditional rigor in his most recent texts (see Derrida 1988, 114, 147–48). This is, of course, not a proof that Derrida's own self-interpretation is more authoritative than Rorty's. But it does suggest that Rorty's position might best be understood as a certain *outcome* of an attempt to take seriously the rigor that Derrida's texts claim for themselves. Thus this book has the task of being the "indispensable guardrail" to those readings that are examples of the deconstruction they set out to establish; it must hold deconstruction to the minute and laborious standards of scholarship (cf. *OG*, 124/83; Gasché, 268) that it demands of itself. Derrida himself has recently called for such a reading:

> Let it be said in passing how surprised I have often been, how amused or discouraged, depending on my humor, by the use or abuse of the following argument: Since the deconstructionist (which is to say, isn't it, the skeptic-relativist-nihilist!) is supposed not to believe in truth, stability, or the unity of meaning, in intention or "meaning-to-say," how can he demand of us that we read *him* with pertinence, precision, rigor? How can he demand that his own text be interpreted correctly? How can he accuse anyone else of having misunderstood, simplified, deformed it, etc.? In other words, how can he discuss, and discuss the reading of what he writes? The answer is simple enough: this definition of the deconstructionist is *false* (that's right: false, not true) and feeble; it supposes a bad (that's right: bad, not good) and feeble reading of numerous texts, first of all mine, which therefore must finally be read or reread. (Derrida 1988, 146)

But the problem cannot be dealt with at the general level of intentions alone. In focusing on *argumentative* strategies, we subject the text—for example, *Speech and Phenomena*— to a logical critique, a seemingly normal enterprise. But this enterprise is problematic in the present case, as one of the most basic questions raised by that text itself is "How can we justify the *decision* which subordinates a reflection on the sign to a logic?" (*SP*, 6/7). The project of such a logical critique might well create the appearance of being itself immune to question, but it would create that appearance by ruling out of court the question that inquires into the *justification* of this decision. Thus, by its own criterion, the appearance of immunity would have to be declared to be mere illusion: the emperor of logicality has no clothes.

Derrida's question has, however, put his own project in a curious position. On the one hand, he asks the—from the point of view of logic (that is, the point of view of "the idea of knowledge and of the theory of knowledge" [*SP*, 3/5]) — absolutely inescapable question concerning the *justification* of a decision. One might say that for the tradition of Western metaphysics, the idea of knowledge simply is the (originally Socratic) demand for infinite justification,[5] a demand that governs both Plato's ascent from the cave into the luminous and infinitely satisfying presence of the Forms, on the one hand, and Humean skepticism, on the other. Thus the reflexive application of the demand for justification to this demand itself is inescapable. But is this the point at which the demand threatens to expose itself as being ungrounded, an exposure that will inevitably occur with the application of its own standard to itself? As Derrida notes, "we do not impute such a *decision* to Husserl; he explicitly assumes it—or rather he explicitly assumes its tradition and its validity" (*SP*, 6/7). The explicit assumption is thus anything but an explicit decision. An explicit decision would immediately confront Husserl with the demand for justification, whereas the assumption, even if explicit, would allow the necessity of the demand to remain hidden by the apparent self-evidence of the assumption, a self-evidence that Derrida refers to as a "metaphysical heritage" of the commitment to presence and knowledge (*SP*, 3/5). Thus one might suspect a hidden logic in the fact that Husserl never presents the decision as a decision, with its attendant demand for justification, for this would immediately reveal the circularity of his project: to attempt to justify the decision would be to move within the decision, which would thereby be shown not to have been subjected to the serious justificatory scrutiny required by Husserl's own demand for a lack of presuppositions (*LI* II.1, 19/I, 263). This is in fact the conclusion Derrida draws: "Husserl *had* to postpone, from one end of his intinerary to the other, all explicit meditation on the essence of language *in general*" (*SP*, 6/7, emphasis added). And while Derrida will attempt to deconstruct the very idea of knowledge itself, he will *use* the categories of knowledge in the course of that deconstruction: "What is at issue . . . is to *see* the phenomenological critique of metaphysics betray itself as a moment within the history of metaphysical assurance" (*SP*, 3/5, emphasis added). The assurance of deconstruction is thus itself a moment of metaphysics.

On the other hand, Derrida's text itself, which is dedicated to demonstrating that Husserl's very project demands the repression of this question, raises the possibility that "the concept of sign precedes logical reflection, is given to it, *and is freed from its critique*" (*SP*, 6/7, emphasis added). If this should turn out to be more than a mere possibility, we would discover that the sign is never in fact completely "subordinated" to logic, that an exclusive concern for *arguments* always misses much of what is going on in a text, although an attention to argumentative strategy that is constantly aware of the ruling decision as such should be able to show this precisely by attending to the arguments themselves. This is a preeminently deconstructive approach: a careful attention to arguments, if it refuses to move within the decision to give primacy to logic and knowledge (that is, to arguments), can uncover the hidden movement within those arguments themselves. In this sense, deconstruction is not something one does, it is something one can become aware of. The argumentative text deconstructs itself.

To what extent is Derrida himself committed to argumentation in the course of "his" deconstruction? If we accept Garver's suggestion that what Derrida shows is that, far from the *telos* of language being logic, language is in the first place essentially rhetorical (see Garver, xxiif.), we may wonder whether Derrida's own arguments—and he is committed to argument on one level, as it is precisely by allowing the Husserlian arguments to unfold themselves fully that he will show them to deconstruct themselves—will not turn out to have an intrinsically rhe-torical dimension. By now we are not surprised by this suggestion, and we can understand that the discovery of such a rhetorical dimension would be anything but an embarrassment to Derrida himself. Such a rhetoric would have to be care-fully distinguished from the superficial sophistry that "makes the better argu-ment appear worse and the worse argument appear better," since this sophistry refuses to submit itself to the rigor of logic, argument, and justification at all, whereas the deconstruction of a text committed to the primacy of logic and jus-tification must be accomplished using that text's very own tools.

In taking my task to be that of a critical reading, I hope to avoid what Rudolf Bernet has called the "unfruitful business" of trying to "nail Derrida [by means of] supposed errors of interpretation in his reading of Husserl" (Bernet 1986, 52). Bernet's is an interesting and, at first glance, curiously defensive statement. Coming as it does from an experienced editor and scholar of Husserl, it surely should not be taken as an attempt to immunize Derrida from certain kinds of scrutiny. In calling this business "unfruitful," Bernet is saying, I take it, not that Derrida is immune to such errors (indeed, we shall see that Derrida is quite vul-nerable to them), but rather that the correlate of a defensive immunization of Derrida's text would be a single-minded concentration on errors that would miss the thrust of Derrida's endeavor. Both elements are necessary: critical attention to the rigor of Derrida's interpretation of Husserl and an openness to a challenge that might threaten the very sense of Husserl's enterprise. I hope that this ap-proach will protect me from the charge of going to the dogs along with, as Wood sees it, the general lot of Derrida's critics.

In this book I shall examine a variety of strategies that Derrida uses in *La voix et la phénomène* and in the sections dealing with Aristotle and Saussure in *De la grammatologie*. These two texts of 1967 stand at the center of Derrida's early deconstructive attack on what he calls the "logocentric" and more specifically "phonocentric" tradition, which he identifies with Western metaphysics in gen-eral. I shall thus be emphasizing the rigor of argumentation rather than the liter-ary quality of Derrida's writings. In addition, I shall make no attempt to measure the path Derrida has taken following these texts of the late 1960s and the distance that might now separate him from them. One could conjecture that he might cur-rently see little reason to interest himself in a critical reading of these early texts, perhaps reacting with a Carnapian "But my grandfather wrote that!" The lack of interest evidenced in his manifestly bored and condescending response to Gadamer's attempt to understand, criticize, and enter into dialogue with decon-struction (Derrida 1989a and 1989b) might point in this direction. On the other hand, more recent comments in "The Time of a Thesis" (Derrida 1983) and the Afterword to *Limited Inc* (Derrida 1988, 147–48) would seem to indicate that he has not disowned his early-born.

Deconstruction

Derrida does not provide a theoretical discussion of deconstruction in *Speech and Phenomena*. Indeed, the first appearance of the term is rather abrupt: "With the difference between real presence and presence in representation as *Vorstellung*, a whole system of differences involved in language is implied in the same deconstruction" (*SP*, 57–58/52). Thus, as far as *Speech and Phenomena* is concerned, we can approach the sense of deconstruction only by looking at the concrete context in which it appears. There is, however, a prehistory to Derrida's introduction of the term into philosophical discussion. In *Being and Time*, Heidegger poses "the task of the de-struction (*Destruktion*) of the history of ontology,"[6] a task that is necessary because Western metaphysics since Plato has been governed by a fatal misapprehension of Being itself (Heidegger 1975, 30/21). Rather than simply moving within the framework of Western ontology, the destruction must return to "the original experiences in which the first and subsequently guiding determinations of Being were gained." Destruction has to investigate the "original 'wellsprings' " of the tradition, the "birth certificate" of its fundamental concepts. The violence of the destruction of metaphysics is necessary in order to retrieve and restore a more fundamental experience of Being, and this can take place only by "a loosening of the sclerotic tradition and a dissolving of the concealments produced by it" (Heidegger 1927, 21/66, 22/67). We cannot simply discard—Cartesian style—our traditional concepts, for they structure the very way we experience the world and Being itself. There is no pure beginning we can simply advert to, for it would always already be "pervaded by traditional concepts" (Heidegger 1975, 31/22). All understanding is hermeneutical, interpretive. And all interpretation is guided by a horizon of preunderstanding: "It is for this reason that there necessarily belongs to the conceptual interpretation of being and its structures . . . a *destruction*, that is, a critical deconstruction (*Abbau*) of the traditional concepts, which at first must necessarily be employed, down to the sources from which they were drawn" (Heidegger 1975, 31/22–23, translation altered). This *Abbau* or unbuilding, deconstruction, destructuring, is a curious project.[7] Just as philosophy cannot start from an absolute, pure, uncontaminated beginning, the conceptual tools that must be used in the destruction of ontology are inevitably implicated in what is to be deconstructed: we have to use the very language we want to destroy. There is no primal experience we can simply turn to, no neutral language, no neutral critical tools. We thus have to dismantle an understanding of Being that determines our entire epoch, an understanding that has covered over the originary experience of Being to be retrieved.

This understanding of Being Heidegger calls the "metaphysics of presence," a prejudice that operates on two levels. On the level of our own self-understanding, it leads us to understand ourselves in terms of the present and neglect our being-toward-the-future. Given the ontological structure of human beings or

Dasein as beings essentially oriented toward the future as to their own possibilities, both Heidegger and Sartre say that human beings are not what they are, and are what they are not. And this leads to a second level: we identify Being itself with presence. What is real is what is present to us in the present. What is past is not any more; what is future is not yet. Being is experienced as what is available and thus manipulable in the present. Heidegger, however, claims that the very presence of something as something is conditioned by an absence (Being) that makes that presence itself possible. The task of deconstruction is the task of retrieving the experience of this absence that makes presence possible.

Derrida takes up this Heideggerian project, but radicalizes it.[8] Unlike Heidegger, Derrida does not appeal to a more primordial living experience or to Being, for to speak of such an experience is inevitably to appeal to a kind of presence—something Heidegger himself indeed falls prey to:

> Henceforth, it was necessary to begin thinking that there was no center, that the center could not be thought in the form of a present-being, that the center had no natural site, that it was not a fixed locus but a function, a sort of nonlocus in which an infinite number of sign-substitutions came into play. This was the moment when language invaded the universal problematic, the moment when, in the absence of a center or origin, everything became discourse . . . that is to say, a system in which the central signified, the original or transcendental signified, is never absolutely present outside a system of differences. The absence of the transcendental signified extends the domain and the play of signification infinitely. (Derrida 1978b, 280)

Thus we never have the things themselves, Being itself, but only "an endless shifting from sign to sign which can never be terminated or fixed." We are left with a "non-center" (Kearney, 116).

Logocentrism

The term "logocentrism" appears often in Derrida and in secondary works on Derrida, but it is generally used simply as a working expression whose sense is unproblematic, and is rarely thematized.[9] The Greek term *logos* derives from the verb *legein*, meaning first "to gather, pick up, lay together," and then "to recount, tell, say, speak."[10] *Logos* bears a number of related meanings: "A *logos* may be an utterance, as the words spoken, or a statement, either in the sense of an act of asserting that something is the case or in the sense of that which is asserted" (Nuchelmans, 15). In philosophical thought *logos* came to take on the meaning of reasonable speech, of argument, the latter being a typical translation of *logos* in Socratic dialogues. It can thus signify reason itself, and it is this development that led to the word "logic" and to the suffix "-logy," meaning "science of.'' The word also came to play a crucial role in Christian thought: ''When all things began, the Word [*logos*] already was'' (John 1:1–2, New English Bible).

Discussions of *logos* play important roles in both Husserl and Heidegger, and a brief look at some of these texts will allow us to give a first suggestion of what ''logocentrism'' might be.[11] Heidegger discusses *logos* in many places, but we can restrict ourselves to a few remarks concerning three texts. His first published discussion is found in ''The Concept of *Logos*,'' §7.B of *Being and Time*, which appeared in early 1927 in Husserl's *Jahrbuch für Phänomenologie und phänomenologische Forschung*, volume 7. Heidegger asks about the ''primary content'' of the concept of *logos*, noting that translating *logos* as speech is inadequate as long as we do not define what speech means. Later ''translations''—that is, interpretations—of *logos* as ''reason, judgment, concept, definition, ground, relation,'' are arbitrary, and conceal the meaning of speech. According to Heidegger, ''*logos* as speech really means *dēloun*, to make manifest 'what is being talked about' in speech. Aristotle explicates this function of speech more precisely as *apophainesthai*.[12] *Logos* lets something be seen (*phainesthai*), namely what is being talked about''(Heidegger 1927, 32/78–80). Heidegger draws an explicit connection, which Derrida exploits in the texts we shall be discussing, between speech as allowing to be seen (*das Reden [Sehenlassen]*) and speaking (*das Sprechen*), vocalization in words. ''*Logos* is *phōnē*, indeed *phōnē meta phantasias*—vocalization in which something always is sighted'' (Heidegger 1927, 32–33/80).

The possibility of truth and falsity is a function of *logos* as letting something be seen: ''The 'being true' of *logos* as *alētheuein* means: to take beings that are being talked about in *legein* as *apophainesthai* out of their concealment; to let them be seen as something unconcealed (*alēthes*).'' For the present discussion, the most important claim Heidegger makes here is that ''because 'truth' has this meaning, and because *logos* is a specific mode of letting something be seen, *logos* simply may not be acclaimed as the primary 'place' of truth'' (Heidegger 1927, 33/80–81). Heidegger rather identifies the Greek sense of the true with *aisthēsis*, sense perception. Thus any understanding of truth that takes it to be most fundamentally a matter of *logos*—whether *logos* is translated as speech, judgment, or reason—would be a *logos*-centered position: logocentric. As such it calls for de-struction.

A second crucial text is found in Heidegger's *Introduction to Metaphysics*, which was presented as a course of lectures in 1935 and published in 1953. Whereas the discussion in *Being and Time* was oriented toward Aristotle, here Heidegger primarily discusses Heraclitus. Heidegger is concerned to free language from its exclusive determination as *logos*. Language as *logos* has the task of bringing that which is *deinon*, overpowering and strange, under control by ordering and making sense of it: ''Originary speech opens up the being of beings in the structure of its collectedness. This opening is collected in a second sense, according to which the word preserves what was originally collected and so administers the overpowering power, the *physis*'' (Heidegger 1953, 131/144, translation altered). Clearly, *logos* is secondary to *physis* (usually translated as "nature"), and "it is by no means evident that language is logos" (Heidegger 1953, 131/144). As Gerald L. Bruns puts it, "Language is not logocentric" (Bruns, 119).

Heidegger returned to the topic of *logos* in 1944, this time in the context of a lecture course entitled "Logic: Heraclitus's Theory of the Logos" (published in Heidegger 1979). The results of this investigation were then incorporated into the essay "Logos (Heraclitus, Fragment B 50)," which appeared in 1954. In this essay Heidegger notes that there is a long tradition, extending back to antiquity, of interpreting Heraclitus's *logos* "as *Ratio*, as *Verbum*, as cosmic law, as the logical, as necessity in thought, as meaning and as reason." But Heidegger immediately puts this tradition into question: "Again and again a call rings out for reason to be the standard for deeds and omissions. Yet what can reason do when, along with the irrational and the antirational all on the same level, it perseveres in the same neglect, forgetting to meditate on the essential origin of reason and to let itself into its advent?" (Heidegger 1954a, 200/60). This is not the place for an extended discussion of this rather dark statement. But this much is already clear: if we count on reason, assuming that it is autonomous and self-grounding, we will be guilty of the forgetfulness in question. One might call such a position "logocentrism": the assumption that the *logos* is centered, self-grounding.

As in *Being and Time*, Heidegger begins his discussion of *logos* with *legein*:

> Who would want to deny that in the language of the Greeks from early
> on *legein* means to talk, say, or tell? However, just as early and even
> more originally—and therefore already in the previously cited
> meaning—it means what our similarly sounding *legen* means: to lay
> down and lay before. . . . How does the proper meaning of *legein*, to
> lay, attain the signification of saying and talking? (Heidegger 1954a,
> 200, 203/60, 63)

He then denies that we find here an extension or transformation of the "proper" meaning: "The original *legein*, laying, unfolds itself early and in a manner ruling everything unconcealed as saying and talking. *Legein* as laying lets itself be overpowered by the predominant sense, but only in order to deposit the essence of saying and talking at the outset under the governance of laying proper." Partially distancing himself from the discussion in *Being and Time*, he goes on to claim that

> the essential speaking of language, *legein* as laying, is determined
> neither by vocalization (*phōnē*) nor by signifying [*Bedeuten*]
> (*semainein*). Expression and signification [*Ausdruck und Bedeutung*]

have long been accepted as manifestations which indubitably betray some characteristics of language. But they do not genuinely reach into the realm of the primordial, essential determination of language. (Heidegger 1954a, 204/63–64)[13]

Speaking and hearing must of course be "embodied" ("obwohl das Vernehmen nur lebt, indem es leibt"), but the specific sense apparatus involved has nothing to do with, for example, the essence of hearing as "gathered hearkening" (Heidegger 1954a, 206/65).

Husserl discusses *logos* in "Outset from the Significations of the Word *Logos*: Speaking, Thinking, What Is Thought," §1 of *Formal and Transcendental Logic*, which appeared in 1929 in volume 10 of the *Jahrbuch*.[14] Starting with "the more original significations of *legein*—namely: 'to lay together,' 'to set forth,' and then, to set forth by means of the word, by means of speech" (*Hua* XVII, 22/18), Husserl traces the most important meanings of *logos*: word, speech, the affair-complex referred to in speaking, the sense of the sentence and even the act of thinking itself; then reason itself, the ability to think rationally. This text is of special interest because it leads to a clear statement of what Derrida would call a "logocentric" position. In a first approximation, any position that claims a primacy and autonomy for logic, cognition, and science will be logocentric, and Husserl provides a classical formulation of such a position. After sketching out the idea of a formal logic, Husserl concludes:

We may say that logic is the *self-explication of pure reason* itself or, ideally, the science in which pure theoretical reason accomplishes a complete investigation of its own sense and perfectly objectivates itself in a system of principles. In this system pure reason or, correlatively, logic is related reflexively to itself; the self-explication of pure reason is itself a purely rational activity and comes under the very principles that thereby attain explication. (*Hua* XVII, 34/30–31)

This is precisely what Derrida challenges, namely, that reason can perform a complete investigation of its own sense. His claim will be that since reason is not self-grounding, the self-explication of reason cannot be a purely rational activity. It will be committed to dogmatic assumptions that will make themselves felt as such in the course of the investigation. The articulation of the tensions that arise in the text dedicated to this self-explication amounts to the deconstruction of the logocentric claim.

Part I
Husserl and the Philosophy of Presence:
Speech and Phenomena

Chapter 1
Speech and Phenomena: The Introduction

The Introduction to *Speech and Phenomena* sketches out the general framework within which the argument of the book will unfold, and it must be read carefully with an eye both to the general direction Derrida will take and to the specific strategies he will use. Here he has two main concerns. First, he briefly emphasizes the *continuity* one finds in Husserl's work, in spite of its extensive development and transformation over the years. This emphasis is crucial, as Derrida will concentrate much of his energy on the first paragraphs of the first of the *Logical Investigations*, which appeared in 1901 and was in Husserl's own estimation his first genuinely phenomenological work. It is possible to draw conclusions concerning phenomenology in general from a reading of such an early text only if one can say that the later works "develop without break" the basic ideas of the early work, which can thus be said to contain "the germinal structure of the whole of Husserl's thought" (*SP*, 1/3).

Second, the main task of the Introduction is to introduce and tie together a series of concepts and questions, thus staking out the framework within which the book will unfold. Here Derrida first asks whether there is not a "metaphysical presupposition" (*SP*, 3/4) at work in phenomenology in the assumption of the fundamental legitimacy of intuition as a source of knowledge (cf. *Hua* III.1, 51/44). What is at issue here is the status and value of *presence* (which Derrida immediately ties to the *present*), and with it the status of the very idea of knowledge itself. This issue is immediately tied to Husserl's thesis of the ideality of meaning, as it is the presence of sense that is at issue (*SP*, 3/5). The legitimacy of presence, of intuition, as a source of knowledge presupposes that the content

3

of cognition can be repeated indefinitely in the identity of its presence—for example, that we can return to our propositions as the same in ever new acts of thinking. This repetition involves time, and the locus of this presence is the living present of consciousness, that present in which objects can be made present to consciousness and in which consciousness is present to itself. The metaphysical presupposition that Derrida suggests is at work in phenomenology here takes the form of the presupposition of a pure presence in a pure present, a presupposition Derrida will confront with the possibility of "an irreducible nonpresence as having a constituting value" (*SP*, 5/6). Such a nonpresence (both in the sense of absence in general and in the sense of the past), he will argue, is a condition of the possibility of anything that can be called presence, and thus affects the status and value of presence itself as the source of knowledge; indeed, it requires a transformation of the very concept of knowledge. Presentation is most fundamentally re-presentation, and is thus grounded not in itself but in that which is not present, not presented, but absent and past.

Phenomenology itself contains a critique of traditional metaphysics as a blind construction, and the Derridean project is not to be an external critique of phenomenology. Such a critique would presuppose an external ground or point of view, which could in turn itself only be metaphysical. One might say that metaphysics is the very idea of a ground or justifiable (and thus ultimately self-justifying) point of view. The task is rather "to see the phenomenological critique of metaphysics betray itself as a moment of metaphysical assurance" (*SP*, 3/5). This strategy might seem surreptitiously to reimport metaphysical moments, as the very notion of "seeing" such a betrayal brings in principles of cognition. But the crucial thing here is that phenomenology should betray *itself*: it is a matter of measuring phenomenology against its own, supposedly nonmetaphysical (in the sense of degenerate speculation) standards. Those standards will turn out to be metaphysical in the sense phenomenology wishes to criticize. And if it turns out that phenomenology's critique of metaphysics is justified (in its own terms), then the metaphysical moments in phenomenology itself will fall to the phenomenological critique.

The suggested transformation of the concept of knowledge simultaneously puts into question the project of subjecting language to a purely logical critique. If language is the medium or tool of cognition, and pure logical consistency is thus the natural *telos* of language, then there must be a mode of language in which its propositional structure is present as such and thus available to a logical critique. This is, according to Derrida's reading of Husserl, "living speech, the spirituality of the breath as phōnē" (*SP*, 9/10). Derrida develops a double strategy for dealing with this commitment to the primacy of living speech.

On the one hand, precisely the phenomenology that is committed to the ideality of meaning is thereby committed to being "a philosophy of *life*" (*SP*, 9/10), a philosophy of consciousness. But this life, as the medium in which meaning comes to presence, cannot be the empirical life of human consciousness, which is part of and thus conditioned by the world. If the empirical life of consciousness were as such the essential medium of cognition, our access to ideality and thus to logical structure itself would be a function of empirical, contingent, and genetic factors: epistemology would be reducible to psychology or the sociology of knowledge. Husserl demonstrated the skeptical consequences of psychologism in exhaustive detail in the Prolegomena to Pure Logic, volume I of the *Logical Investigations*. This critique calls forth the distinction between life qua mundane, that is, life considered as a conditioned part of the world, and life qua transcendental, that is, life considered solely as medium of access to the world. For Husserl, the normative power of presence depends on the viability of this distinction. But by the same token, the distinction itself depends on the normative power of presence, as it must be capable of being drawn cleanly and purely, of being brought to presence and fixed in literal concepts. Derrida confronts this assumption with "the analogical character of the language which must sometimes be used to announce the transcendental reduction" (*SP*, 11/12), and goes on to suggest that "language never escapes analogy . . . it is indeed analogy through and through" (*SP*, 13/13; this is put in the form of a hypothetical: "*If* language . . . ").

On the other hand, the commitment to the primacy or autonomy of logic requires the thesis of the primacy of the voice, the "essential tie between *logos* and *phōnē*" (*SP*, 14/15). Phenomenology asserts the primacy of consciousness as the "universal medium of access to whatever exists for us and is considered by us as valid" (Gurwitsch 1974, 212), but this primacy is, on Derrida's reading, a function of the primacy of the voice, the "living vocal medium" (*SP*, 14/15). Husserl radicalizes the privilege of the *phōnē* in what Derrida calls the "phenomenological voice," in which a purified speech is present to itself in a completely unmediated manner: in such speech the voice "hears/understands itself" (*s'entendre*) (*SP*, 15/16, translation altered; the French term bears both meanings simultaneously in this context). Such speaking is a "hearing" (and thus self-relation, self-consciousness) that is identical with understanding: in such speech we find the pure presence of meaning itself. Here thinking is in possession of that which is thought. This leads to a tension in Husserl's phenomenology, since on the one hand he is committed to a prepredicative, and thus prelinguistic, stratum of experience, while on the other hand self-consciousness and self-presence, Derrida argues, require language. Thus "the element of consciousness and the element of language will be more and more difficult to differentiate. Will not their indiscernibility introduce nonpresence and difference (mediation, signs, referral back, etc.) in the heart of self-presence?" (*SP*, 15/15). This leads Husserl to a balancing act between consciousness/presence on the one hand and language/nonpresence on the other: "The voice simulates the conservation of presence" (*SP*, 15/15). But it can only simulate this presence, and when this simulation finally reveals itself as "the simulation of language" itself (*SP*, 15/16), phenomenology's commitment to presence as the ultimate cognitive principle will turn out to be a speculative construction that deconstructs itself.

The Assumption of Continuity

In the very first lines of the Introduction to *Speech and Phenomena*, Derrida states one of the fundamental presuppositions underlying his project in the book. While not denying the often dramatic changes Husserl's phenomenology underwent between the publication of the *Logical Investigations* in 1900 and Husserl's death in 1938, Derrida is at pains to emphasize the continuity in Husserl's work: the "conceptual premises" of the *Investigations* remain at work even in the latest texts (*SP*, 1/3). This claim accords with Husserl's own self-interpretation. In 1913, looking back on his own development, he called the *Investigations* a " 'break-through,' not an end but rather a beginning" (*LI* I, viii/I, 43). But as Husserl notes in his draft for a foreword to the second edition of the *Investigations*, in a breakthrough work one typically finds a mixture of old and new, and in this case the author himself was not entirely in command of the new elements; much remained to be brought to full clarity (Husserl 1939, 124). The working out of those unclarities led to dramatic new developments, to radical shifts and corrections. But it remains possible, Husserl insists, to see these developments as the consistent and progressive working out of one basic enterprise, an enterprise whose completion Husserl thought would require generations of investigators.

Thus Derrida is surely on firm ground in his insistence on continuity, but vigilance is required in the application of that assumption to specific cases. For example, Derrida writes that "*Ideas I* and *Formal and Transcendental Logic* develop without break the concepts of intentional or noematic sense" (*SP*, 1/3), a statement that neglects the fact that the concept of noematic sense is not found in the *Investigations* (cf. *LI* I, xiv/I, 48). And it is not just the term that is missing: the theory of meaning that Husserl develops in the *Investigations*, according to which the meaning of an expression is a universal whose instances are acts of meaning (*LI*, II.1, 100/I, 330), was rejected later, as Husserl took some care to point out (Husserl 1968, 10; Husserl 1938, 314/261–62; cf. Parpan, 163–76). And yet one can still emphasize continuity here, for as Husserl also says, in the *Investigations* "the noetic concept of meaning is one-sidedly stressed, though in many important passages the noematic concept is principally dealt with" (*LI* I, xiv–xv/I, 48). Thus Husserl's own analyses were more advanced than his conceptual framework, and the development of the noematic concept of meaning can be seen as bringing to clarity what he was already doing.

The assumption of continuity is again at work when Derrida says that in §7 of the Introduction to volume II of the *Investigations* Husserl "proceeds to what is in effect a phenomenological reduction" (*SP*, 2/3). The phenomenological reduction was not developed until 1907, and Husserl quite rightly considered it something dramatically new. The section in question does not contain a phenomenological reduction. What Husserl does in §7 amounts to what he would later call an eidetic reduction along with an epochē of objective science (and metaphysics) (*Hua* VI, §35), not a phenomenological reduction. But Husserl was also justified in finding a transcendental import in the analyses of the *Investigations*, and thus one could say that §7 presents a deficient functional equivalent of the later reduction. We risk serious misunderstanding if both sides of this situation are not clearly noted. These two examples show that the assumption of continuity requires careful scrutiny in each case so that we may see just where the continuity is and what its limits are.

The Decision for Logic

The presupposition of continuity governs the entire strategy of *Speech and Phenomena*, for Derrida argues that the "essential distinctions" that Husserl lays out in the first chapter of the first of the *Logical Investigations* "rigorously command all the subsequent analyses" (*SP*, 2/4), and it is these distinctions that constitute the central object of Derrida's book. He places such emphasis on the essential distinctions of the First Investigation because he thinks that it is precisely at that point that he can most fruitfully pose his general question:

> Do not phenomenological necessity, the rigor and subtlety of Husserl's analysis, the exigencies to which it responds and which we must first recognize, nonetheless conceal a metaphysical presupposition? Do they not harbor a dogmatic or speculative commitment which, to be sure, would not keep the phenomenological critique from being realized, would not be a residue of unperceived naïveté, but would *constitute* phenomenology from within, in its project of criticism and in the instructive value of its own premises? (*SP*, 2–3/4–5)

The *Logical Investigations* are dedicated to developing "an objective theory of knowledge and . . . a pure phenomenology of the experiences of thinking and knowing" (*LI* II.1, 2/I, 249). This leads to a more specific form of Derrida's question: "Is not the idea of knowledge and of the theory of knowledge in itself metaphysical?" (*SP*, 3/5). And although this metaphysical commitment would constitute phenomenology from within, and thus would not and could not be discovered as a presupposition within phenomenology—that is, by use of the phenomenological method—it should be possible, Derrida suggests, "to see the phenomenological critique of metaphysics betray itself as a moment within the history of metaphysical assurance." Again, this cannot simply amount to an application of the phenomenological critique of metaphysics to phenomenology itself; but the very movement of phenomenology should betray the fact that "the recourse to phenomenological critique is metaphysics itself" (*SP*, 3/5).

What is metaphysics for phenomenological critique itself? What defines this metaphysics, in Husserl's eyes, as "the perversion or the degeneracy" of an authentic metaphysics (*SP*, 4/5)? Husserl defines authentic metaphysics as "ultimate cognitions" in contrast to the "speculative excesses" of "a historically degenerate metaphysics" (*Hua* I, §60; quoted at *SP*, 4/5–6). Thus Derrida must demonstrate that the commitment to ultimate cognitions is itself a metaphysical commitment *in the sense of a dogmatic or speculative commitment*. And one might suspect that the idea of ultimate cognitions and the idea of knowledge will be inseparable on this analysis.

The six investigations that comprise volume II of the *Logical Investigations* are studies in the theory of objective knowledge. The necessity of such studies had been argued in the first volume of the *Investigations*, the Prolegomena to Pure Logic. That critique of the reigning psychologism in the philosophy of logic argued for the necessity of a pure logic, as opposed to a psychologized logic, as the fundamental theory of science. Only such a logic can develop the principles that make possible the "unitary objective reference" and "ideal validity" of scientific thinking (*LI* I, 228/I, 225, translation altered). The subject matter of logic is not acts of thought as such, but rather the propositional contents of those acts, "the logical judgement [as] the identical asserted meaning, which is one over against manifold, descriptively quite different, judgement-experiences" (*LI* II.1, 4/I, 251). This content is thus defined as an ideal unity in contrast to the reality of the act of judging: "My act of judging is a transient experience: it arises and passes away. But what my assertion asserts, the content *that the three perpendiculars of a triangle intersect in a point*, neither arises nor passes away. It is an identity in the strict sense, one and the same geometrical truth" (*LI* II.1, 44/I, 285).

It is for this reason that Husserl could say that the only genuine path in the theory of knowledge is idealism. But such an idealism is not, Husserl claims, a Platonic realism that hypostatizes the universal as something that "really exists *externally* to thought" (*LI* II.1, 121/I, 350). Idealism is rather "a theory of knowledge which recognizes the 'ideal' as a condition for the possibility of objective knowledge in general, and does not 'interpret it away' in psychologistic fashion" (*LI* II.1, 108/I, 338). Meaning is that which can be the content of an open multiplicity of acts of thinking. As Derrida puts it, the ideal is that which "may be indefinitely *repeated* in the *identity* of its *presence*," and this numerical identity constitutes the "irreal" or "nonworldly" character of ideal meanings (*SP*, 4/6). Husserl defines the ideality of meaning as "the complete opposite of reality or individuality" (*LI* II.1, 102/I, 331), and if "world" is understood in the sense of "world of reality," then it is true that meaning is nonworldly. But care must be taken if we are to avoid serious confusion.

When Husserl introduces the transcendental turn in his phenomenology, he says that consciousness as thematized within the phenomenological reduction is "not a piece of the world" (*Hua* I, 64/25), in contrast to consciousness as thematized in reflection as a region of objects appearing within the world. Meaning is not "nonworldly" in this sense, and indeed Husserl's later work explicitly demonstrates the manner in which the world functions as the horizon for the constitution of meaning, both judgmental meaning in general and the specific idealizing achievements of mathematics and the natural sciences. In §7 of the *Investigations*, Husserl calls the question of the existence of "the external world" a metaphysical question (*LI* II.1, 20/I, 264), one with which phenomenology is not concerned, because, as an eidetic science, its results are not dependent on the existence of particulars exemplifying the essential structures in question (*LI*, II.1, 22/I, 265–66).

In his late work *The Crisis of European Sciences*, Husserl explicates these different modes of thematizing consciousness in terms of what he calls "the paradox of human subjectivity." On the one hand, consciousness is part of the world. On the other hand, consciousness is the universal subject for the world: the world is that which appears to consciousness. This leads Husserl to ask, "How can a component part of the world, its human subjectivity, constitute the whole world, namely, constitute it as its intentional formation . . . while . . . the subjects accomplishing . . . are themselves only a partial formation within the total accomplishment?" (*Hua* VI, 183/179; cf. *Hua* IX, 336f.). Husserl responds to this paradox by developing the epochē as a method that allows the philosopher to thematize consciousness purely *as* consciousness of the world by "bracketing" all questions of existence, including the existence of consciousness as object in the world, turning the world into a phenomenon for transcendental, nonmundane, constituting consciousness (*Hua* VI, §§53 and 54).

Thus the ideality of meaning should not be confused with the nonworldly status of transcendental consciousness. Both can be legitimately described as nonreal, but in different senses. The ideality of meaning is defined in terms of its supertemporality (*Überzeitlichkeit*), and even Husserl's explication of supertemporality as "omnitemporality (*Allzeitlichkeit*), which . . . is a mode of temporality" (Husserl 1938, 313/261) explicitly distinguishes it from the essential temporality of acts of consciousness. When Derrida speaks of "ideal presence to *an ideal or transcendental consciousness*" (*SP*, 8/9, emphasis added) and of "the acts of repetition, *themselves ideal*" (*SP*, 8/10, emphasis added), he appears to conflate the nonworldliness of transcendental consciousness and the ideality of meanings (and other ideal objects), calling acts of consciousness ideal and meanings nonworldly.

In addition, care must be taken with Derrida's statement that ideal meaning is that which "may be indefinitely *repeated* in the *identity* of its *presence*" (*SP*, 4/6). This statement is not false, but it does run the risk of appearing to make the normal function of meaning that of being an object for consciousness. Husserl states that "an act of meaning [*Akt des Bedeutens*] is the determinate manner in which we refer to our object" (*LI* II.1, 49/I, 289), and the ideal meaning is the universal, the species of the acts or meaning-intentions (*LI*, II.1, 100/I, 330). Meaning is the general *manner* in which objects are intended, a manner that can be repeated indefinitely in an open-ended number of acts. In these acts we are concerned with objects, not meanings (though of course those objects can themselves be meanings); in the primary sense, it is objects that come to presence in the varying modalities of nonfulfillment and fulfillment, absence and presence:

> If we perform the act and live in it, as it were, we naturally refer to [*meinen*] its object and not to its meaning. If, e.g., we make a statement, we judge about the thing it concerns, and not about the statement's meaning, about the judgement in the logical sense. This latter first becomes objective to us in a reflective act of thought, in which we not only look back on the statement just made, but carry out the abstraction (or better, the Ideation) demanded. (*LI* II.1, 103/I, 332, translation altered)

If, however, our object is an ideal object such as a number or a geometrical state of affairs, it is clear that its ideality is constituted by the possibility of returning to it, making it present, again and again as one and the same in different acts and varying modes of givenness. This presence to consciousness—and here we rejoin Derrida's Introduction—presupposes the living present, the temporal field of and for consciousness, and the living present must itself be constituted in and for consciousness: the presence of the ideal requires the self-presence of transcendental life.

Presence does play a privileged role in Husserl's analyses, a role that Husserl considers necessary for any analysis of cognition and truth. The very sense of a knowledge claim implies a distinction between merely thinking that something is the case and in the broadest sense coming to see that it is (or is not) indeed the case. The difference between merely intending something and seeing that things are indeed the way one held them to be, between empty intending and its fulfillment, is constitutive of the very concept of truth. As Ernst Tugendhat put Husserl's guiding insight:

> If that which is objectively intended [in a given act] were always given in the same manner, then we would have no occasion to inquire into truth and falsity. Only because we have the peculiar possibility of intending something that is not "directly" given to us, and again because this same intended object *can* be directly given, does talk about true and false mean anything. Thus, the sense of "true" seems to be grounded in a unique difference between different possible *modes of givenness of the same* objects. (Tugendhat 1967, 30)

The very sense of "truth" and "falsity" is based on the formal difference between empty and fulfilled intending. This means that presence is defined functionally in terms of the contrast between meaning the same thing, now in its absence, now in its bodily presence. The primordiality of presence is defined in
terms of this contrast and other related contrasts such as the presence found in
imagination and in the various stages of incomplete or inadequate givenness of
the object (see *Formal and Transcendental Logic*, §16, on modes of clarity). The
important thing here is that intuition, presence, primordiality, evidence, and so
on are given a primarily functional definition.

But the temporal self-constitution of consciousness is not the only condition
for the constitution of ideal objectivity. The ideal is that which is available in
principle to all other possible subjects as one and the same: objectivity is the correlate of intersubjectivity (see the Fifth Cartesian Meditation). And now Derrida
can offer a further specification of his thesis. Phenomenology is the study of the
modes of givenness of world and objects to consciousness, the study of the ways
objects come to be present to consciousness in varying modes of presence and
absence. Derrida's thesis is that

> at the heart of what ties together these two decisive moments of
> description [temporalization and the constitution of intersubjectivity] we
> recognize an irreducible nonpresence as having a constituting value, and
> with it a nonlife, a nonpresence or nonself-belonging of the living
> present, an ineradicable nonprimordiality. (*SP* 5/6–7)

Nonpresence is constitutive of objectivity in two respects: (1) objectivity presupposes memory and thus re-presentation as a modification of presentation;
re-presentation is thus a condition of the possibility of presentation, one which
"conditions [presentation] by bifurcating it *a priori*" (*SP*, 5/7); and (2) the
objectivity of presentation is made possible by appresentation (itself a modification of presentation) of the other who cannot be directly presented. Thus Derrida
does not question presence in its own terms, does not attack its value (since it is
constitutive of the very meaning of cognition and thus of Derrida's own claims).
His aim is to point out that this presence is not founded in presence, in the ideal
of self-presence that had been the dream of metaphysics up to and including the
reflexive grounding of the principles of cognition in the Cartesian *cogito* and the
Kantian "I think." Derrida does not so much deny those principles as principles
of presence as claim that according to the phenomenological analysis of that
presence itself, it is founded on a "lack of foundation [that] is basic and nonempirical," an essential nonpresence, an "ineradicable nonprimordiality"
(*SP* 5/7). In this sense, the very ideal of a transcendental grounding of knowledge
will turn out to be strictly speaking impossible (though not for that reason any
less necessary in its own terms—and there are no others): the idea of "ultimate
cognitions" is a dogmatic commitment, a metaphysical presupposition.

The strategy of Derrida's deconstruction of Husserl's account of the sign requires that Husserl's text be put on the defensive from the very beginning: "First, how can we justify the *decision* which subordinates a reflection on the sign to a logic? And if the sign precedes logical reflection, is given to it, and is freed from its critique, from whence does it come?" (*SP* 6/7). Now, in one sense the sign does precede logical reflection, as even the phenomenology of knowledge is a thematization and critique of functioning cognition. But Derrida's suggestion is more radical: his question suggests that prior (logically prior) to being taken up into the movement of cognition and subjected to logical principles, the sign already functions, subject to principles (if that is the right word) of its own. In that case, the assumption that language is essentially an instrument or medium of cognition would be a blind presupposition, and the epistemic analysis of language would claim an authority it cannot possess.

It must be asked, however, whether Derrida is really confronting Husserl with unacknowledged decisions. Does Husserl really attempt to "determine the essence and origin of language"? We will later find reason to think rather that Husserl looks upon language only as an instrument of knowledge, without denying that there are other dimensions. Husserl is interested in the essence of cognition, of the logical, and is interested in language only qua medium of cognition. Note too that in asking his question Derrida is moving within metaphysics: his question can be posed only in terms of a *distinction* between logicality and the sign, along with an *ordering relation* of precedence, thus bringing in the entire framework of originality versus derivation, freedom versus subjugation, condition versus conditioned, and so on that is to be deconstructed along with the tradition of metaphysics.

These themes must be kept in mind, but for now let us focus on the charge that Husserl's phenomenology of knowledge is governed by a certain tradition of the primacy of logic. Derrida backs up his charge by pointing to what he alleges are the "limitless" consequences of such an assumption:

(1) "Husserl *had* to postpone . . . all explicit meditation on the essence of language *in general*" (*SP*, 6/7), presumably because such reflection would have resulted in a disturbance of the entire project of phenomenology itself.

(2) Husserl could not raise the question of the transcendental *logos*, the question of the possibility and validity of transcendental discourse itself. Husserl's insistence that he can fix the meaning of his terms, freeing them from their historical commitments and ambiguities, is naive, and this naïveté is indicative of a commitment that cannot withstand direct scrutiny.

Thus Husserl the logician and phenomenologist interested in cognition is "interested in language only within the compass of rationality," and to that extent he determines "logos from logic" (*SP*, 6/8). But is Husserl really determining the essence of language? Need he say that the logical is the *telos* or norm of language? Or can he be content to elucidate the commitments implicit in the cognitive use of language?

At this point Derrida offers an example of the way in which this commitment leads Husserl astray. In the Fourth Investigation Husserl begins to develop what he calls "the old idea of a universal and, more specifically, a priori grammar" (*LI* II.1, 295/II, 493), which would be a part of the pure logic demanded by the Prolegomena. According to Derrida, Husserl's concern with logic has the result that "the generality of this meta-empirical grammar is not sufficient to cover the whole field of possibility for language in general; it does not exhaust the whole extension of language's *a priori*" (*SP*, 7/8). The rules of pure grammar make it possible to recognize "whether discourse is really a discourse, whether it makes sense, whether falsity and the absurdity of contradiction (*Widersinnigkeit*) have not rendered it unintelligible [*inintelligible*], have not deprived it of the quality of meaningful discourse [*discours sensé*], thereby rendering it *sinnlos*" (*SP*, 7/8, translation altered). Husserl's concern with logic and cognition means that he can deal only with the dangers of falsity and the absurdity of contradiction, which render discourse unintelligible. This restriction is necessary, for "this grammar concerns only the *logical a priori* of language; it is *pure logical grammar*" (*SP*, 7/8).

Now, this account simply does not square with what Husserl's pure logical grammar is all about. In his general characterization of that grammar, Husserl writes:

> Within pure logic, there is a field of laws indifferent to all objectivity to which, in distinction from 'logical laws' in the usual pregnant sense, the name of 'logico-grammatical laws' can be justifiably given. Even more aptly we can oppose the pure theory of semantic forms [*der reinen Formenlehre der Bedeutungen*] to the pure theory of validity which presupposes it. (*LI* II.1, 295/II, 495)[1]

These "laws of complex meanings set the requirements of merely significant unity, i.e. the a priori patterns in which meanings belonging to different semantic categories can be united to form one meaning, instead of producing chaotic nonsense [*Unsinn*]" (*LI* II.1, 295/II, 493). Following up on this distinction between logic in the normal sense and a pure grammar that does not yet raise questions of validity, Husserl writes that

> one must not confound the senseless (or nonsensical) [*das Sinnlose (das Unsinnige)*] with the absurd (or 'counter-sensical') [*mit dem Absurden*

(dem Widersinnigen)], though we tend to exaggerate and call the latter 'senseless,' when it is rather a sub-species of the significant. The combination 'a round square' really yields a unified meaning . . . , but it is apodictically evident that no existent object can correspond to such an existent meaning. But if we say 'a round or,' 'a man and is' etc., there exist no meanings which correspond to such verbal combinations as their expressed sense. *(LI* II.1, 326/II, 516–17)[2]

Judgments that are absurd or countersensical in Husserl's sense are false or even contradictory, but they still have a sense—that is, they conform to the elementary laws of composition studied by pure grammar. They are in this very broad sense well formed. The curious thing is that Derrida recognizes precisely this in several later passages of *Speech and Phenomena* (see *SP*, 80/71, 100–102/89–92).[3] For example:

One can speak without knowing. And against the whole philosophical tradition Husserl shows that in that case speech is still genuinely speech, provided it obeys certain rules which do not immediately figure as rules for knowledge. Pure logical grammar, pure formal semantic theory, must tell us *a priori* on what conditions speech can be speech, even where it makes no knowledge possible. *(SP*, 100/89–90)

Derrida's misunderstanding of Husserl's position is disturbing, as his comments are offered as evidence for the claim that Husserl thematizes language only from the point of view of rationality, determining *logos* from logic. In other words, his claims about Husserl's pure grammar are designed to support the claim that Husserl's phenomenology is logocentric and that such logocentrism is based on an unfounded exclusion of other possibilities: "The delineation of the logical *a priori* within the general *a priori* of language does not set apart a region; rather it designates, as we shall see, the dignity of a telos, the purity of a norm, and the essence of a destination" *(SP*, 8–9/9). Derrida's suggestion is clear: the telos is based on a prejudice, an unjustifiable decision. But we shall have to look elsewhere for support for this suggestion.

Life as Constituting Medium

Derrida's thesis now takes on a new form. Because, as he hopes to show, presence is constituted by nonpresence, a phenomenology constituted by its devotion to presence as a norm and telos will find its central phenomenon constantly threatened and will react with a series of modifications designed to save the primordiality of presence. When the actuality of presence is threatened, Husserl will appeal to presence as "an Idea in the Kantian sense." Ideality is constituted in the "and so forth" *(undsoweiter)*; it is a function, not of simple presence, but of "the infinity of permissible repetitions" *(SP*, 8/9). This infinity of repetition is potential repetition, by me and others—repetition in my presence and beyond my presence. Thus Derrida can ask whether the repetition constitutive of ideality "is a certain relation of an 'existent' to his death"(*SP*, 8/10). If this is the case, then a certain absence, here identified as death, would appear within the very medium of constitution, the transcendental life of consciousness.

Derrida has already suggested that nonpresence has a constituting value within presence; now he suggests that "language is properly the medium for this play of presence and absence," of life and death (*SP*, 9/10). Language, in living speech, seems to unify life (speaking) and ideality (the ideal unity of the expressed meaning); it is the very medium of repetition. Derrida's point here can be explicated using the now familiar terminology of types and tokens. While language can be defined as a system of linguistic types (Saussure's *langue*), Husserl's insight is that we cannot understand what a type is without reference to the repetition of possible tokens of the type: the type (ideal meaning) simply is that which can be repeated or realized in a multiplicity of tokens, and to be a token is to realize a type that is essentially realizable in other tokens. There is no such thing as a "pure type," defined without reference to possible tokens, and to bring a type into play is to deploy a token. (In Saussurean terms, this means that the study of *langue*, the abstract language system, has to start, directly or indirectly, from *parole*, from concrete speech, something that Saussure never doubted.) Similarly, to bring a type to presence as a thematic object is to deploy a token, but a token of a different type, since the meaning in which an ideal meaning is made an object is not the same meaning. When a meaning is thematized, "the meaning in which [the] species is thought, and its object, the species itself, are not one and the same" (*LI* II.1, 102/I, 331, translation altered). It is not at all clear, however, that for Husserl language is the primary medium for the play of presence and absence. There is a play of presence and absence in language for Husserl, but it is far from clear that for Husserl language is essential to this play. We shall return to this point.

The introduction of the theme of language reinforces the focus on life that has already made its appearance in the discussion of the constitutive function of repetition for the sense of ideality: the dual theme of ideality and presence, of the possible presence of ideal objects to consciousness, finds its most original presentation in the phenomenon of "living speech," in the voice. This introduces the theme of the voice that will dominate much of Derrida's interpretation of Husserl. For the moment, however, Derrida concentrates on the more general concept, that of life in general.

Husserl often speaks of the life of consciousness, and this life can be thematized as a phenomenon within the world, as the life of human consciousness, and as a transcendental phenomenon, that is, in its function as constituting the world (including itself *as* a mundane phenomenon). Now, in terms of these distinctions, we can ask which structures of mundane consciousness are essential and which accidental, and we can go on to ask which structures are not only essential to the mundane phenomenon but also exercise a transcendental function. Phenomenology is a philosophy of life, according to Derrida, because, in contrast to the suggestion he has just made concerning a constitutive relation to death, it recognizes death as nonessential and thus nontranscendental; the "source of sense," the transcendental function, is the act of living (*SP,* 9/10).

Derrida raises the question of the unity of the concept of *living* across these various distinctions (essential/accidental, transcendental/mundane). His thesis is that "the unity of living, the focus of *Lebendigkeit* which diffracts its light in all the fundamental concepts of phenomenology (*Leben, Erlebnis, lebendige Gegenwart, Geistigkeit,* etc.), escapes the transcendental reduction and, as unity of worldly life and transcendental life, even opens up the way for it" (*SP,* 9/10).[4] In other words, he will argue that there is an essential contingency, which he will call "death," that is constitutive, that exercises a transcendental function. The argument seems to be based on a simple semantic point. Given the structure

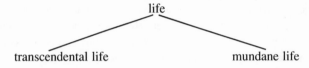

there must be a unitary meaning of "life" that precedes the distinction between the transcendental and the mundane, a ground for the unity of the mundane and the transcendental, a ground that thus itself escapes the transcendental. If we reply by emphasizing the radical heterogeneity of the mundane and the transcendental, insisting that the appearance of the word "life" in the transcendental context indicates either ostensive definition or metaphorical usage, then, as Derrida notes, "it is upon the possibility of this relation that the whole weight of the question falls" (*SP,* 9–10/10). In other words, such a reply would have to provide either a theory of ostensive definition (which Derrida calls an "indicative relation") that would show how transcendental meaning can accrue to the word without importing its pretranscendental, mundane meaning (which would take us back to the problem of unity) or a theory of metaphor that would show (1) how literal meaning is possible and (2) how what begins as a metaphorical usage (the metaphorical use of an originally mundane word in a transcendental context) can also have literal meaning. In either case, it will be the concept of *life* that makes the ostensive definition or metaphor possible. Derrida will argue that language itself is essentially analogical (*SP,* 11/12) and that the transcendental itself, the *logos* of the transcendental, cannot purify itself of its origins in the mundane.

Derrida's strategy here is to pose a dilemma. Either there is a unitary meaning of "life," in which case this meaning escapes the reduction while opening the way for it (Husserl doesn't—indeed can't—raise this question), or there is no unity, only metaphor or ambiguity. But then what makes the metaphor possible? Answer: the concept of *life*. This would be viciously circular. What, however, does "escapes the reduction" mean? Mundane life *appears* within the reduction *as phenomenon*. The transcendental "is" only as constituting the mundane. But perhaps this is precisely Derrida's point.

Even Husserl's attempt to make a radical distinction between a phenomenological psychology and transcendental phenomenology would then be doomed to failure. His famous doctrine of the parallelism of the psychological and transcendental realms is formulated as an answer to a skepticism that in a certain sense all of modern philosophy attempts to overcome.[5] For Husserl, Descartes' fundamental insight is that

> everything objectively real, and ultimately the entire world, is something that exists for us as thus and so only as the actual or possible *cogitatum* [i.e., that which is thought] of our own *cogitatio* [thinking], as the possible experiential content of our own experiences. . . . True being is thus for us a title of actual and possible cognitive achievements. (*Hua* IX, 329)

Descartes determined the ego of this thinking as thinking substance, as the soul, whose distinctness from the body and whose possible immortality could be ascertained; Locke identified the thinking ego with the human mind (*Hua* IX, 330). Both approaches lead to psychologism, the view that our essential medium of access to the world is human subjectivity, with its mundane and thus contingent, conditioned characteristics. The world of experience is thus merely the world as it happens to appear to us. Descartes attempted to avoid the skeptical conclusion by anchoring our innate ideas in the creative power and goodness of God.[6] In Locke the skeptical consequences begin to come out more clearly, and in Hume they appear full-blown.

Husserl responds with a *functional* distinction. We can consider consciousness as a mundane existent. In this case we can make it the object of empirical psychology or the object of an a priori phenomenological psychology. The latter investigates the essential structure of psychic reality purely as such, independently of its relations to the physical world. The essential methodological tool of such an investigation is the phenomenological-psychological reduction. Here the psychologist must "thematically disengage" all reference to extramental reality: as a phenomenological psychologist, "I must cease to take into account the entire real world that was and is in continual ontic acceptance in my natural life" (*Hua* IX, 312). In addition, the psychologist must perform the eidetic reduction: phenomenological psychology investigates consciousness, not with regard to its contingent, empirical properties, but rather "with reference to all possible (thinkable) *real* worlds" (*Hua* IX, 335, emphasis added). Yet such a psychology remains "transcendentally naive" and therefore subject to a highly refined version of skepticism. If we consider consciousness purely as a factual reality in our world, we arrive at an *anthropological skepticism*, which invokes the contrast between the way the world appears to us and the way it might appear to other possible conscious beings. If we subject the region of the mental to an eidetic analysis, we can still speak only of the appearing of the world to real or possible "souls," that is, conscious beings who are part of the worlds they experience. Such a pure psychology remains a positive science that takes the world as something pregiven (*Hua* IX, 335). It can tell us only about the ways any possible world must appear to conscious beings who are part of that world, and this leaves room for a skeptical distinction between the way the world appears to such subjects and the way the world is in itself.

Husserl argues, however, that we may replace the interest motivating pure psychology—namely, an interest in the souls that are to be found in the world as pregiven (*Hua* IX, 335)— with a transcendental interest motivated by the insight "that the world for us is '*the*' world, the world that is there [*vorhandene*], exists, and is thus and so determined for us, *in* this consciousness, as appearing, intended, displayed [*ausgewiesen*], etc., in it" (*Hua* IX, 332). Even the world itself is what it is for us, has the very sense of existing for us, only in the life of consciousness. Thus it is possible to radicalize the psychological reduction, to drop the thematization of conscious life as something present in the world and thematize consciousness as constituting the very sense of the world itself. As Husserl puts it, with the transcendental turn we "radically inhibit" our apperception of the world as existing world and take the world as a "mere phenomenon." On this account, the transcendental reduction is a "higher-level and radicalized epochē" (*Hua* IX, 341). It leads to the insight that the results of pure phenomenological psychology have a validity that goes beyond the framework of that psychology itself, that the essential structures of any possible consciousness are not merely constitutive for the experience of a world in which such a consciousness appears. Rather, such structures are constitutive of the very phenomenon of the world itself. Thus Husserl can claim that in the transcendental epochē the entire content of pure psychology remains preserved as a transcendental content (*Hua* IX, 341–42).

As Derrida notes, the parallelism between the region of the purely psychic (as thematized in pure psychology) and the transcendental does not lead to an "ontological double" (*SP*, 11/11). Husserl sometimes employs an ontological terminology, as when he states that "like any meaningful question, the transcendental [question] presupposes a ground of unquestionable being in which all means for the solution must be contained" and speaks of "the transcendental field of being" (*transzendentale Seinsfeld*) (*Hua* IX, 337–42).[7] But in accordance with the fundamental insight of phenomenology, *any* sense of being must ultimately be traced back to a mode of givenness, and this is what we find: "The transcendental field of being, like the method giving access to it, is a *parallel* to the phenomenological-psychological field, with the method giving access to it, [namely] the psychological reduction'' (*Hua* IX, 342). The transcendental field is strictly a correlate to the method giving access to it, and its sense of being must be investigated in terms of that method, namely, the transcendental reduction. It would be a mistake to take this distinction to refer to two separate regions that happen to be structurally parallel to one another. What we have is rather one and the same ''thing,'' namely, consciousness, thematized now from one (psychological) point of view, now from another (transcendental) point of view. Thus ''parallel signifies here a parallel correspondence in every respect concerning particulars and connections, a totally unique way of being different while not being external to one another or separated in any natural sense''; the transcendental is ''a new, absolute, transcendental *sense*'' of consciousness (*Hua* IX, 342; see also 343–44; *Hua* VI, §§53–54, §§69–72; *Hua* XVII, §99). The distinction is thus in this sense functional, not ontological.

Given this, it is surely questionable to speak of the transcendental as a ''protoregion'' (*archi-region*) (*SP*, 10/11). Similarly, the term ''duplication (*Verdoppelung*),'' which Derrida uses to characterize Husserl's position (*SP*, 11/11), can easily be misleading, as Husserl uses the term to set up the *problem* of the relationship between the psychological and the transcendental. Thus he speaks of ''the transcendental illusion [*Schein*] of duplication'' (*Hua* IX, 336; see also 338, 342). Derrida seems to take this into account by stressing that the duplication in question is a ''duplication of sense'' and not an ''ontological double'' (*SP*, 11/11), but it is precisely the radical difference in sense that constitutes the illusion of duplication.

In spite of his insistence that there is no ontological duplication, Derrida clearly has a stake in describing the transcendental as a ''protoregion,'' using spatial metaphors such as ''outside the world'' and ''alongside, right next to the other'' (*SP*, 14/14). Just how misleading this description is can be seen by looking at Husserl's Afterword to the *Ideas*, which originally appeared in 1930.[8] According to this text, in the transcendental-phenomenological reduction ''psychological subjectivity loses precisely that which gives it validity as something real in the naively experientially pregiven world; it loses the existential sense [*Seinssinn*] [of being a] soul of an existing body in the pregiven spatiotemporal nature.'' In the epochē we are able to thematize ''the universal phenomenon 'world for consciousness [*Bewußtseinswelt*] purely as such.' '' Once again, Husserl does use ontological terms in describing the field of transcendental experience as ''an infinite, self-contained, absolutely self-sufficient realm of beings . . . —that of pure or transcendental subjectivity'' (*Hua* V, 145). But his discussion quickly makes it clear that the sense of such talk of ''beings'' is dependent on the manner in which subjectivity is thematized. ''Within my field of transcendental phenomena I am no longer theoretically taken [*in theoretischer Geltung*] as human ego, no longer [taken as] a real object within the world taken as existing; rather I am exclusively taken as subject *for* this world.'' The crucial thing is *how* the ego is taken: ''the transcendental I'' is ''the I *as* . . . absolutely in itself and for itself 'prior' to all mundane being'' (*Hua* V, 146).

Given this priority of the mode of givenness, it is not surprising that the transcendental reduction is described, not as a shift in object, but as a ''transformation of sense'' in which the theoretical content (*Gehalt*) of phenomenological psychology becomes transcendental phenomenological content (*Hua* V, 146). The ''parallel'' is between phenomenological psychology and transcendental psychology, not between two ''objects.'' Thus Husserl can write that the entire theoretical content of psychology is completely unphilosophical, whereas '' 'the same' content in the transcendental attitude, thus understood as transcendental phenomenology, [is] a philosophical science.'' The source of the difference lies in the shift in *attitude*: ''Here we do in fact find the chief difficulties in understanding, as it must seem completely unreasonable that such a 'nuance,' which grows out of a mere change in attitude, is to have a great, indeed a decisive, significance for all genuine philosophy'' (*Hua* V, 147). Thus here too what looks like a material distinction between objects or realms turns out to be a difference in attitude or mode of givenness.

Again, in §14 of the *Cartesian Meditations*, which Derrida also refers to, Husserl speaks of a parallel between pure psychology of consciousness and transcendental phenomenology of consciousness, calling this distinction a ''nuance'' that concerns the *sense* of the psychological and transcendental-phenomenological explorations of consciousness, ''though the contents to be described on the one hand and on the other can correspond.'' The two disciplines study ''parallel, substantively identical data [*inhaltlich gleichen Daten*],'' taken in the one as concerning actuality, the world presupposed as existing, and in the other as concerning the world ''only as an actuality-phenomenon'' (*Hua* I, 70–71/32, translation altered).

Derrida interrogates the sense and possibility of such a fundamental and enigmatic difference. The very claim to a difference that is not ontological (Derrida calls it ''a difference in fact distinguishing nothing'' [*SP* 10/11], a phrase that would surely require some justification in view of Husserl's careful attempt to trace that difference back to a difference in the way consciousness is thematized) leads Derrida to state in the form of a conclusion what can only be a thesis (though as it appears in an introduction, perhaps this statement is meant to be understood as a thesis). As the transcendental is not a ''metaphysical phantom'' of the empirical,

> this leads us to denounce the purely theoretical image and analogy of the ego [*Je*] as the absolute spectator of its own psychic self [*moi*] and to expose the analogical character of the language that must sometimes be used to announce the transcendental reduction as well as to describe

that unusual "object," the psychic self as it confronts the absolute transcendental self. (*SP*, 11/12, translation altered)

And this thesis is fundamentally a thesis about language: "In fact no language can cope with the operation by which the transcendental ego constitutes and opposes itself to its worldly self, its soul, reflecting itself in a *verweltlichende Selbstapperzeption* [mundanizing self-apperception]" (*SP*, 11/12).

Derrida generally keeps fairly strictly to this functional sense of the transcendental, although he can play with it a bit loosely: "if the world needs the *supplement of a soul*, the soul, which is in the world, needs this *supplementary nothing* which is the transcendental and without which no world would appear" (*SP*, 13/13). This assertion is questionable on two counts. In the first place, in what sense does the world "need" the "supplement" of a soul? Is the very idea of a world without conscious beings contradictory? I know of no good Husserlian reason to say any such thing. (Clearly the *entertainment* of such a possibility requires consciousness, but these are two different things.)[9] In the second place, to speak of a "supplementary nothing," aside from the problems noted earlier with Derrida's use of the word "nothing," is misleading. In what sense is the transcendental supplementary? Consciousness has a transcendental function that can be uncovered, but there is no sense in which it can be said to be supplementary. Or does Derrida mean to suggest the possibility of a worldly psyche that does not exercise a transcendental function? If so, he should give at least some content to his suggestion. Something similar would hold of his use of the term "nonconsistency" (*inconsistance*: inconsistency) (*SP*, 13/13) for the difference.

At this point, Derrida once again returns to his thesis concerning language, stating it this time in terms of a possibility: "If language never escapes analogy, if it is indeed analogy through and through, it ought . . . freely to assume its own destruction and cast metaphor against metaphor"(*SP*, 13/13). In other words, if all language is metaphor (an assertion Husserl would not have accepted), and if Husserl's introduction of the distinction between the psychological and the transcendental must make use of metaphors in the traditional and naive sense that allows the metaphorical to be contrasted with the literal, then we must play off the metaphorical nature of language against these absolutely necessary metaphors, metaphors that constitute the very light of possible knowledge and truth. What is at stake in this "war of language against itself" (language as analogy versus the possibility of literal language, versus the very possibility of the becoming-literal of language) is "the possibility of sense and world" in the sense of metaphysics, a sense that depends on maintaining the distinction between the literal and the metaphorical. Here we find another stage of Derrida's thesis:

This war . . . takes place in this *difference* [between the psychological and the transcendental], which, we have seen, cannot reside in the world but only in language, in the transcendental disquietude of language. Indeed, far from only living in language, this war is also the origin and residence of language. Language preserves the difference that preserves language. (*SP*, 13/14)

These assertions are problematic. In the first place, the "we have seen" is gratuitous; "we" have seen no such thing. Derrida has asserted (with the assurance that we will not be surprised to hear it) that language is the medium of the play of presence and absence constitutive of the very sense of ideality (*SP*, 9/10). We have also been told, but have not necessarily seen, that language cannot cope with the distinction between the transcendental and its mundanizing self-apperception (*SP*, 11/12), presumably because it must have recourse to metaphor (*SP*, 11/12), something which, if true, will clearly undermine Husserl's account of ideality and his defense against transcendental psychologism. But we have not "seen" that the difference between psychology and the transcendental is constituted by language—and Husserl would have flatly rejected any such assertion (perhaps to his detriment). Thus, rather than being taken in by the illusion of an established conclusion, we should read this statement as a thesis to be proved. However unclearly, Derrida is suggesting a relationship in which a principle (language) not only conditions but is conditioned by that of which it is the principle (the difference between the psychological and the transcendental), so that the latter in turn itself functions as principle.

How is all of this dwelling on the distinction between the psychological and the transcendental made to pay off? The first thing to notice is the manner in which Derrida moves from the parallelism between the disciplines of psychology and transcendental phenomenology to a parallelism between the "objects" of those disciplines. Whereas in the Afterword to the *Ideas* Husserl speaks of the " 'nuance' [that] grows out of a mere change in attitude," a "nuancing" that concerns the difference between pure psychology and transcendental phenomenology (*Hua* V, 147, 148), Derrida, having earlier assured the reader that the duplication of sense is "no ontological double" (*SP*, 11/11), now shifts from talking about a parallel between psychology and transcendental phenomenology to speaking of a parallel between the objects of these sciences. In addition, the language used to describe this parallel is strongly spatial: "the parallels, one of which is in the world and the other outside the world without being in another world, that is, without ceasing to be, like *every parallel, alongside, right next to the other*" (*SP*, 13–14/14). Thus, despite his earlier assurance, which was fully in accord with Husserl's intentions, Derrida now insinuates a difference between parallel objects, objects that "like every parallel" must exist alongside, next to each other. Asserting that we must "stringently assemble and protect in our discourse these frivolous, subtle . . . 'nuances,' " Derrida nevertheless describes them in such a way as to distort their meaning.

Against the background of his discussion of these parallels, Derrida introduces another thesis: "But the strange unity of these two parallels, that which
refers the one to the other, does not allow itself to be sundered by them and, by
dividing itself, finally joins the transcendental to its other; this unity is *life*" (*SP*,
14/14). Psyche is life as self-relationship—the unitary self that divides itself and
joins itself to its other. Consciousness is self-relationship, self-presence, and
Derrida suggests that consciousness is not the only form of this self-relationship.
" 'Living' is thus the name of that which precedes the reduction and finally escapes all the divisions [for example, mundane/transcendental] which the latter
gives rise to" (*SP*, 14/14–15). Living in this sense, as "its own division and its
own opposition to its other," is not so much the origin of discourse as the origin
of the *insecurity* of discourse, the point at which discourse is no longer grounded,
made possible in its truth, by the transcendental distinction, the point at which
the light flickers. This is the point at which the difference between the psychological and the transcendental is no longer capable of grounding discourse, of
"assur[ing] its possibility and rigor within the nuance" (*SP*, 14/15). Such a concept of life, as the unity of the parallels, producing them, can have its home neither in the philosophically naive attitude of straightforward life, the natural attitude, nor in the transcendental attitude. It is thus "ultratranscendental." As that
which makes language—the medium for the play of presence and absence constitutive of ideality (*SP*, 9/10), but also that which cannot cope with the transcendental difference (*SP*, 11/12) and which presumably for that reason "has never
been inscribed in language"—possible, this concept requires *another name* than
"life" in the mundane sense. (This name will turn out to be *différance*.)

What is the structure of the argument here? Starting from the triad

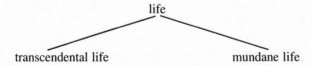

Derrida argues that "life," as the unity of transcendental and mundane, that
which asserts its unity in the face of their duality, which in producing that duality
("dividing itself") binds them together (thus making their difference a mere nuance, a mere difference of sense and attitude), relates them to each other (and
they are of course the same, so the relation is a self-relationship, which is the
formal structure of life itself). This life cannot have the attributes of mundane life
(or of transcendental life either, for that matter). And it is a "strange unity"—for
how can it be said to be a unity in any normal sense? It would indeed be the origin
of self-relationship itself, more original than the transcendental ego, as it would
have to be the source of transcendentality itself (the source of the *difference* be-

tween the mundane and the transcendental). This "life" would indeed require another name, and any name we suggest for it will have to be borrowed.

This ultratranscendental concept of life will escape "the self-presence of transcendental life" (*SP*, 5/6); it will be the source of the living present itself. It will in this sense be the reason why questions of presence continually reappear in phenomenology, why presence is continually threatened, as Derrida earlier claimed (*SP*, 8/9), forcing continual modifications of the factor of presence. Phenomenology's defense against this threat, as Derrida has already suggested, will be living speech as that "which best seems to preserve ideality and living presence in all its forms" (*SP*, 9/10). In living speech we have the most pregnant form of life, of presence and self-presence, of the presence of meaning to consciousness and the presence of consciousness to itself. Thus Derrida finds in phenomenology an attempt to protect the spoken word, an attempt to defend "an essential tie between *logos* and phōnē." Such an endeavor is understandable "when we remember that consciousness owes its privileged status . . . to the possibility of a living vocal medium" (*SP*, 14/15). But what we remember is Derrida's earlier claim, which still remains to be demonstrated.

Derrida finds an intimate connection between self-consciousness and language, as self-consciousness requires a transcendent object (this seems to be an echo of Kant's Second Analogy, but it is also true for Husserl). It is thus never foreign to, or anterior to, the *possibility* of language, presumably because language exhibits the same structure: it only appears in relation to an object, whose presence it can keep and repeat. Against Husserl's attempt to distinguish a preexpressive (and thus prelinguistic, though for Husserl language is not necessary for expression in the sense of the *Ideas*) stratum of experience, Derrida claims that the difference between the contribution of consciousness and that of language is ultimately indiscernible. Why? Because "the possibility of constituting ideal objects belongs to the essence of consciousness" (*SP*, 15/15). In what sense is this possibility essential to consciousness? Does Derrida want to claim that any consciousness is essentially capable of constituting ideal objects, of making idealities the thematic objects of consciousness? Does Husserl claim any such thing? To be sure, consciousness for the Husserl of the *Ideas* onward is essentially the correlation of noesis and noema, and the noematic sense is ideal. But the noema of an act of consciousness is not the object of that act. It can become an object only in an act that reflects upon the noematic sense of the first act. Indeed, the constitution of ideal objects, including states of affairs as objects, would seem to be a relatively high-level achievement of consciousness.

Derrida's tactic is clear: he seeks to insinuate language into the very functioning of consciousness itself, to discern language as the very medium of constitution. Language, representation, will "introduce nonpresence and difference (mediation, signs, referral back, etc.) in the heart of self-presence" (*SP*, 15/15). Presence is threatened once again, and the emphasis on the voice that Derrida will attempt to demonstrate in Husserl is thus interpreted as an attempt to meet the threat of language, of nonpresence. The threat is met by taking language, which is essentially nonpresence and difference, in a form that seems to preserve presence—the voice as the inner voice, the "phenomenological voice." But the voice is not presence; it only "simulates the conservation of presence" (SP, 15/15). In other words, Derrida's claim is that self-relationship resides in language, and thus only simulates presence. This simulation, if it can be demonstrated, will show that the threat to which it is the response is not simply "a difficulty of the system" that might be dealt with by modifying the system. It is not a problem or contradiction internal to the system, an illusion correctable within the system, but is rather constitutive of the system itself (of its very systematicity, we might suggest, relying more on Of Grammatology than on Speech and Phenomena). The simulation is a necessary simulation, for it is the simulation of language itself, the source of the concepts of illusion,[10] phantasm, and hallucination.

On Derrida's reading, this "difficulty" is not peculiar to Husserl's phenomenology, though it does take on its most radical form there. The privilege of the phōnē is essential to the entire history of metaphysics as the metaphysics of presence. But in Husserl's work, it is not the audible voice that is privileged, not the mundane embodiment of speech, but "the voice phenomenologically taken . . . [namely] the intentional animation that transforms the body of the word into flesh" (SP, 15/16). We will have to investigate precisely what Derrida means by "the voice phenomenologically taken," but it is clear that the phenomenological voice will exercise a transcendental, nonmundane function. It will be that instance of the voice which is present to itself, present in its own "hearing/understanding itself [s'entendre]—in the absence of the world" (SP, 15–16/16, translation altered). But precisely here Derrida catches sight of a naïveté, for the voice moves in the medium of words as unities of signifying sound and signified meaning, and this presupposed unity will itself have to be interrogated as to its constitution, "broken down" in a deconstructive analysis that will move in an unresolved tension in phenomenology between "the purity of formalism and the radicality of intuitionism" (SP 16/16).

The task is to examine a "truism" that has governed metaphysics and thus phenomenology without ever being made thematic, namely, "that the privilege of presence as consciousness can be established . . . only by virtue of the excellence of the voice" (SP, 16/16). Metaphysics and phenomenology are committed to logocentrism and phonocentrism. This prejudice cannot be corrected within metaphysics, for it is constitutive of metaphysics as such. Similarly, as Derrida will later insist, overcoming this prejudice is not a simply a matter of spotting an error in metaphysics and moving beyond it to a nonmetaphysical account, for metaphysics will turn out to be anything but one alternative among others, something we can simply drop.

Summary

Looking back over the Introduction to *Speech and Phenomena*, it is important to note the extent to which it is dominated by a series of dichotomies. The ruling dichotomy is the one said to be fundamental to metaphysics itself: presence versus nonpresence or absence. This dichotomy gives rise to or governs a series of dichotomies fundamental to the project of phenomenology. They are governed by the basic dichotomy in various ways—for example, as direct instantiations of presence/absence or as differences in the relative fullness or originality of different kinds of presence. Thus we find:

    knowledge/(nonknowledge)
    ideality/reality
    presentation/representation
    self-presence/appresentation
    sense/nonsense
    life/death
    living speech/(writing)
    transcendental life/empirical life
    transcendental phenomenology/phenomenological psychology
    literal/indicative or metaphorical[11]

Phenomenology, as will quickly be seen, gives an originary value to the term on the first side of each dichotomy. In claiming to find "an irreducible nonpresence as having a constituting value" (*SP*, 5/6), Derrida claims to upset the entire system of dichotomies, and we shall have to watch carefully as the distinctions Husserl takes such care to draw begin to undermine themselves in the course of Derrida's reading.

Chapter 2
"Sign and Signs"

Chapter 1 of *Speech and Phenomena* contains an initial probing of some of the "essential distinctions" with which Husserl begins the first of the *Logical Investigations*. Husserl distinguishes between two fundamental kinds of signs: expressions (*Ausdrücke*), which mean (*bedeuten*) something or express a meaning (*Bedeutung*); and indications or indicative signs (*Anzeichen*), which do not express a meaning. An indicative sign indicates the presence or existence of some object, but it does not express anything: the track of an animal indicates the past presence of the animal, but it does not express the proposition that the animal passed this place. In this sense, while there may be a fake track, put there to mislead a pursuer, indicative signs are neither true nor false. They do not express anything that could be true or false; they are not discursive. Expressions, on the other hand, mean something: an assertion not only refers to something, it says something about it. Thus there is a distinction between the content and the object of the expression.

As Derrida emphasizes, the distinction between indication and expression is not a distinction between different signs, but rather a distinction between the functions a sign can exercise. Indeed, in communication one and the same utterance functions indicatively and expressively at the same time. The words uttered *intimate* or *manifest* (*kundgeben*) the cognitive acts of the speaker; that is, they function as indications that the speaker is living through certain acts of thought. But at the same time the words *express* the ideal content of those acts, the thoughts themselves. The hearer both takes the speaker to be having certain lived experiences and understands what is being said. Communication requires both dimensions: "meaning—in communicative speech—is always bound up [*allzeit* . . . *verflochten*] with such an indicative relation" (*LI* II.1, 24/I, 269). From the logical point of view, however, it is the expressive function alone that is crucial. Logic is concerned not with the pragmatics of communication, but with the logical structure of the meanings expressed. Thus Husserl must distinguish or separate aspects that are always bound up with one another in communicative speech, and he does this by pointing to a speech that is not communicative, the speech in which the speaker addresses no one other than herself.

Meaning as "Wanting-to-Say"

Derrida begins his discussion of Husserl's "essential distinctions" with some remarks on translation. The most important issue here concerns the German verb "*bedeuten*—to mean." This term presents problems in French, for while in German one can speak of *bedeutsame Zeichen* and in English of "meaningful signs," the French *signe signifiant* is redundant. Thus in his discussion of Husserl Derrida will have to "propose solutions halfway between commentary and translation," and we will have to pay careful attention to the way these solutions influence his discussion.

The key to the translation Derrida will offer lies in the alleged centrality of spoken language in Husserl. "It will then be quickly seen that, for Husserl, the expressiveness of expression—which always supposes the ideality of a *Bedeutung*—has an irreducible tie to the possibility of spoken language (*Rede*)" (*SP*, 18/18). Derrida has prepared the way for this statement in his Introduction (see *SP*, 9/10, 14–15/15–16), but the "it will then be quickly seen" seems to refer more to that Introduction than to Husserl. That consciousness owes its privileged status to "the possibility of a living vocal medium" was asserted in the Introduction (*SP*, 14/15), but not demonstrated to be a Husserlian thesis. Here Derrida seems to anchor his claim by referring to Husserl's use of the German word *Rede*, which he translates as *discours parlé*, or "spoken language." The word *Rede* appears in the opening sections of the First Investigation, but it is far from clear that its use involves a priority of spoken language, of a living vocal medium. Indeed, when it appears in §5, it is carefully embedded within the statement that what is being said is for the purpose of "provisional intelligibility" (*LI* II.1, 30/I, 275). This issue will continue to occupy our attention: Derrida will often assert a priority of speech for Husserl, but his justification for this assertion will not appear until chapter 3 of *Speech and Phenomena*. For now, we must simply note that this claim provides the background for his translation decisions.

Derrida's translation of *bedeuten* is *vouloir-dire* or "want to say,"[1] which does mean "mean" in the sense of "what I mean, what I want to say" as well as "what a word means" ("Que veut dire ce mot?" means "What does this word mean?''). An indicative sign does not "want to say" anything; it expresses nothing, has no meaning. It merely indicates. An expression, on the other hand, "wants to say" something, and it does so because somebody, the speaker or writer, "wants to say" something and uses those words to do so. This translation seems to be an appropriate expression of the "communicative intent" of the speaking subject, and it is speech and the speaking subject that Derrida has in mind. In communication, the speaker utters a sound or makes a mark "with the intention [*Absicht*] of 'expressing himself about something' through its means; he must endow it with a sense in certain acts of mind, a sense he desires to share with his auditors. Such sharing becomes a possibility if the auditor also understands the speaker's intention [*Intention*]'' (*LI*, II.1, 32–33/I, 276–77). The speaker "wants to say" something with the words he or she utters, and in a derivative sense the words uttered "want to say" something. Thus the connotation of willing in *vouloir-dire* seems quite appropriate for signs uttered with communicative intent.

But Husserl is not really interested in giving a Gricean-style analysis at this point, though he has many of the elements required. He is concerned with formal logic, not with the pragmatics of communication. He therefore wants to include all speech and portions of speech as expressions, "whether or not such speech is actually uttered, that is addressed with communicative intent [*kommunikativer Absicht*] to any persons or not'' (*LI*, II.1, 31/I, 275). The importance of this becomes clear when we note that the English and French translations of the passage quoted in the preceding paragraph use the single word "intention" or *l'intention* to translate two different German words, *Absicht* and *Intention*, and that in Husserl's usage the word *Intention* does not have connotations of willing.[2] In the Fifth Investigation Husserl equates the "intentional relation" of acts with their "intention"; the intention is an "act character" (*LI* II.1, 367–68/II, 554–55). "The term 'intention' presents the peculiarity of acts by means of the image of *aiming*, and so fits the numerous cases that are naturally and understandably ranked as cases of theoretical aiming. But the metaphor does not fit all acts equally'' (*LI* II.1, 378/II, 563, translation altered). And when it comes to speaking of acts, "we must steer clear of the word's original meaning: *all thought of activity must be rigidly excluded*'' (*LI* II.1, 378/II, 563).

Thus the translation of *bedeuten* by *vouloir-dire* must be treated with care, and similar caution is required in the case of Derrida's translation of *Bedeutungsintention* ("meaning-intention") by *l'intention du vouloir-dire* (*SP*, 23/22). Derrida generally leaves the substantive *Bedeutung* ("meaning") untranslated, but he does offer "*what* a discourse or somebody *wants to say* [ce que quelqu'un ou un discours veulent dire]'' as a translation of *Bedeutung*, concluding that "what is conveyed, then, is always a linguistic sense, a discursive content" (*SP*, 18/18).

Meaning and Language

In confirmation of his reading, Derrida immediately relates this sense of expression, according to which an utterance expresses the meaning thought by the speaker, to another sense from §124 of the *Ideas*, where Husserl introduces a distinction between sense (*Sinn*) and meaning (*Bedeutung*) not drawn in the *Investigations*. As Derrida summarizes Husserl's discussion, "*Bedeutung* is reserved for the content in the ideal sense of *verbal* expression, spoken language, while sense (*Sinn*) covers the whole noematic sphere right down to its nonexpressive stratum" (*SP*, 19/19, translation altered). According to this distinction, *meaning* is used to characterize speech, whereas *sense* is used more broadly. Thus we speak of the meaning of words and of the sense of the object perceived as such. However, Derrida's interpretation of this passage requires some comment.

In the first place, Derrida misinterprets §124 of the *Ideas* both in *Speech and Phenomena* and in "Form and Wanting-to-Say: A Note on the Phenomenology of Language."[3] Husserl does introduce the terms *bedeuten* and *Bedeutung* in terms of "the linguistic sphere, that of 'expressing,' " but it quickly becomes apparent that this is intended merely as a way into a field of phenomena that have no intrinsic relation to language. Husserl begins with a distinction between "the sensuous, so to speak, the corporeal side of expression, and its nonsensuous or 'mental [*geistigen*]' side," only to leave the former out of consideration (*Hua* III.1, 285/294). This turn away from the sensuous side is not to be understood as a mere leaving it out of thematic consideration for the time being; the term "meaning" in the phrase " '*logical*' or '*expressing*' meaning" (*Hua* III.1, 285/294, translation altered) has no intrinsic relation to language at all. In Husserl's example, I may see an object and then explicate what I see according to the schema "This is white." "This process does not require the slightest bit of 'expression,' either expression in the sense of verbal sound or anything like a verbal signifying [*Wortbedeuten*], which is also capable of being present independently of the verbal sound (as when the sound is 'forgotten')" (*Hua* III.1, 285/295, translation altered). Even without any reference to verbal meaning, in such a case we have something "*expressible by means of 'meanings'* " (*Hua* III.1, 286/295). Thus when Husserl writes that "*logical meaning is an expression*," this has nothing at all to do with language. The verbal sound is an "expression" only in the derivative sense that it expresses the meaning; the primary sense of "expressing" lies in that meaning itself.

This reading is confirmed by §94 of the *Ideas*, which has the title "Noesis and Noema in the Realm of Judgment." In the course of distinguishing between "what is judged" (*das Geurteilte*)" and "what is judged about" (*das Beurteilte*), Husserl suggests that for the sake of simplicity, we can "disregard the *higher stratum* pertaining to verbal 'expression' " (*Hua* II.1, 216/228, emphasis added; see also 288/297).

Does this mean that Husserl changed his view between the *Logical Investigations* and the *Ideas*? Does the continuity thesis fail in this case? In his discussion of the First Investigation, Derrida has two strategic goals that are relevant here. In the first place, he argues that meaning "is always a linguistic sense, a discursive content" (*SP*, 18/18), and it is this thesis that he finds "confirmed" by §124 of the *Ideas*. This is important because, as we saw in chapter 1, Derrida is concerned to maintain both that language is the medium for the play of presence and absence constitutive of ideality (*SP*, 9/10) and that it is the medium of the self-presence of consciousness itself. It now turns out that this thesis has to be asserted against Husserl's explicit intention. Second, Derrida argues that "for Husserl, the expressiveness of expression—which always supposes the ideality of a *Bedeutung*—has an irreducible tie to the possibility of spoken language (*Rede*)" (*SP*, 18/18), which picks up the theme of the voice from the Introduction (*SP*, 14/15). We will deal with the second claim shortly. For the moment, it is important to see that in the *Ideas* not only does Husserl not reserve the power of expression, and thus logicality, for *spoken* language, but logicality is not reserved for language at all. The continuity thesis, however, has in fact not broken down: Derrida's interpretation of the *Investigations* is plausible only because he neglects a text that appears in close proximity to the essential distinctions of the First Investigation, namely, the Introduction to the second volume of the *Investigations*.

The Introduction begins by noting that it is often recognized that logic must begin with linguistic discussions. But Husserl's statements concerning the relation between language and thought remain curiously indefinite and uncertain. His opening statement is immediately followed by a quotation from John Stuart Mill, according to which "language is evidently one of the principal *instruments or helps* of thought" (Mill, *Logic*, bk 1, chap. 1, §1, quoted at *LI* II.1, 1/I, 248). Thus, far from being the medium of logicality, language is the instrument of thought, a help to thought. Husserl goes on to note, however, that Mill finds a "deeper ground for this necessity," namely, that a discussion of language is the only way to investigate the meaning of propositions, and such discussion stands, in Mill's words, "at the threshold" of logic. At the threshold, but only at the threshold. Linguistic discussions are "philosophically indispensable preparations" for pure logic, as it is only with their "aid" (*Mithilfe*) that we can attain clarity about the objects of logic (*LI* II.1, 2/I, 249). This is true because "all theoretical research, though by no means solely conducted in acts of verbal expression or complete expression, none the less terminates in such statement" (*LI* II.1, 3/I, 250). Such expression—and here Husserl is clearly thinking of *written* expression—enables cognition to become an "abiding possession." To be sure, some judgments may be dependent on linguistic expression for pragmatic reasons, but this by no means indicates that thought *essentially* moves in the medium of language:

> *Whatever the connection of thought with speech may be, whether or not*
> the appearance of our final judgements in the form of verbal
> pronouncements has a *necessary grounding in essence*, it is at least
> plain that judgements stemming from higher intellectual regions, and in
> particular from the regions of science, could barely arise without verbal
> expression. (*LI* II, 13–14/I, 250, emphasis added.)

Language is a pragmatic necessity, both because of the limits of individual memory and because of the intersubjective and historical character of theoretical research. But that is as far as Husserl is willing to go at this point.

Thus the objects of logic, ideal assertoric meanings, "are, in the first instance, . . . given to it in grammatical clothing" (*LI* II.1, 4/I, 250), where "grammatical" is coextensive with "linguistic." Because this is our mode of access to these objects phenomenology begins with an analysis of signs, but Husserl is careful to point out the dangers of allowing grammatical analysis to replace "the authentic analysis of meaning" (*LI* II.1, 12/I, 257, translation altered). Husserl admits that there is "a certain parallel between thinking and speaking" (*LI* II.1, 13/I, 257), but the parallel is very imperfect. The phenomenology of linguistic forms cannot replace the phenomenology of meaning-experiences, the phenomenology of thought. Language is a tool, an often imperfect one, and the tool must be reformed in line with its task. To the extent that this task is that of giving expression to thought, we must analyze thought itself, distinguishing what is essential for thought from the often contingent features of its imperfect expression.

Derrida never discusses this text, which undermines his claim that for Husserl the logical is the a priori *telos* of language, its proper destination. Husserl was a logician and epistemologist, and he was primarily interested in language as the instrument of cognition, but he did not for that reason deny that language has many functions.

The "Interweaving" of Indication and Expression

As Derrida emphasizes, the difference between indication and expression is functional, not substantial: "It is functions and signifying relations, and not terms, that are indications or expressions" (*SP*, 20/20, translation altered). This leads to "the center of the problem," which turns on the fact that one and the same use of a sign can involve both the indicative and the expressive function. Derrida will argue that this fact ultimately signifies that the distinction between indication and expression itself cannot be maintained in its essential purity, and the initial key to this demonstration is to be found in the fact that according to Husserl, in such a use of a sign, the expressive function is not simply an additional function that the sign may take on, as Husserl initially seemed to suggest in saying that "signs in the sense of indications (ear-marks, traits, etc.) *do not ex-*

press anything, unless they fulfill a significational function [*Bedeutungsfunktion*] in addition to [*neben*] the function of indicating (*LI* II.1, 23/I, 269, quoted by Derrida at *SP*, 20/20: "à moins qu'ils ne remplissent outre la fonction d'indiquer [*neben*, à côté de . . .] une fonction de *Bedeutung*"). Rather, "meaning [*bedeuten*: to mean; Fr. *le vouloir-dire*]—in communicative speech—is always interwoven [*allzeit . . . verflochten ist*; Fr. *est toujours entrelacé*] with such an indicative function" (*LI* II.1, 24/I, 269, translation altered).[4] In communication, the expressive function *depends on* the indicative function.

Given Derrida's goals, he has a vested interest in the interpretation of this sentence. He first writes that the "two functions may be interwoven or entangled [*s'entrelacer, s'enchevetrei*]" and then speaks of "an intimate involvement, an entanglement [*Verflechtung*] [*d'intrication intime, d'enchevetrement*]" (*SP*, 20/20). The choice of the word *enchevetrement*, "tangle" or "confusion," gives the interpretation a solid push in the desired direction. Husserl's words *verflochten* and *Verflechtung* are derived from the verb *flechten*, meaning "to braid, plait or weave." The word *Verflechtung* can have the figurative meaning of "entanglement," but its more literal meaning is "interlacing," and *verflochten* would carry the more literal meaning of "interlaced" or "interwoven." Now, to say that the two functions are "interwoven" is indeed, as Derrida points out, to go far beyond saying that a sign can have a signitive function *in addition to* its indicative function. But to read *Verflechtung* as signifying "entanglement" (*enchevetrement*) rather than "interlacing" or "interweaving" is to prejudge the issue at hand by suggesting that it may be impossible to untangle the two functions. At the very least, Derrida needs to offer reasons for the appropriateness of this translation, especially if it turns out, as it will, that this translation leads in directions counter to Husserl's express intentions. The point is not that the translation is simply wrongheaded, but rather that it must be based on arguments rather than function as the unargued premise for further demonstrations.

Unfortunately, it seems to serve the latter function in Derrida's text. He is quick to press the advantage this translation gives him: "We know already that *in fact* the discursive sign, and consequently the wanting-to-say [*le vouloir-dire*], is *always* entangled [*toujours enchevetré*], always *caught up* [*pris*] in an indicative system" (*SP*, 20/20, translation altered). This sentence is problematic in two respects. In the first place, Husserl nowhere says that meaning is *always* interwoven with indication. The phrase in question reads, rather, "daß das Bedeuten—in mitteilender Rede— . . . ," that is, "meaning—in communicative speech— . . . " Derrida uses his own modification of the French translation, and given his translation decisions, it quite properly reads "le vouloir-dire (*bedeuten*)—dans le discours communicatif (*in mitteilender Rede*)— . . . " Clearly, it is not discourse pure and simple, not simply "the discursive sign" (*le signe discursif*) (in the supposedly explicative transformation Derrida immediately introduces), but discourse, speech, the discursive sign *as used in communi-*

cative speech or discourse, in which we find indication and the meaning function interwoven. Derrida is quick to correct this insinuation, writing, *"In fact and always (allzeit verflochten ist)* to the extent to which the meaning is taken up in communicative speech" (*SP*, 21/20), but the insinuation is already in place, and Derrida will exploit it. He immediately follows his correction with the claim that "each time an expression is in fact produced, it has a communicative value [*comporte une valeur de communication*]" (*SP*, 21/20, translation altered). Thus his claim is clear, even if it has not been argued: the apparent restriction of the phrase "in *communicative* discourse" is no restriction at all. Since, as we shall see, this goes against Husserl's express intentions, we shall have to take this assertion as a thesis to be argued.

In the second place, Derrida wastes no time in exploiting the overtones of his word "entangled." Having used the two words "entangled" and "caught up" alongside one another as expressions of one and the same state of affairs, Derrida can exploit the connotations of the one while using the other: "Caught up is the same as contaminated [Pris, c'est-à-dire contaminé]" (*SP*, 21/20). Thus, in the course of only a few sentences, Derrida has moved from Husserl's claim that the two functions are "interwoven" in communicative discourse, through the insinuation that such interweaving is entanglement, to the conclusion that meaning is *contaminated* by indication *any time* an expression is produced (because any such expression will have a "communicative value").[5] The only move in this transformation that Derrida even vaguely suggests might be more than a straightforward and unproblematic explication is the unargued assertion that whenever a sign is produced it has "communicative value," and even here there is no attempt to specify the precise sense, much less the implications of this claim. (It might, for example, mean that any use of a sign has a communicative potential, which would be plausible enough; but this would not mean that it functions communicatively. As will become clear shortly, Derrida assumes a much stronger interpretation of his claim.)

When Derrida continues, it is "this interweaving," and not the entanglement, that is said to be in need of clarification, but this project of clarification has already been powerfully prejudiced, and Derrida will exploit this prejudice. The essential distinction between expression and indication is, Derrida claims, "purely *de jure* [*juridique*]," asserted in the face of the "*de facto* necessity [*nécessité factuelle*] of entanglement" (*SP*, 21/20). But in the first place, it is not clear what the term "*de facto* necessity" is supposed to mean here. It might mean that there is a purely contingent, empirical law according to which all expressive use of language by human beings also involves indication. This law would state an anthropological fact about human beings, and would have no particular validity beyond that context. But this is simply not what Husserl has in mind when he speaks of the interweaving of indication and meaning in communicative speech. He means rather, as he says, that indication plays an *essential* role in *communication*, that it is essential to the very structure of communication as such. That is the clear significance of the "always." As Husserl writes, "communicating is *made possible by* the listener's understanding the intention [*Intention*] of the speaker" (*LI* II.1, 33/I, 277, translation altered, emphasis added), and the indicative function of the spoken or written expressions produced by the speaker or writer is what makes this understanding possible. Thus "all expressions in *communicative* speech function as *indications*." The interweaving is *essential* for communicative speech.

In the second place, Derrida's assertion of a *de facto* necessity of "entanglement" for all uses of signs presupposes not only the thesis stated at the end of his preceding paragraph—namely, that any expression that is produced has a communicative value—but also a certain assumption about the implications of that thesis. He is assuming that the communicative value he attributes to expressions even when they are not produced with communicative intent implies that in those expressions there is a necessary entanglement of indicative and meaning functions. Such an entanglement would be the expression of certain essential relations, relations that would presumably presuppose the "rigorous distinction of essence." Once again, we must recall that this is asserted in the face of Husserl's express statement of the opposite.

This rather confused use of the distinction between the *de facto* (*factuelle/le fait*) and the *de jure* (*juridique/le droit*) sets up the crucial thesis of the book: the separation (not distinction) between the *de facto* (*le fait*) and the *de jure* (*le droit*), existence and essence, reality and intentional function, which provides the very structural framework for a phenomenology that would be an eidetic and transcendental discipline, is not something available that is then applied to language as one case among others. Rather, it "does not exist prior to the question of language" (*SP*, 21/21); language is the condition of its very discovery. In its most precise form, the thesis is that the *de jure* value of "a distinction between fact and intentional right depends entirely on language and, in language, on the validity of a radical distinction between indication and expression" (*SP*, 21/21, translation altered).[6] The implication is clear: if the radical distinction between indication and expression cannot be maintained, the distinctions that constitute phenomenology will be undermined, and phenomenology along with them.

This thesis has been prefigured in a variety of ways in the Introduction. In some cases the connection is clear, while in others the connection remains to be demonstrated. For example, what Derrida calls the decision to subordinate the sign to logic (*SP*, 6/7) presupposes the distinction between indication and expression, as indication is an empirical, nondiscursive matter, whereas signs are subject to the ideal laws, relations, and norms of logic. If all expressions are also indicative as the very condition of their exercising an expressive function, then it would seem that logic will never be pure, that the sign will always be subject to extralogical constraints. By the same token, the presence of the ideal identity of meaning in repetition will also be threatened by contingency, by changing contexts, and so on (*SP*, 8/9). Indication will be the moment of absence and death (*SP*, 9/10), of contingency and nontruth in transcendental life. Similarly, if all expression is infected by indication, a purely transcendental *logos* (*SP*, 6/7–8) will be a chimera, and with that the very distinction between the psychological and the transcendental becomes unstable. The "nothing" that distinguishes them, without which no language can be dedicated to the service of truth, would turn out to be nothing at all, with the result that all language would be "deformed by some real contact" (*SP*, 12/12). Again, Derrida notes the analogical character of the language that announces the reduction (*SP*, 11/12) and suggests that language is analogy through and through (*SP*, 13/13). It is clear that if the distinction, and indeed separation, between indication and expression cannot be sustained, we will have an "insecurity of discourse" (*SP*, 14/15), a *mere* simulation of the conservation of presence (*SP*, 15/15).

Expression as a Form of Indication

With this thesis in place, we can join Derrida as he returns to the Husserlian text, a return that should provide the needed clarification of the thesis. Repeating his misleading claim that every expression is caught up in an indicative system, Derrida entertains the possibility, rejected by Husserl, that expression is a species of the genus "indication." This might seem plausible. Since, as Derrida has already noted, a sign can exercise an indicative function without being an expression, whereas, as he keeps insinuating against Husserl's express intent, expression is inevitably indicative, there might be two kinds of indications: those that do and those that do not express a meaning. In this case, Derrida claims, speech would be "but a form of gesture" (*SP*, 21/21), as to mean or "want to say" would be a form of indication.

Derrida will discuss gesture later (*SP*, 37–41/35–38), but at this point nothing has prepared the reader for this statement. Husserl mentions gestures in §5 of the First Investigation, where he excludes from expression in his technical sense "facial expression and the various gestures which involuntarily accompany speech without communicative intent, or those in which a person's mental states achieve understandable 'expression' for his environment, without the added help of speech" (*LI* II.1, 31/I, 275). Now, even when words are uttered with expressive intent, their indicative function is not that of a gesture in this sense. Spoken words have an indicative function when "they serve the hearer as signs of the 'thoughts' of the speaker, i.e. of his sense-giving experiences," when "the hearer *intuitively* takes the speaker to be a person who is expressing this or that" (*LI* II.1, 33, 34/I, 33), and it is part of the communicative intention of the speaker that the hearer do so. If Derrida's claim has any determinate meaning, we will have to wait to see what it is.

The important thing about the general suggestion that expression is a species of indication is that this would amount to a thesis about "the essence of language *in general*," a topic that Derrida in the Introduction claims Husserl "*had* to postpone" (*SP*, 6/7, emphasis added). Derrida will soon suggest that this postponement is taking place right before our very eyes in this Husserlian text (*SP*, 23/23). Thus although the suggestion is, as Derrida immediately notes, rejected by Husserl, and although it is introduced by a claim that Husserl rejects (a claim that Derrida will soon argue directly and not just by insinuation), the reader can begin to recognize a Derridean thesis—*All expression is indication*—that would imply that the "radical distinction" between expression and indication cannot be maintained, with, presumably, all of the consequences we have just seen Derrida suggest.

But, of course, Husserl would not concede any of this: he is committed to showing that expression is *not* a species of indication. His strategy is to show that although expression is normally bound up with indication, it can appear without such interweaving.[7] This, Derrida asserts, requires a form of expression that is not communicative at all, for the communicative use of words is entangled, intertwined, contaminated (Derrida strings these three words together once more) with indication. Derrida gives two reasons for this entanglement. These reasons are worth noting, as one might have thought that Husserl was committed to only one of them. In the first place, a communicative utterance, as we have seen, indicates to the hearer that the speaker is having certain experiences, is acting with a certain intent, and these experiences "cannot fall in the intuition" of the auditor (*LI* II.1, 34/I, 278). But this is not all, for, second, in communication "the ideal content of the meaning and spirituality of expression are here united to sensibility" (*SP*, 22/22). This latter claim will play a certain role in Derrida's argument. For the moment we can ask whether it is really the case for Husserl that the sensible sign *indicates* its meaning. Derrida here suggests only that sensibility necessarily brings in indication, by which he presumably means not the mere possibility of indication but a functioning indicative relation. This issue will concern us shortly.

Husserl turns to "solitary mental life," where, he thinks, expressions exercise their function of meaning without indicating anything. Derrida finds this move paradoxical: the "ex-pressiveness" of meaning (*ex-* out plus *pressare* to press) can be isolated only "when the relation to a certain *outside* is suspended" (*SP*, 22/22). This outside is the outside of the other, with whom the speaking subject can communicate. In the soliloquy of solitary mental life I am not turned to the other, and in this sense the other might be said to be "suspended." This might indeed seem paradoxical: the expressive essence of language, the medium of communication *par excellence*, can be thematized in its purity only when its communicative function, its relation to an other, is suspended.

But it quickly becomes apparent that Derrida is putting a great deal more weight on the word "suspended" than this: "What we just called a paradox is in fact only the phenomenological project in its essence," the project of accounting for the existential sense of every possible kind of being, "the *obj*ectivity of the *obj*ect (*Gegenstand*) and the *pres*ence of the *pres*ent (*Gegenwart*)" (*SP*, 23/22), in terms of the constituting function of consciousness. Consciousness is the absolute, because it is self-constituting (this is a central theme of Husserl's *Lectures on the Phenomenology of Internal Time-Consciousness*, to which Derrida will devote several chapters). Thus the objective sense of objects is to be described "from the standpoint of 'interiority,' or rather from a self-proximity, an *ownness* (*Eigenheit*)" (*SP*, 23/22), an interiority that is intentional through and through and that can be revealed in its functional purity only in the transcendental reduction.

Derrida touches here on a number of the fundamental themes of transcendental phenomenology, such as the tracing of noematic sense back to its noetic constitution and the self-constitution of consciousness. But one theme stands out, namely, the reference to ownness. The inclusion of the German term *Eigenheit* makes the reference to the "reduction to the sphere of ownness" in the Fifth Cartesian Meditation unmistakable (see *Hua* I, §44). This reduction has been criticized repeatedly, often by authors whose Husserlian sympathies are beyond question.[8] Thus the claim that it constitutes "the phenomenological project in its essence" will require demonstration.

Before moving on, Derrida pauses to comment on the stage his reading of Husserl has reached. Husserl's position as it has developed can be given, he thinks, two readings. "*On the one hand*, Husserl seems to repress, with dogmatic haste, a question concerning the *structure of the sign in general*" (*SP*, 23/23). The very distinction between two different kinds of signs presupposes at least a precomprehension of the essence of the sign in general. The charge of repression accords with, and should be read in conjunction with, several of Derrida's earlier statements—especially the reference to the meditation on the essence of language in general that Husserl *had* to postpone (*SP*, 6/7). By now we can expect to find Derrida arguing that the question is repressed because pursuit of it would inevitably lead to the very entanglement and contamination that Husserl must at all costs avoid.

Now, in one sense Husserl not only does not avoid this question, but answers it in the second sentence of §1 of the First Investigation. Derrida quotes: "*Every* sign is a sign for something (*für etwas*), but not every sign has a 'meaning,' a 'sense' that the sign 'expresses' " (*LI* II.1, 23/I, 269; *SP*, 24/23, emphases added). But Derrida is not satisfied, for "this would suppose we implicitly knew what 'being-for' means." He proceeds to give a series of what he presents as synonyms or explications of this "being for": "being-in-the-place-of" and "substitution or reference" (*SP*, 24/23). The expressive sign "points to"

(*Hinzeigen*) its meaning and "indicates" (*Anzeigen*) the speaker's psychic experiences (*LI* II.1, 35–35/I, 279). There must be a sense of "*Zeigen* in general, which points to the invisible and may then be modified into *Hinzeigen* or *Anzeigen*" (*SP*, 24/23). Thus a sign—*any* sign—is a sign for something, stands in the place of that thing, substitutes for it, refers to it, points to that which is invisible or absent.

The Unity of the Sign in General

Derrida now states the thesis whose way he has been preparing: "One can already guess—perhaps we shall verify it further on—that this '*Zeigen*' is the place where the root and necessity of all 'interweaving' of indication and expression is manifested" (*SP*, 24–25/23–24). Given our reading thus far, this "one can guess" is misplaced. What we might well guess is that Derrida would *suggest* this, both in the sense of suggesting the thesis and in the sense of suggesting that we, his readers, can guess (the validity of) the thesis. But has he given us reason to guess any more than this? The insinuation that we should be guessing what he suggests that we guess is a powerful impetus to find ourselves in fact guessing it, but the urge can be resisted.

All of this, however, is only one possible reading of Husserl's position (though Derrida will clearly make use of it). There is an alternative: "May we not interpret this *on the other hand* as critical vigilance?" (*SP*, 25/24). The first reading moved within a presupposition—namely, that there must be some essential unity of the sign in general—and we could interpret Husserl as refusing to make that assumption. "Is this not precisely to refuse or deny precomprehension as the apparent starting point because it would be a prejudice or presumption?" (*SP*, 24/23). Stated in this generality, such a move would amount to a challenge to the hermeneutic circle. Note that this reading does not so much deny the fact of precomprehension (Heidegger's *Vorverständnis*) as challenge its right. Might it not turn out that what seemed to be a precomprehension of a unity is in fact a mere verbal ambiguity? And indeed, Husserl speaks of "two concepts connected with the word 'sign' " (*LI* II.1, 24/I, 269; *SP*, 25/24).

The presumption of unity has deeper philosophical roots as well. If we ask "*What* is the sign in general?" we move in the space of Greek ontology, the space of Western metaphysics in general. The Socratic question "What is it?" assumes that there is a unitary answer to the question, an answer that will turn our confused opinions, the unclarity of our prereflective precomprehension, into a knowledge that will enable us to recognize things for what they really are.[9] In giving such an answer, we would regiment our often ambiguous words to the truth of the things themselves, language to the genuine "what it is" of things, what we say to the insight of thought, and, in a gesture familiar from the *Phaedrus*, writing to speech. If there is a truth *about* the sign in general, and if our linguistic usage is to be regimented to this truth, this truth itself cannot be a function of, be constituted by, signs.

Derrida is here setting up a conditional that will be crucial for his overall argument:

If there is a unitary truth about the sign in general, then the sign is not the condition of truth,

in which case

If the sign is the very medium of truth, then there is no truth about the sign in general.

This argument is constructed in terms of a logic or grammar of the original and the derivative, that which precedes and that which is subsequent. Thus either truth precedes the sign, in which case the sign merely signifies the truth, or "the sign precedes what we call truth or essence," in which case we cannot speak about "the truth or essence of the sign" (*SP*, 26/24). Whichever way we go, we are assuming the validity of a dichotomy; the only question is the proper ordering relation within the dichotomy. The argument faces the reader with an either/or, and the strategy will be to confront metaphysics with a dilemma, one that can be resolved only by admitting the untruth of metaphysics itself. One has to wonder, however, whether the dilemma is seamless: is there any prospect of taking the dilemma by the horns, of denying the exhaustiveness of the alternatives? Must we really subject sign to truth or truth to sign? Is it possible to assert that thought moves in the medium of language without assuming that language is a distorting medium, constituting and fracturing the possibility of truth at one and the same moment? Is it possible to assert that language is the medium of cognition and thus of the very possibility of truth without having to admit that there is no truth about language? These questions will have to be kept in mind as we follow the movement of Derrida's reading.

For the moment, Derrida gives what he takes to be a possibly Husserlian formulation of the reading under consideration. How and why might Husserl say that there is no truth or essence of the sign? Perhaps, suggests Derrida, by playing off the fact that to be a sign is a functional predicate, the sign being as such the result of "an intentional movement," against the category of "a thing in general (*Sache*)," of a "being" with its own being (*SP*, 26/25). Perhaps the question "What is it?" cannot be asked in this case; perhaps, indeed, as Derrida elsewhere argues, it is the sign that *produces* the question "What is . . . ?" and thus the very possibility of an answer (see *OG*, 31/18).[10]

Now, there is something deliberately odd about this suggestion. In light of Husserl's famous slogan in the *Logical Investigations*—"We want to go back to the 'things themselves' [*die 'Sachen selbst'*]" (*LI* II.1, 6/I, 252)—the reading under consideration would amount to a recognition that there is "something" that we cannot go back to, that we cannot thematize as "it itself," that cannot be brought to an original givenness. This something, the sign, would be the constitutive condition of original givenness (which has sense only as the source of an answer to the "What is it?" question) and would, for that very reason, escape the givenness it makes possible. But all of this moves counter to the Husserlian strategy itself. If the sign is ruled by the structure of an intentional movement that itself owes nothing to the sign, then the suggested conclusion does not follow: the instrumentality of signs will be a matter (*Sache*) for phenomenological investigation.

Indeed, perhaps we need to look more carefully at the phrase "if one considers the sign as the structure of an intentional movement." For Husserl, the sign-function has its source in an intentional movement, in the apprehension of the sign that animates it, gives it meaning. Derrida's suggestion is different: the sign would *be* the structure of an intentional movement, would constitute it as such. What Derrida attributes to Husserl, however, is not this thesis, but a conditional: "May we not think—as Husserl no doubt did—that if one considers the sign as the structure of an intentional movement, it does not fall under the category of a thing in general (*Sache*), it is not a 'being' whose own being would be questioned?" (*SP*, 26/24–25). What is the source of this "no doubt"? Why should we attribute this claim to Husserl? The advantage of doing so is clear: if it can be shown that the sign is indeed the structure of intentionality, then it follows that the sign is not a matter (*Sache*) for phenomenological investigation, is not a "being" whose being can be questioned. It will instead be the source of the very question concerning being, the "What is . . . ?" question, a source that cannot fall under the question it makes possible.

Derrida finds evidence for such a reading, evidence of an attention "to what—although it has no truth in itself—conditions the movement and concept of truth" (*SP*, 26/25), in the *Logical Investigations*, the *Ideas*, and other works up to the late essay "The Origin of Geometry." In the *Investigations*, Husserl states that "theoretical research . . . terminates in such [complete] statement[s]" or expressive acts. But as we have seen, this assertion is followed immediately by a refusal to take any stand at all concerning "the connection of thought with speech" (*LI* II.1, 3/I, 250). Derrida quotes from the *Ideas*: "Logical meaning (*Bedeutung*) is an expression" (*Hua* III.1, 286/295; *SP*, 26/25). But as we saw earlier, the expressivity at issue in that text has nothing to do with signs. Finally, in "The Origin of Geometry" language does play a crucial role in making possible a science of ideal objects, a systematic science pursued by generations of researchers. But this is merely an elaboration of the pragmatic dimension of the sign already sketched out in the *Investigations* in the very sentence that precedes Husserl's refusal to take a stand on the relationship between thought and speech.

Derrida sees Husserl as caught in a dilemma. On the one hand, phenomenology returns from the world to the active life of consciousness, which "produces truth and value in general through its signs" (*SP*, 27/25). (Note again the assumption that the sign is *essential*, something Husserl refuses to assert in the *Investigations* and denies in the *Ideas*.) On the other hand, this (supposed) centrality of the sign stands in a certain tension with the motif of presence. This relationship between the sign and presence will define the field of Derrida's concern in *Speech and Phenomena*.

Now, against this entire set of interlocking suggestions, I would argue that we cannot simply wait to see whether Derrida can successfully show that expression cannot function without indication. I would argue rather that even if meaning is *always*—essentially and not merely *de facto*—interwoven with indication, their essential differences can nevertheless be thematized and analyzed. The fact that Husserl thinks that the former can sometimes appear without the latter is not decisive.

Chapter 1 of *Speech and Phenomena*, like in the Introduction, is dominated by a series of distinctions or separations. Thus we have:

expression/indication
spoken/(written)
de jure/*de facto*
essence/existence
intentional function/reality
intentional right/fact
inside/outside
own/other

And again, as in the Introduction, we find the claim that one of these distinctions—that between indication and expression—is the condition of possibility of the others. Not surprisingly, the separability of indication and expression will turn on issues of presence: the purity of expression and the purity of presence will be intimately bound up with, if not entangled with, each other.

Chapter 3
"The Reduction of Indication"

Derrida's short second chapter follows Husserl as he attempts to demonstrate that indication is not essential to expression. Indication must be "set aside, abstracted, and 'reduced' " (*SP*, 28/29). Indication involves a unity of motivation, which Husserl defines as including logical demonstration as well as indication in the strict sense. This general account employs concepts (*Sein, Bestand*) broader than those appropriate to indication in the strict sense (*Existenz, Dasein, Realität*). The latter is distinguished from logical demonstration, which concerns not reality or real existence but idealities and ideal necessities.

Only ideal contents can be linked together in logically necessary ways. Motivations and acts, even acts that grasp necessary, logical relations, are contingent, empirical, and thus belong to the realm of indication. When we ask about the "showing (*Weisen*) in general" that would underlie both the *Beweis* of logical demonstration and the *Hinweis* of indicative allusion, we find that the two are always interwoven with one another: the acts involved in logical demonstration are linked indicatively. It is this indicative realm that is subject to the various "reductions," and their possibility depends on the possibility of separating indication and expression. Indication is to expression as the psychic (which is mundane) is to the transcendental. The method of reduction is thus rooted in speech itself. However, we must add, it is so rooted only to the extent that speech gives itself out as being in command of what it says, of its meaning. But, Derrida concludes, "one could almost say that the totality of speech is caught up in an indicative web" (*SP*, 33/31).

Indication and Its "Reduction"

As we have seen, Derrida finds a "reductive" move at work in the exclusion of indication from the concerns of logic and the theory of knowledge. "Indication must be set aside, abstracted, and 'reduced' as an extrinsic and empirical phenomenon, even if it is in fact closely related to expression, empirically interwoven with expression" (*SP*, 28/27). This statement of Husserl's task requires some comment. In the first place, the word "empirical" is carefully chosen to bring in the opposition between the factual and the eidetic, and perhaps the distinction between the empirical and the transcendental as well. But neither of these oppositions is of immediate relevance in this context. It is simply not the case that, as Derrida tried to insinuate in chapter 1, on Husserl's account expression and indication are always interwoven as a matter of empirical fact (as opposed to eidetic necessity). Husserl claims rather that a specific form of indication (*Kundgabe*) plays an essential role in communication, but is not essential for the expressive function in general.

In the second place, the term "reduction" is carefully chosen to set up a series of suggestions, or more properly theses, that Derrida will begin to develop in this chapter. A great deal is at stake, for Derrida wants to argue that the exteriority or extrinsic character of indication—that is, precisely what is now being termed its "reduction"—is essential to the possibility of both the eidetic and the transcendental reductions (*SP*, 31/30). These suggestions will appear more plausible if the term "reduction" is already in play before the suggestions make their appearance. It appears three times, in three different forms, in the first paragraph, and its first two appearances are in quotation marks: Husserl's treatment of indication is " 'reductive' "; indication must be " 'reduced' "; and such a "reduction" is difficult (*SP*, 28/27). Derrida's use of quotation marks alerts the reader to the fact that the term "reduction" is being used in a special, technical sense. But is this a Husserlian sense?

There are a number of Husserlian candidates: eidetic reduction, psychological phenomenological reduction, transcendental reduction, reduction to ownness. The term "reduce" as Derrida uses it here seems to involve the eidetic reduction: something involved in all real examples of expression turns out, when we freely vary the phenomenon of expression through a series of purely imaginary examples, to be inessential. The transcendental reduction seems at first glance less relevant, as the point is not to "bracket" the functioning of indication, to suspend *our* belief (qua phenomenologists) in either the indicating sign or the indicated object or state of affairs. Such a "reduction" would be in order if we wanted to study the constitution of indication, to give a transcendental analysis of indication and its role in the constitution of the world we experience. But aside from the fact that the first thematic formulation of the epochē came some seven years after the publication of the *Logical Investigations*, indication as such is not Husserl's real concern in the First Investigation.

Finally, the term is given some explication by being presented as part of a series: "set aside, abstracted, and 'reduced.' " The "and" alerts the reader to the fact that these are not alternative expressions for the same thing, but rather a series of operations all of which must be performed. Things can be set aside as not being the topic under discussion, or as not being relevant to the topic. What is set aside may indeed be essentially related to the topic: we can always discuss one essential aspect (in Husserl's technical terminology, one *moment*) of a phenomenon while "setting aside" other essential aspects. This does not mean that we can actually separate the two, that one can exist independently of the other; but they can be thematized independently of one another. (It goes without saying that such a discussion would at some point need to broaden its scope and inquire into the interrelations between the two aspects of the larger whole.) To abstract can also mean to put something out of thematic consideration, to view it as not being of immediate relevance.

Derrida will attempt to show that the reduction—that is, the separation or distinction in principle between indication and expression—fails (and along with it the possibility of the "other" reductions), and this for several reasons. He will argue that Husserl fails in his attempt to show that expression can function in the absence of the specific indicative function of *Kundgabe*. And he will go on to argue that "indicative adherences [*adhérences*], sometimes of other kinds, continually reappear further on, and getting rid of them will be an infinite task" (*SP*, 28/27, translation altered). This sets up the general thesis that will govern much of the analyses to come:

> Husserl's whole enterprise—and far beyond the *Investigations*—would be threatened if the *Verflechtung* [interweaving] which couples the indicative sign to expression were absolutely irreducible, if it were in principle inextricable and if indication were essentially internal to the movement of expression rather than being only conjoined to it, however tenaciously. (*SP*, 28/27)

Derrida here uses a term that in Husserl appears in a very specific context (expression is "interwoven" with indication in communicative speech—this is the function of *Kundgabe* discussed in §§6–7 of the First Investigation) in a much more general way, for indicative functions other than *Kundgabe*. Even if it were granted that his thesis is correct in the case of *Kundgabe*, it would not follow that it is necessarily correct in the other cases. This point is absolutely crucial: Derrida must *demonstrate* rather than simply assume that indicative relations, when present, "contaminate" the expressive function.

Indication and Motivation

Indication and Writing

For Husserl, indicative signs can be natural or artificial, the latter including, on Derrida's reading, "all the instruments of conventional designation [*tous les instruments de désignation conventionelle*]" (*SP*, 29/27). Given this analysis, Derrida claims in a footnote, Husserl could have used writing as an example of indication. Now, while the theme of writing has been one of Derrida's favorites, especially in *Of Grammatology*, the companion volume to *Speech and Phenomena* (see Part II below), one has to ask why Husserl would have to include "writing in general" under indication. That Husserl does not do so is clear: the physical expression includes not only sounds but written signs (*LI* II.1, 31/I, 276). In addition, it should be noted that Derrida's phrase "all the instruments of conventional designation" is not a fair rendition of Husserl's text. Husserl writes that "only in the case of indications deliberately and artificially brought about, does one speak of designation [*Bezeichnen*]" (*LI* II.1, 24/I, 270, translation altered).[1] Thus "designation" here refers to conventional *indication*, and not to the full range of conventional signs. It is unclear why writing in general would fall under this rubric, and if it is taken to do so, one might wonder why speech would not be just as clear a case. *Phonetic* writing, qua phonetic, might be thought to be indicative of the spoken word, but this would not satisfy Husserl's own criteria for indication: an isomorphism does not necessarily imply an indicative function.[2]

Indication and Demonstration

The following paragraphs of Derrida's chapter (*SP*, 30–32/28–30) must be read with care. They discuss passages from the final paragraph of §2 and the first sentences of §3 of the First Investigation, and it is crucial that the reader be familiar with these passages themselves. In the final paragraph of §2 Husserl analyzes indication in terms of the circumstance that cognizance of the being or obtaining of one thing provides "a noninsightful motive" (*ein nichteinsichtiges Motiv*) for the belief in or presumption of the being or obtaining of something else (*LI* II.1, 25/I, 270). Husserl then discusses cognitive motivation in general terms, determining the objective correlate of motivation as a connection between two things or states of affairs: "certain things *may* or *must* obtain [*bestehen*], *because* [*weil*] other things have been given" (*LI* II.1, 25/I, 270, translation altered). This general account of cognitive motivation covers much more than the motivation that functions in indication, for the account of indication contains a careful qualification: the motive at work in indication is not based on insight into logical relations, so the objective correlate of the experience of indication can never be that something *must* be the case in any strict sense, though indication can produce a (perhaps quite justified) conviction that something does exist or is the case.

Husserl notes the generality of this account in the first sentences of §3: "We have sketched the phenomenological situation so generally that what we have said applies as much to the 'demonstration [*Beweisen*]' of genuine inference and proof as to the 'pointing [or indicative allusion: *Hinweis*en]' of indication" (*LI* II.1, 25/I, 271, translation altered).[3]

Derrida does not follow the order of Husserl's text, preferring to begin his discussion not with the analysis of indication but with the treatment of motivation. He rightly points out that Husserl's account of motivation is very general, that the objects and states of affairs in question must be understood in the broadest possible sense and are not restricted to real things. Whereas in his initial examples of indication Husserl speaks of "existence" (*Existenz*) (canals on Mars indicate the existence of intelligent life; bones indicate the existence of prediluvian animals [*LI* II.1, 24/I, 270]), in his general determination of motivation and in his account of indication he speaks of *Sein* and *Bestand* (Derrida writes *l'être ou la consistance*, which Allison translates as "being or subsistence"), which cover both real and ideal objects, the existence of things and the obtaining of states of affairs.[4] Derrida assures us that the difference between *Sein* and *Bestand*, on the one hand, and *Dasein*, *existieren*, and *Realität* (factual existence, to exist, and reality), on the other, will turn out to be of great importance.

The word *Bestand* can have several meanings. The only suggestion made by Dorion Cairns in his *Guide for Translating Husserl* that is relevant in this context is "existence." For the verb *bestehen* he suggests "to exist, to be, to obtain," noting that *subsister* was used by Suzanne Bachelard in her French translation of *Formal and Transcendental Logic* (Cairns, 20–21). *Bestehen aus* means "to consist of, to be composed of," and *Bestand* takes on related meanings. "To subsist" is a widespread translation of *bestehen*, especially in discussions of the Austrian philosopher Alexius Meinong. In his use of the word *consistance*, Derrida presumably does not mean logical consistency. He seems rather to be working from *consister*, "to consist, to be made of." Thus *consistance* would be the makeup of a thing or fact.

Up to this point Derrida's discussion presents few real problems, but now things take a curious turn. As we have seen, he begins not with the analysis of indication, but with what he calls the "definition"[5] of motivation, noting, as does Husserl, its very general character. But when he then moves on to Husserl's analysis of indication, which in Husserl's text precedes the account of motivation, he reads that analysis in terms of the account of motivation, and therefore assumes that the analysis of indication has the same generality as the account of motivation. The move is quite explicit. Immediately following his discussion of motivation Derrida writes:

> Husserl *thus* [emphasis added] defines the essential character which
> most generally incorporates all of the indicative functions:

> In these we discover as a common circumstance the fact that certain objects or states of affairs *of whose obtaining* [*consistance*] (*Bestand*) *someone has actual knowledge* indicate (*anzeigen*) to him *the reality of certain other objects or states of affairs*, in the sense that *his belief in the being* (*Sein*) *of the one is experienced as a motive* (though a noninsightful motive) *for the conviction or presumption of the being of the other*.

> But this essential character is still so general that it covers the whole field of indication and even more. Or rather, since it is certainly an *Anzeigen* that is described here, let us say that this common character goes beyond indication *in the strict sense*. (*SP*, 29–30/28–29, quoting *LI* II.1, 25/I, 270; translation of Husserl altered)

To read the generality of the account of motivation into the definition of indication is to distort Husserl's text, as the definition of indication refers not to motivation in general but to noninsightful motivation, and the insight in question is clearly insight into *logical* connections. Rather than relating Husserl's remark (in the first sentence of §3) about the "generality" of his sketch of the phenomenological situation to the immediately preceding sentences (at the end of §2) on the "because" of motivation, which does indeed cover more than indication, Derrida relates that remark to the definition of indication itself.

Once this is done, we have a definition of a genus, which we might call *indication in general*, that would cover as its species *indication in the strict sense* (that is, indication in Husserl's sense) along with something else. Whatever this something else might be, on this reading it will be a form of indication. And it is immediately clear what this something else is: it is the demonstration (*Beweis*) of logical proof, which Husserl distinguishes from the pointing or indicative allusion (*Hinweis*) of indication. Both demonstration and indicative allusion function by means of a "because" of motivation, but only demonstration involves insight into the necessity of the connection. On Derrida's reading, such demonstration would be a species of indication in general. Husserl, of course, would recognize what Derrida calls "general motivation," but not the indication in general that would be the genus of indication in the strict sense.

On Derrida's reading, it is this distinction between indication in general and indication in the strict sense that is to explain the importance of distinguishing between *Sein* and *Bestand*, on the one hand, and *Existenz*, *Dasein*, and *Realität*, on the other. The suggestion seems to be that indication in general or "general motivation" concerns the broad range covered by *Sein* and *Bestand*, whereas indication in the strict sense concerns *Existenz*, *Dasein*, and *Realität*, which is to say, real as opposed to ideal objects. We would thus have the following classifications:

General motivation
indication in general:
  Sein, Bestand

(1) insightful motivation
demonstration (*Beweis*):
  ideal necessities
  ideal objects

(2) noninsightful motivation
indication in the strict sense, indicative allusion (*Hinweis*):
  empirical and contingent relations
  empirical existents, individuals
  Existenz, Dasein, Realität

This set of classifications is immediately put to work in the next paragraph of Derrida's chapter. Alan White has pointed out a curious error in this paragraph (White, 56–57):[6] whereas for Husserl, in logical proof it is the ideal contents, the propositions, that are linked by logical relations, by ideal necessities, Derrida attributes to Husserl the claim that in a proof, "the 'because' links together the evident and ideal necessities which are permanent and which persist beyond every empirical *hic et nunc*" (*SP*, 30/29). In other words, according to Derrida it is the propositions linked in a proof, the premises themselves, not the links between the propositions or the syllogism as a whole, that are ideal necessities. It remains to be seen whether this is a momentary carelessness or points to a systematic misreading.

This misreading is followed by a second. After quoting Husserl's description of the ideal rule that governs logical proof, Derrida writes: "Motivations linking together lived experiences, as well as *acts* which grasp necessary and evident idealities, ideal objectivities, may belong to the contingent and empirical order of 'nonevident' indication; but the relations which unite the *contents* of ideal objects in evident demonstration are not cases of indication" (*SP*, 30/29, translation altered). This sentence is quite curious. For Husserl, what is linked by the "because" that is the objective correlate of cognitive motivation is either something functioning as an indication and what it indicates, or something functioning as a premise and what it implies. In neither case is it the acts that grasp these relations. There is, as Husserl notes, a motivational relation between the acts, but this does not mean that one act indicates or implies the other. The distinction between the real and the ideal, or between the act and its content, is not parallel to the distinction between indicative allusion and proof. The lived experiences are properly described as insightful or noninsightful, and it makes no sense to say that an act of insightful—that is, logically evidential—thinking should "belong to the contingent and empirical order of 'nonevident' indication."

At this point we begin to see a kind of snowball effect at work in chapter 2. Derrida's misreading of Husserl's analyses of indication and motivation leads him, against Husserl's text, to claim that Husserl defines a sense of indication more general than that of "indication in the strict sense." He then reads Husserl's use of terms such as *Sein* and *Bestand* in terms of this distinction, claiming that indication in the strict sense is appropriately explicated in terms of *Existenz*, *Dasein*, and *Realität*. It follows that there can be no indication at work when we are dealing with ideal objects, as there is a strict correlation between *Beweis* and ideal objects, on the one hand, and *Hinweis* and empirical existents, on the other. But nothing in Husserl's text supports such a claim. Indeed, it is clear that what at one stage of the development of mathematics might have been an *indicative* relation between, for example, an algebraic equation's being of an uneven order and its having at least one real root (see *LI* II.1, 27/I, 272) might at a later stage be proven to be a necessary relation. As Aron Gurwitsch has pointed out, all that one can say is that indication presupposes that the indicating and the indicated "both pertain to the same plane":

A fact conceived as relevant to the natural environment can only serve as sign [in the sense of indication] for events pertaining to the same order and, more specifically, a sound one perceives as emitted by a living and especially a human being can only signal vital or psychic events. Analogously, a mathematical fact can only announce other mathematical facts, etc. (Gurwitsch 1985, 91)

It thus begins to appear that Derrida's misreadings are not isolated careless errors. We have already noted how Derrida's interpretation of both the tradition of metaphysics in general and phenomenology in particular is dominated by a series of distinctions or separations that are themselves dominated by the basic distinction between presence and absence. Derrida sees the entire framework of phenomenology as governed and made possible by the separation between expression and indication. In the present passage, he takes the distinction between proof and indicative allusion to be the key to a series of other distinctions, in particular the distinction between the necessary and the contingent and that between the ideal and the real. Thus wherever ideality is in question, we should find necessity and proof, not contingency and indication. This set of dichotomies dominates the paragraph in question (*SP*, 30–31/29), and to it Derrida adds another: the distinction between the ideal content of an act and the act of cognition itself. The "because" of proof links together idealities; the rule governing this link exhibits the "supraempirical generality" of proof (*LI* II.1, 26/I, 271) as opposed to indication. If we follow out the logic of this system of distinctions, the "because" of indication would then have to link together realities, and the rule governing that link would have to be contingent and empirical. But the acts that grasp ideal necessities are real, not ideal, and thus "belong to the contingent and empirical order of 'nonevident' indication" (SP, 30/29). This sets up a simple argument: Proof concerns ideal contents and necessities. Proving is a matter of acts of thought that are real, not ideal, and that thus belong to the order of non-evident indication. Therefore, proof always involves indication.

On Derrida's reading the entire system of distinctions at work here is governed by the distinction between expression and indication. He has already strongly suggested that expression is always contaminated by indication. This is merely confirmed by the present suggestion that indication might "intervene in a demonstration . . . on the side of psychic motivations, acts, beliefs, etc." (SP, 31/29)

As Derrida notes, for Husserl demonstration is not a kind of indication. But is it indication in general or indication in the strict sense that is in question in the Derridean reading of these distinctions? This is the issue Derrida approaches when, against the background of the distinction between *Hinweis* and *Beweis*, he poses the question as to the unitary meaning that makes that distinction possible. What is "showing [*monstration*] (*Weisen*) in general" (SP, 31/29), the genus of the species distinguished by the specific differences of insight and lack of insight? The genus would presumably be found in the general phenomenon of motivation and in the "because" that is its objective correlate (*LI* II.1, 25/I, 270–71, translating *weil* as "because"). But given Derrida's interpretation of Husserl's definition of indication in terms of an indication more general than "indication in the strict sense," we can expect to find more at work.

The question concerning "showing (*Weisen*) in general" is analogous to the one posed in chapter 1 concerning the sign and its *Zeigen* (SP, 24/23), and it quickly becomes apparent that for Derrida these questions are essentially connected. He immediately relates the present question to the problem of "interweaving," thus reactivating his suggestion that indication might turn out to "contaminate" the purity of expression: "Indeed, we know now that for the order of signification in general, the whole of psychic experience, with regard to its *acts*, even when they intend idealities and objective necessities, contains only indicative concatenations. The indicative sign falls outside the content of absolutely ideal objectivity, that is, outside truth" (SP, 31/29–30, translation altered). This confirms what we have begun to see as the broader contour of Derrida's strategy: if the acts involved in signification in general contain only indicative concatenations, then logical proof will be "contaminated" by indication. And indication, whose function is not a matter of insight, falls outside the truth.

This requires comment. In the first place, what Derrida calls "the problem of 'interweaving' " is the result of his own imposition of a semantic slide from "interwoven" through "entangled" to "contaminated," along with his repeated refusal to pay consistent attention to Husserl's limitation of such interweaving to *communicative* speech, as well as of the suggestion that expression might be a species of indication. This needs to be recalled every time Derrida makes use of this "problem" as a by now well-established result, as it is clear that he is building up the rhetorical framework that will make his conclusion appear plausible. Our task here is to keep that apparent plausibility visible as a possible problem.

The Overarching Universal of Deconstruction

Let us assume for the moment that the pointing of *Hinweis* as noninsightful showing does necessarily contaminate the proof of insightful demonstration. In this case we would have an interesting logical state of affairs, one that offers us our first real opportunity to stand back and get a preliminary fix on where Derrida's analysis seems to be heading. Instead of the genus/species relation

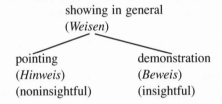

showing in general
(*Weisen*)

pointing   demonstration
(*Hinweis*)   (*Beweis*)
(noninsightful)   (insightful)

we would have a situation in which the traditional, metaphysical distinction between insight and lack of insight is a distinction within (Derrida would say "inscribed within") a more original sense of lack of insight.

In *Spurs: Nietzsche's Styles*, Derrida describes deconstruction as a general strategy of focusing on conceptual oppositions. Within these oppositions (truth/falsity, being/nonbeing, presence/absence; in the present case expression/indication, proof/indicative allusion, and so on), deconstruction attends to the concepts regarded as secondary in traditional, metaphysical thought. Deconstruction proceeds first by a *reversal* of the opposition, giving priority to the supposedly secondary term. But this is not sufficient: the opposition is not to be simply reversed; "the *Umdrehung* must be a transformation of the hierarchical structure itself" (Derrida 1979, 81). Thus, reversal is followed by a second phase of "reinscription, displacement, or reconstruction" (Gasché, 171). "In this second phase the hitherto repressed traits of concepts, or traits held in reserve, are restored to their generality, to their power of generalization, and to their generative force" (Gasché, 172). The point is not, in other words, to take a traditional hierarchy and simply reverse it, giving priority to the other term. That is the initial gesture. In the opposition expression/indication, Husserl finds the possibility of insight only in the former. Derrida executes a certain reversal: expression is contaminated by indication, is a specific form of indication. Indication must therefore be the principle that allows us to account for expression. As pointing out is now to be the principle of expression *and* indication, of rational connection *and* mere association, however, two things follow immediately: (1) the "pointing out" that is now principle cannot be simply identical with the pointing out that moves within association as opposed to the insight of logical thinking, and (2) this "pointing out" cannot serve as a rational principle, cannot lead to a rational accounting of its own possibility and truth. The very possibility of such an account has itself been deconstructed.

This result amounts to a reversal of the most fundamental logical form in Hegel's speculative logic. Josef König has called this form the "embracing or overarching universal" (*das übergreifende Allgemeine* (König, 33–34).[7] A universal, as distinguished from what we would ordinarily call a concept, is "a self-subsuming, self-explanatory principle," and it can be this only by exhibiting a reflexivity such that it refers "to itself by virtue of properties that it bestows on itself in virtue of bestowing some properties on others" (Pinkard, 77–78). Thus, "the universal as the conception [*Begriff*] is itself and its opposite, and this again is the universal itself as its posited determinateness; it embraces its opposite and in it is in union with itself. Thus it is the totality and principle of its diversity, which is determined wholly and solely by the universal itself" (Hegel, *Logic*, 281/606). This is the very structure of a self-grounding, systematic whole. It is also the structure of subjectivity itself: the thinking self constitutes itself as having thoughts (the Kantian "I think" that accompanies all my representations, the analytic unity of apperception) only by virtue of constituting the object of thought as having certain properties (the synthetic unity of apperception). For Hegel, this structure is transparent to thought and is thus the ideal case of explanation (cf. Pinkard, 77–80).

Now, the result Derrida is suggesting can be given a Hegelian formulation (though this formulation would violate the very center of the Hegelian system) in the following way: proof$_t$ and pointing out$_t$ (in the sense of the *t*raditional distinction) are both species of pointing out. In other words, pointing out would be the genus of itself and its other, the genus of both insightful and noninsightful "showing" in the traditional sense. The insightful would be a species of the noninsightful and would thus never escape it. Logical purity would be a chimera.

The background for Derrida's move can be found in Heidegger, for example in his claim that "truth, in its essence, is un-truth" (Heidegger 1950, 43/54). Heidegger is careful to point out that

> the proposition 'the essence of truth is un-truth' is not, however,
> intended to state that truth is at bottom falsehood. Nor does it mean that
> truth is never itself but, viewed dialectically, is also its opposite. Truth
> occurs precisely as itself in that the concealing denial, as refusal,
> provides the steady provenance of all lighting, and yet, as dissembling,
> metes out to all lighting the indefeasible severity of error. (Heidegger
> 1950, 43/55)

This structure cannot be as appropriately described as a deconstructed overarching universal, nor can all of Derrida's similar results.)[8]

Now, this situation has its peculiarities. Above all, Derrida must *use* the traditional distinction in order to arrive at his result: all of the traditional tools of analysis and demonstration will be used in taking apart Husserl's attempt to establish a distinction between indication and expression. Husserl's attempt will be measured against the very standards of demonstration itself, as traditionally understood. The failure of this attempt will not itself constitute a demonstration of Derrida's own thesis; it will at most *point to* that thesis. The Derridean thesis itself asserts that there can be no insight in the traditional sense into the truth of any thesis. Husserl's failure will at most *point to* the "truth" of Derrida's thesis. The word "truth" has to be used in scare quotes here, as the traditional, metaphysical concept of truth has now been displaced into logical quicksand by the displacement of the distinction between insight and lack of insight. Derrida would (or could) follow Heidegger by writing the traditional term *sous rature*, "under erasure" (cf. *OG*, 31/19; Spivak, xivf.): t̶r̶u̶t̶h̶. We cannot do without the term "truth," any more than we can do without the term "demonstration." But these terms have lost their metaphysical security. "D̶e̶m̶o̶n̶s̶t̶r̶a̶t̶i̶o̶n̶" (B̶e̶w̶e̶i̶s̶) still means "demonstration," but it no longer carries all of the connotations of "demonstration$_t$," the traditional, metaphysical concept of demonstration defined by its opposition to mere "pointing to" (*Hinweis*). The crossing-out of "d̶e̶m̶o̶n̶s̶t̶r̶a̶t̶i̶o̶n̶" points to (but does not demonstrate) the trace of pointing-to that contaminates all proof.

Derrida often insists that what he sometimes calls "infrastructures" — for example, *différance*, *archē*-trace, supplement, iterability, re-mark, *pharmakon*, hymen — are not really or simply concepts at all (see Derrida 1981a, 9). They can be compared to what Hegel would call *Begriffe* or conceptions. Terry Pinkard explains the difference between concepts and conceptions as follows: "A concept is nonexplanatory and is expressed by a term. A conception is explanatory and is expressed by a proposition; conceptions, however, express beliefs within a system of beliefs" (Pinkard, 13). The crucial thing to keep in mind here is that the *sous rature* should be the result of a demonstration that meets all of the traditional requirements even as it shows that they cannot be maintained: it is by the constant endeavor to provide rigorous interpretation and argument that one "shows" that such argument can at most "point to" something. Thus far, however, *Speech and Phenomena* has yet to provide a single rigorous reading or argument.

It now becomes clear why Derrida was at pains to introduce the word "reduction" into his account of Husserl's treatment of indication, and why a "contamination" of expression by indication would threaten the very enterprise of transcendental phenomenology (*SP*, 28/27): "Having its 'origin' in the phenomena of association, and always connecting empirical existents in the world, indicative signification in language will cover everything that falls subject to the 'reduc-

tions': factuality, worldly existence, essential nonnecessity, nonevidence, etc.''
(*SP*, 31–32/30). We will have occasion to investigate this claim in some detail.

Chapter 4
"Wanting-to-Say as Soliloquy"

In chapter 3 of *Speech and Phenomena*, Derrida grants Husserl the claimed separation of expression and indication in order to follow what Husserl is able to do on this basis. What does it mean to call expressions meaningful signs, *bedeutsame Zeichen*, signs that "want to say" (*veulent-dire*) something? Derrida spells this out in two major steps. The first (A) is dominated by the claim that meaning (*Bedeutung*) is a function of oral discourse. The second (B) develops the further claim that it is not in oral discourse in general, but in the interior monologue of soliloquy, that purity of expression can be found.

(A) On Derrida's reading, it is oral discourse that transforms the sign into an expression that means or "wants to say" something. What then is involved in calling a sign an "expression" that "wants to say"? Derrida's answer has three moments: (1) ex-pression is *exteriorization*; (2) expression is *voluntary* exteriorization; and (3) the interpretation of *meaning* occurs properly only within oral discourse as a wanting-to-say.

These determinations repeat the exclusion of indication on a deeper level, for now Husserl begins to exclude the physical side of the sign, and not just a specific function of that side, from the essence of expression. Not just the communicative function, but rather the physical side itself is the involuntary that would contaminate the purity of the voluntary wanting-to-say. The ideal meaning whose ideal laws are studied by logic is rooted in the wanting-to-say of lived experience, in expression as opposed to indication, in the voluntary with its self-presence as opposed to the involuntary, in the soul as opposed to the body, in the pure spiritual intention as opposed to the physical sign, in the explicit as opposed to the implicit, in presence as opposed to absence.

(B) All of this shows that it is not merely oral discourse that is the true medium of pure expressivity. Not only the physical side of expression, but everything that would be a moment of non-self-presence in the living present of consciousness must be excluded: worldly existence, the natural or empirical, sensibility, association, and so on, as well as the other subject, who falls outside my sphere of ownness. In all of these exclusions, what is at issue is presence. Wherever something that is less than fully present plays a role, we find indication at work, whereas in pure expression the content, the meaning, is present to inner intuition. Here we find the final *inside*: meaning is present to the self in a present not yet contaminated by world, space, or nature or by the relation to the other. Thus the isolation of pure expression requires a turn to the way expressions function in "solitary life," in interior monologue. Here there is no physical sign, no communication with oneself. Interior monologue moves in a completely irreal medium, with no place left for an indicative function. Ultimately, this would mean that there is no place for genuine signs in soliloquy, for Husserl, in a telling slip, begins to admit that indication is definitive of signs as such. Derrida concludes that the distinction between expression and indication begins to break down.

Expression and Oral Discourse

As we have seen, Derrida begins by reaffirming his claim that expression is attached to the living voice in a privileged manner: "*Bedeutung* [meaning] doubtless comes to the sign and transforms it into expression only by means of speech, oral discourse" (*SP*, 34/32, translation altered). Why should this be the case? Why "doubtless," and why "only"? As we have seen, Derrida has prepared the way for this statement by his claims that it is "living speech, the spirituality of the breath as *phōnē*" that best seems to preserve ideality (*SP*, 9/10), that there is "an essential tie between *logos* and *phōnē*" such that "consciousness owes its privileged status . . . to the possibility of a living vocal medium [*la vive voix*]" (*SP*, 14/15), that Husserl "will radicalize the necessary privilege of the *phōnē*" (*SP*, 15/16), and that "the expressiveness of expression . . . has an irreducible tie to the possibility of spoken language" (*SP*, 18/18). The first of these claims is rather carefully phrased, though even there we have noted the lack of a serious attempt at justification; but the rest amount to assertions for which no justification is offered. Here again in chapter 3, the "doubtless" is not immediately supported by any argument. (The quotation from Husserl that immediately follows adds nothing.) Derrida will in fact attempt to provide a justification in the pages to come.

Why speak of signs that "want to say," and why are they called "expressions"? Derrida gives three answers.

(1) "Ex-pression is exteriorization. It imparts to a certain outside a sense which is first located in a certain inside" (*SP*, 34/32, translation altered). This is already clear from the root meaning of the term "expression," which comes from the Latin *ex-* (out) plus *pressare* (to press). Derrida will follow Husserl's attempt to come up with a clear isolation of the "inside" in question. What is this inside?

In the first instance, the inside/outside is that of *bedeuten/Bedeutung*, to mean and the meaning meant. But in what sense do we have "a sense which is first located in a certain inside"? "The *bedeuten* intends an outside which is that of an ideal ob-ject" (*SP*, 34/32). (It is noteworthy that here Derrida uses the German term and not his suggested translation. Why not "The wanting-to-say intends an outside which is that of an ideal ob-ject'? or "The wanting-to-say intends an outside which is that which it wants to say"?) Thus it is the act of meaning, the meaning-intention, the wanting-to-say, that is the most intimate inside, and it is thinkable only with reference to what it wants to say, which Derrida interprets as an ideal ob-ject. This inside/outside must constitute a whole that can account for meaning and the purity of expression.

If we look at Husserl's account of the act of meaning, we find that the act of meaning intends its object, which is not the same as its ideal meaning: "An expression only refers to an objective correlate *because* it means something [*bedeutet*], it can be rightly said to signify or name the object *through* its meaning [*Bedeutung*]," and "the object never coincides with the meaning" (*LI* II.1, 49/I, 287, 289). As Derrida recognizes, ideal meaning is not a real part of the meaning-intention; it does not constitute an "inside" in the sense of real immanence. A reading that sought to remain within the account of the ideality of meaning of the *Investigations* might say that the ideal meaning, as the species of a multitude of possible acts of thinking the same thing, is an ex-pression of the intentional function of the acts. When, in the *Ideas*, this account is abandoned in favor of the noematic theory, the "inside" of sense would have to be redefined in terms of what Husserl will later call the "transcendental immanence" of the noematic. But Derrida takes it one step further in this context: the "inside" is the inside of "solitary mental life."[1]

This leads to a second "going-forth" of sense beyond itself, in which the preexpressive sense, which is "inside" in the first sense, is ex-pressed in logical meaning. Derrida here appeals to §124 of the *Ideas*, and we have already discussed his misinterpretation of that text. It should be recalled that Derrida insists that meaning "is always a linguistic sense" (*SP*, 18/18), an assertion that fits neither the position of the *Logical Investigations* nor that of the *Ideas*. For the Husserl of the *Ideas*, the preexpressive sense is "expressed" by logical meaning, which need not itself involve linguistic expressions. This would then give rise to a third form of ex-pression: the meaning is given linguistic expression by signs.

Husserl calls the expression found in logical meaning "unproductive": it is the conceptual or predicative articulation or, as Gurwitsch puts it, the thematization of that which is given prepredicatively (cf. Evans 1984, 108–11). But as Derrida notes, Husserl is clearly uneasy with the term "unproductive": "The stratum of expression is . . . not productive. Or, if you will: its productivity, its noematic achievement, exhausts itself in expressing and in the form of the conceptual that this brings in." This is a true productivity, a *geistige Formung*; it is that which makes critical thought and science possible (*Hua* III.1, 287–88/ 296–97, translation altered). As Gurwitsch realized, this account requires a theory of conceptualization neither Husserl nor Gurwitsch developed.

For the moment, two points should be noted. First, traditional accounts of conceptualization speak of "abstracting" the concept from given particulars. But a broadly "Kantian" account would emphasize that concepts are essentially relational: a concept presupposes a conceptual framework (cf. Evans 1984, 74f.). Concepts would not so much simply "express" a preconceptual sense as bring a conceptual framework to bear on the interpretation of the preconceptual: the sphere of judgment would have a specific autonomy and productivity (cf. Evans 1984, 113). Second, if it could be shown, as Wilfrid Sellars claims in his "psychological nominalism," that "the conceptual element in all the phenomena singled out by mentalistic [that is, intentional] expressions is a matter of the use of verbal symbols" (Sellars 1974a, 261), then Husserl's separation between "logical meaning" and "word meaning" (*Wortbedeuten*) would be untenable, and we might discover a completely new form of "productivity" of expression. As Derrida notes, we shall have to return to this.

Derrida ends this discussion with a renewed appeal to the voice: expression is "the going-forth-beyond-itself of an act, then of a sense, which can remain in itself, however, only in speech, in the 'phenomenological' voice" (*SP*, 35/33). It is not just that oral discourse is the medium of expression; a "phenomenological" voice is required. This is clarified in Derrida's second point.

(2) "Expression is a voluntary exteriorization." It is the decision to exteriorize something that is present in the "inside." Such a voluntary act requires a self-transparency and self-command: "In expression the intention is absolutely explicit" (*SP*, 35/33). It cannot be limited by the empirical elements of indication—the real body of the sign and the existence of the object indicated. Such explicitness is available only in an internal voice, a voice not subject to the vicissitudes of the real sign and the indicative dimensions it brings with it.

Where does the "absolutely" come from? Derrida's term implies that we are clear about what we mean, that the self-presence of consciousness is a realm of transparency. Does Husserl suggest any such thing?

(3) Finally, Derrida draws a connection here between *bedeuten* as wanting-to-say and oral discourse (*discours oral* [*Rede*]), on the one hand, and interpretation as listening, on the other. Since what the saying means or wants to say is "left up

to whoever is speaking" (*SP*, 36/34), the meaning can be apprehended only in a listening in which the speaking is present, not in a reading in which the writer is absent. Given the emphasis in points (1) and (2) on solitary mental life and the internal voice, it is clear that true understanding will be an internal listening to oneself: meaning is present, explicit, only in the self-listening of inner speech.

Derrida claims to find here "a common fund of metaphysical implications" in Husserl's project (*SP*, 36/34). Although he does not draw explicit attention to it, the first of these metaphysical presuppositions would seem to be the privileged position of the voice. In his brief remarks on interpretation or understanding as listening and thus as the correlate of oral discourse, Derrida indicates that *discours oral* translates the German term *Rede* (*SP*, 36/34). This sets the stage for his first concrete evidence for a Husserlian privileging of the voice. He quotes from §5 of the First Investigation:

> We shall lay down, for provisional intelligibility, that all speech [*discours*] (*Rede*) and every part of speech (*Redeteil*), as also each sign that is essentially of the same sort, shall count as an expression, whether or not such speech is actually uttered [*effectivement prononcé*] (*wirklich geredet*), or addressed with communicative intent to any persons or not. (*LI* II.1, 30–31/I, 275, translation altered by David Allison)

This seems clear enough: expressions are spoken signs. They belong, or belong most originally, to speech, talk, oral discourse. But what does Husserl mean by "each sign that is essentially of the same sort"? Could that phrase indicate a broadening of the scope of expressions (recall that all of this is said for the purpose of "provisional intelligibility")? The answer has to be positive, as §6 begins with a partial inventory of what can function as the physical side of the expression: "the sensible sign, the articulate sound-complex, *the written sign on paper* etc." (*LI* II.1, 31/I, 276, emphasis added). It is thus clear that meaning, *Bedeutung*, is not restricted to oral discourse. Derrida does quote the list from §6 (*SP* 40/37), but he makes no attempt to relate it to the question of the voice. But this passage is not the only justification for the priority of oral discourse that he claims to find in Husserl: the entire appeal to soliloquy is to be such a justification, and we will have to watch it unfold.

A whole series of oppositions makes its appearance here, and each time one side has to be separated out for the sake of the purity of the other:

expression/indication
pure spiritual intention/physical sign
Geist or soul/body
will (self-presence)/involuntary
listening/(reading), visibility, spatiality

presence/absence, death
explicit/implicit.

Expression moves in the medium of the left side of these oppositions. The entire right side must be excluded as contaminating the purity of presence and expression, as being the death of the self-presence of expression. Thus involuntary facial gestures must be excluded from expression: regardless of how much they may "say" or reveal about us, they do not *want* to say anything.

Derrida is correct in stating that when Husserl writes that a sign need not be "actually uttered" (*wirklich geredet*: *effectivement prononcé*) in order to be an expression, he is claiming that the physical incarnation of the sign is not essential to the expressive function as such. But Husserl is not claiming that physical incarnation of meaning necessarily implies an indicative function or "belongs to indication" (*SP*, 36/34). He is simply noting that he is not thematizing actual utterance or communicative intent. When Derrida writes, "The effectiveness, the totality of the events of discourse, is indicative, not only because it is in the world, but also because it retains in itself something of the nature of an *involuntary* association" (*SP*, 36/34), he is getting ahead of himself, and the justification will have to come later. At this point, the most that can be asserted is that anything that is actually uttered, whether with communicative intent or not, has an indicative potential, and Derrida has not shown that Husserl's project requires the exclusion of such potential.

Does Husserl's analysis of expressive signs involve him in a "voluntaristic metaphysics" (*SP*, 37/34)? Derrida's suspicion seems to find a striking confirmation in Cairns's conversations with Husserl in the early 1930s. Cairns reports that on 28 December 1931, Husserl spoke about his project of "the carrying out of a universal voluntarism" (Cairns 1976, 61): every act of the ego is a decision, and even the background phenomena of the mind involve a "background decision." On 1 January 1932, Husserl returned to the topic, denying that such a voluntarism leads to an infinite regress. Rather, it leads back to "the necessary construction of situations wherein there is an activity, a doing, which did not presuppose previous doings." For example, in early infancy there is a "self-constituting hyletic flux" of sensations without yet the constitution of objects. Over against this flux there is "a more or less organized kinaesthetic flux which evinces correlations with the hyletic flux." These kinaesthesias involve "something volitional or quasi-volitional" (Cairns 1976, 64). These conversations with Cairns are evidence of Husserl's renewed study of the problems of time-consciousness in the 1930s. In 1933 Husserl wrote about a "universal drive-intentionality [*Triebintentionalität*] that unitarily constitutes every primal present and that *presses on* from present to present in such a way that all content is content of the fulfillment of these drives and is intended prior to its achievement" (*Hua* XV, 595).[2]

It is not clear, however, that these statements confirm Derrida's diagnosis of a voluntaristic metaphysics. Derrida has emphasized the moments of self-presence ("'in the with-oneself or before-oneself'") and of the "explicitness" of intention in the wanting-to-say of expression. Meaning is what the speaker "*wants* to say, what he *means* to say—expressly, explicitly, and consciously" (*SP*, 36/34). This emphasis stands in dramatic contrast to Husserl's claim that "primordiality is a system of drives" that is essentially corporeal, belonging to a "primitive founding stratum of egoless flowing" (*Hua* XV, 594, 598).

Derrida's emphasis on expression as a "going-forth beyond itself" of an inside to an outside suggests a very specific model of voluntary exteriorization. It suggests that something that is in the potential speaker's possession, present to consciousness in "solitary mental life," is voluntarily ex-pressed, exteriorized: first possession, then expression. But this cannot be the last word, for that very possession itself is a *bedeuten*, and thus for Derrida a wanting-to-say. On Derrida's interpretation there will clearly have to be an arena in which wanting-to-say, in expressing itself, does not pass beyond itself but is rather purely present to itself. "Sense wants to signify itself; it is expressed only in a wanting-to-say which is none other than a wanting-to-tell-itself proper to the presence of sense" (*SP*, 37/35, translation altered). Here consciousness is aware of what it wants to say only in a saying that is present to itself purely and without intermediary. The reflexivity here is that of a voluntaristic self-presence, a going-out that is a return. Sense *is* only in this ex-pression. The emphasis on the inside—inner speech and an inner hearing/understanding oneself—is becoming ever more insistent.

On Derrida's reading, Husserl must exclude from expression everything that is not a pure function of wanting-to-say. Anything that might have a life of its own and thus resist the movement of the voluntary, anything whose presence involves a transcendence that cannot be contained in a pure self-presence, threatens the purity of expression itself: "*They are literally the death of that self-presence*" (*SP*, 37/35). Derrida's entire rhetoric of the threat is, at least so far, crucially dependent on his introduction of the threat of "contamination" in chapter 1. It is worth pausing a moment to recall that this rhetoric of threat—"death" (*SP*, 8/10), "contamination" (*SP*, 21/20), "destroy the self-presence of will and spiritual animation which opens up discourse," and "literally the death of that self-presence" (*SP*, 37/35)—is Derrida's, not Husserl's. This is in marked contrast to Saussure's *Cours de la linguistique générale*, of which Derrida provides a reading in *Of Grammatology*. There Derrida can point to the striking vociferousness, the moral accent of Saussure's remarks on the role of writing: "The tone counts; it is as if, at the moment when the modern science of the logos would come into its autonomy and its scientificity, it became necessary again to attack a heresy" (*OG*, 52/34). Saussure's rabid tone, which erupts in the midst of a sober, scientific discourse, becomes the clue to Derrida's deconstructive reading of the *Cours* (see chap. 10 below). In the case of the First Investigation, it is rather the opposite: the calm, measured tone of a *logos* that seems to be taking possession of itself will, on Derrida's reading, turn out to be a desperate struggle to defend the autonomy and purity of expression against an outside that continually erupts at the very core of the inside of presence itself. The general point to be made here is that each reading has to assert and justify itself independently of the pathos of the language, be it Saussure's enraged morality, Husserl's sober self-assurance, or Derrida's insinuation of a rhetoric of threat into that claimed self-assurance.

Derrida next follows Husserl as he excludes facial expressions and bodily gestures—what we would now call "body language"—from expression. The passage that introduces Derrida's discussion should be read carefully, as it is a splendid example of a certain strategy of interpretation. Derrida has just traced the essence of expression back to the presence of a wanting-to-tell-itself, and thus to self-presence. It follows, he notes, that everything that escapes that will is excluded from *bedeuten* and expression. But when "the visible and spatial as such" (*SP*, 37/35) is excluded, does this involve the exclusion of all visibility and spatiality, or merely the exclusion of visibility and spatiality as exercising an indicative function? Derrida seems to assert the former: "What is excluded is . . . in a word, the whole of the visible and spatial as such"; but he then assures the reader that it is the latter that is intended: "As such: that is to say, insofar as they are not worked over by *Geist*, by the will" (*SP*, 37/35). And yet the reader is, I think, left wondering: "Visibility and spatiality as such could only destroy the self-presence of will and spiritual animation which opens up discourse. *They are literally the death of that self-presence*" (*SP*, 37/35). Does the visible and spatial sign as such destroy meaning? Or is it visible and spatial signs as exercising an indicative function in addition to an expressive function (and recall that Derrida has just assured us that "the whole stratum of empirical effectiveness [which is to say: actual utterance] . . . thus belongs to indication") that are the death of meaning—in which case "the death of self-presence" would be merely an overheated way of saying that the indicative function of a sign is not its expressive function? Derrida seems to assert the first claim, then transforms it into the second, and ends the paragraph with formulations that again seem to suggest the first. In fact, he will end up with a clear assertion of the first (*SP*, 86f./77f.).

Derrida's discussion of gesture and its interpretation places a strain on the translation of *bedeuten* as *vouloir-dire*. Husserl writes that facial expressions " 'mean [*bedeuten*]' something to [an observer] in so far as he interprets [*deutet*] them" (*LI* II.1, 31/I, 275). Derrida writes that "this interpretation (*Deutung*) makes *understood* a latent expression, a wanting-to-say (*bedeuten*) that was still held back" (*SP*, 38/36, translation altered). But for Husserl the "meaning" of involuntary gestures and facial expressions is a function of an interpretation, not of a wanting-to-say. Derrida artfully bridges this gap by speaking of "what was murmuring in [nonexpressive signs], in a stammering attempt" (*SP*, 38/36), indicating that in body language we have something that is neither simply a thing that indicates another thing nor deliberate communication. Husserl himself recognizes this, and in §5 he puts *bedeuten* in scare quotes precisely because his technical concept of *bedeuten* and *Bedeutung* is a narrow one that does some violence (*Zwang*) to ordinary usage, and the scare quotes indicate a move back to the broader usage. Derrida's translation resists this, as it builds willing into the very meaning of *bedeuten* in the broad sense.[3] And it is his translation, not Husserl's text, that leads him to say that one who interprets involuntary facial gestures "finds something discursive in another person's gestures" (*SP*, 39/36–37). On Husserl's account, the indicative function of facial expressions is not discursive at all. It is simply a matter of one thing functioning as a natural sign of something else.

This is more than the mere side issue it might appear to be, since it is the background for Derrida's claim that "the distinction between indication and expression cannot rightfully be made as one between a nonlinguistic and linguistic sign" (*SP*, 39/36). The statement is true enough, but not for the reasons Derrida adduces. The distinction between indication and expression is indeed not that between the nonlinguistic and the linguistic, for linguistic signs as such can exercise an indicative function—and do so in the intimating function—and this is a voluntary dimension of their use (the indicative function is not necessarily involuntary). For Husserl, the point is not that body language is a form of language in the strict (in his technical usage, "expressive") sense. The line between expression and indication sometimes passes between language and the nonlinguistic, sometimes between different functions of language itself. And Husserl never dreams of attempting "to exclude all the indicative forms from language" (*SP*, 39/36).

Derrida uses these unclarities to perform another of his genus/species reversals: "At most, then, we can distinguish with Husserl between linguistic signs 'in the strict sense' and linguistic signs in the broader sense" (*SP*, 39/36). Thus we would have

language in general

the explicit;	the nonexplicit;
linguistic signs "in	linguistic signs in
the strict sense"	the broader sense

The quotation that follows does not justify this distinction. Husserl speaks of "meanings [*Bedeutungen*] in the special sense in which verbal signs have meaning [*im prägnanten Sinne sprachlicher Zeichen*]" (*LI* II.1, 31/ I, 275). He distinguishes not between a strict and a broad sense of the *linguistic* sign, but rather between signs in the sense of indication and signs in the special sense of linguistic signs. The root of this confusion is rather simple. When one begins with ordinary usage in order to specify a technical, "restricted sense" (*LI*, II.1, 30/I, 275, translation altered), this does not mean that the broad, ordinary sense is the genus of the technical sense.

For Husserl, the cognitive dimension of language, which is the one that interests him as a logician, is a function of our cognitive endeavors: logic, "what counts for deduction" (in Frege's words), concerns what one can choose to say or assert. It does not follow that "the indicative sphere . . . circumscribes the failure of this telos . . . [and] represents everything that *cannot* itself be brought into deliberate and meaningful speech" (*SP*, 39/36, emphasis added). What is the sense of this "cannot"? Should it not rather be "has not yet," since that which is intimated can be given full propositional expression?

The Exclusion of the World

The second part of chapter 3 pursues the purity of expression beyond the medium of oral discourse in general to a region in which expression is cleansed of every nonexpressive aspect. And the nonexpressive involves more than the physical side of expression. After frequent insinuations that Husserl claims a privilege of the voice as the medium of expression, Derrida finally quotes a passage that shows clearly that Husserl is not committed to any such primacy: examples of the physical side of expression would be "the sensible sign, the articulate sound-complex, the written sign on paper, etc." (*LI* II.1, 31/I, 276; quoted at *SP*, 40/37). But he passes on without any comment on this passage.

Derrida makes a rather disconcerting claim as he begins to follow Husserl's exclusions. "Considering now the nonphysical side of speech [*la face non physique du discours*], Husserl excludes from it, as belonging to indication, everything that belongs to the *communication* or *manifestation* of mental experiences" (*SP*, 40/37). While Husserl does indeed distinguish the "physical side" of expressions from the psychic experiences associated with them, he does not do so in order to turn away from the physical side in favor of the nonphysical side. It is precisely by way of a consideration of the physical side that Husserl first discusses communication and manifestation, and then turns to a use of signs that involves neither. One might think that we have here a simple typographical error or slip of the pen. Perhaps Derrida wrote *la face non physique du discours* when he meant instead *la face physique du discours*. We will find reason to think that Derrida wrote exactly what he meant to write.

Derrida's thesis is that in following Husserl's separation of the expressive from the indicative, we will discover that "in the final analysis what separates expression from indication could be called the immediate nonself-presence of the living present" (*SP*, 40/37). This thesis is perhaps not yet entirely clear, but it has been prepared for, and at least some of its implications are fairly clear. As on Derrida's reading meaning and expression are a function of self-presence, whereas indication is essentially determined as reference to that which is not present, an "immediate nonself-presence of the living present" would mean that the indicative appears at the very heart of expression, that expression cannot be purified of the indicative, that we cannot isolate a realm in which logic would hold sway. Husserl has of course already pointed out that indication is always at work in communication. Derrida glosses this by writing that "in this way words act like gestures" (*SP*, 40/38), but this is precisely not Husserl's point. The "gestures" that Husserl discusses in §5 are involuntary, whereas in communication words are used "when a speaker produces [them] with the *intention* [*Absicht*] of 'expressing himself about something' " (*LI* II.1, 32/I, 276–77).

Derrida's discussion of communication, or rather of Husserl's discussion of communication, requires a few comments. In communication, an uttered or written sign manifests or intimates (this is the indicative *kundgebende Funktion*) the speaker's sense-giving lived experiences and expresses the contents of those acts, their meaning (see *LI* II.1, 46–48/I, 286–89). "But the 'animation' cannot be pure and complete, for it must traverse, and to some degree lose itself in, the opaqueness of a body" (*SP*, 41/38). How is this claim rooted in Husserl's text? It is followed by a long quotation from §7, and the colon indicates that the passage quoted should in some way substantiate the claim. But all that passage says is that in communication every expression exercises an indicative function. There is nothing about opacity, nothing about loss. Once again, the rhetoric of threat and loss, which goes back to the substitution of "contamination" for "interweaving," is at work.

The intimating or manifesting function of the sign in communication does exhibit a certain opacity, an opacity common to indication in general: the acts it intimates are *not present* to the hearer in the sense that they are not lived through by the hearer. The hearer can "see" (in a perfectly correct use of the word) the speaker as thinking this or that only on the basis of the utterances or the facial expressions and other body language of the speaker—only on the basis of an indicative function. Derrida concludes: "The very idea of 'physical,' 'physical side,' is conceivable in its specific difference only on the basis of this movement of indication" (*SP*, 42/39). As we shall shortly see, this distorts Husserl's texts, for it is often quite possible to thematize the "physical side" of signs used in soliloquy, signs that in that context do not exercise an indicative function. Derrida's assumption here seems to be that expression, thought itself, moves in an inside that is not and indeed *cannot* be mediated by physical signs, and that it makes sense to speak of a physical side of signs only when the intimating function is at work.

This is confirmed when Derrida interprets Husserl's move to study "expressions in solitary life" (*LI* II.1, 35f./I, 278f.) in light of the "reduction of transcendental experience to the sphere of ownness" in the *Cartesian Meditations* (*Hua* I, §44). The problem with this connection is that the Fifth Meditation does not define ownness in terms of self-presence. It is instead defined by exclusion of "everything that transcendental constitution gives me as Other [*als Fremdes*]" (*Hua* I, 125/93), where "Other" refers to other egos.[4] The sphere of ownness includes all of my intentionality, but excludes the noematic sense "other ego." This leaves the field of my transcendentally reduced experience, *including the noematic phenomenon "world,"* now stripped of the sense "other ego." This is not a field of pure self-presence. It is not a withdrawal from the world, but rather a certain stratum of the phenomenon "world," namely, the world purely for me. It is not an "interior," a self-presence, but rather the presence of a certain (diminished) sense of the world. Obviously, in both §8 of the First Investigation and §44 of the *Cartesian Meditations* the experience of the other ego as such plays a role, but this is no reason simply to equate them with each other.[5]

As we would expect, it is the issue of presence that interests Derrida in Husserl's discussion of the intimating function of signs. "The notion of *presence* is the core of this demonstration. . . . Whenever the immediate and full presence of the signified is concealed, the signifier will be of an indicative nature" (*SP*, 43/40). Here we must pay close attention to Derrida's use of the terms *signifiant* and *signifié*. He first uses them to refer to indicating sign and indicated object. In the next paragraph he speaks of the "signified content" as what is restored to immediate presence by expression. This is identified with the "content (*Bedeutung*) . . . present . . . in consciousness," that is, "present to an 'inner' intuition or perception." Now, something has gone terribly awry here, since it is lived experiences, *Erlebnisse*, that are said to be given in inner perception, not ideal meanings. (As we have noted, for Husserl it is the referent, not the meaning, that is the object of an act, and if the referent is a meaning, there is a meaning in which it is thought as an object.) This is clear from §7 of the First Investigation: "The hearer perceives the speaker as manifesting certain mental experiences [*psychische Erlebnisse*], and to that extent he also perceives these experiences themselves; he does not, however, himself live through or experience them [*er selbst erlebt sie nicht*], he has not an 'inner' but an 'outer' perception of them" (*LI* II.1, 34/I, 278).[6] Derrida is thus confusing the understanding of meaning (*Bedeutung*) with the immediate awareness that consciousness has of itself. Only the latter is legitimately called "my own self-presence" (self-presence in this sense should not be confused with self-presence in the sense of the presence of the thing itself, in the sense of "itself-present," though the former is a species of the latter).

It is this silent shift from *Bedeutung* to *bedeuten*, only the latter of which is present to inner perception, that allows Derrida to write, "The meaning is therefore *present to itself* [*présent à soi*] in the life of a present that has not yet gone forth from itself into the world, space, or nature" (*SP*, 44/40, translation altered). It is lived experience, conscious acts, that are, in a sense to be discussed in the coming chapters, present to themselves. The meaning (*Bedeutung*) is indeed the meaning of these acts—meaning in the *Investigations* is act-meaning (it is the sense of the sense-giving acts that is communicated)—but to understand the meaning is not to have an intuition of the sense-giving acts. Derrida is constructing an "interior" that is not Husserlian, as will become clear in his analysis of inner monologue.

The point of this construction becomes evident when the rhetoric of threat immediately reappears. The "going-forth" of meaning into the world[7] is an "exile" from self-presence, and "we know now that indication . . . is the process of death at work in signs" (*SP*, 44/40). This process of death appears as soon as communication, the relation to the other, appears: "The relation with the other as nonpresence is thus the impurity of expression" (*SP*, 44/40, translation altered). "Impurity," like "death," here has the connotation of contamination, and it is only as plausible as the earlier "contamination" was. And we are still waiting for evidence of its plausibility. The expressive function is to be distinguished from the indicative or intimating function. That is all. When they appear together there is no contamination, no death. So when Derrida concludes that "in 'solitary mental life' the pure unity of expression as such should at last be restored to me" (*SP*, 45/41), one can only reply that it was never lost. It was merely interwoven with the intimating function of the sign.

But, after all, Husserl does turn to the noncommunicative use of language, to "expression in solitary life." In what sense is the relation with the other then "suspended," as Derrida puts it (*SP*, 44/40)? Derrida's language here is carefully chosen to suggest the phenomenological reduction, and he hastens to build on this suggestion by calling Husserl's turn to "solitary mental life" a "reduction to the interior monologue" (*SP*, 45/41).

Why is this move to solitary life, be it a "reduction" or not, important? In the first place, according to Derrida, it is important because "the physical event of language there seems absent" (*SP*, 45/41). Now, it should be noted that as Husserl originally describes "uncommunicated mental life"[8] in the passage quoted by Derrida, it is not necessarily interior at all, and Husserl is not assuming that the actual utterance of a word in soliloquy brings in an indicative function. In soliloquy, "we are *in general* content with imagined rather than with actual words" (*LI* II.1, 36/I, 279, emphasis added). Soliloquy is equally possible in actual or imagined words, and Husserl's entire point is that it makes no difference. The fact that we can just as well use imagined words simply shows that actually uttered words do not play an indicative function in soliloquy. Derrida's attempt to identify the "physical side" and the indicative function is read into, not out of, the Husserlian text and, indeed, the Husserlian enterprise.

We turn now to what Derrida refers to as a "decisive" argument. Husserl asks: "Shall one say that in soliloquy one speaks to oneself, and employs words as signs [*Zeichen*], namely, as indications [*Anzeichen*] of one's own lived experiences? I cannot think such a view acceptable" (*LI* II.1, 35/I, 279, translation altered). Does this signify the reappearance of indication within the self-relationship of soliloquy? Derrida thinks so: "For it is more and more clear that, despite the initial distinction between an indicative sign and an expressive sign, only an indication is truly a sign for Husserl" (*SP*, 46/42). It is unclear why this is supposed to be more and more clear. Derrida offers two reasons. One is to come later, and will concern the fulfilled expression, the fulfilled intention of the wanting-to-say, which will turn out to "depart" from the concept of the sign. For the moment, the evidence rests on the phrase "as signs, namely, as indications." Derrida takes this to mean that signs *are* indications, which would mean that expressions are a species of indication, in direct contradiction to Husserl's official doctrine. If Husserl is compelled to assert this, it would surely be a devastating blow to the integrity of his official project. But Derrida chooses not to make too much of this: "But for the moment let us consider that as a slip of the tongue, the truth of which will be revealed only as we go on. Rather than say 'as signs, namely, as indications' (*als Zeichen, nämlich als Anzeichen*), let us say 'signs, namely, signs in the form of indications' " (*SP*, 46/42, translation altered).

Now, this is a rather astounding turn of events, for Derrida's magnanimous reformulation is not a correction of a "slip of the tongue" but rather a straight-forward paraphrase of Husserl's obvious meaning. If I say in soliloquy, "Expressions are a type of sign," Husserl's question is whether these words function for me as signs—*and that can only mean as indications*—of my own lived experience of thinking that expressions are a type of sign. Husserl could just as well have left out the explicatory phrase "namely, as indications," in which case the sentence would read, ' . . . employs words as signs of one's own lived experiences." Given everything Husserl has said in the first pages of the First Investigation and especially the immediately preceding sentence, it is clear that the signs in question are indicative signs, *Anzeichen*, and this is what the phrase in question specifies. As John Llewelyn notes, the *nämlich* is specificatory, not appositional (see Llewelyn, 21), and the rest of the paragraph confirms this.

Thus we find a curious strategy at work. Derrida first misreads—indeed, as it turns out, apparently deliberately misreads—the text, but then quickly and with apparent generosity announces that he won't hold this "slip of the tongue" against Husserl. In line with this hermeneutic generosity, Derrida suggests a kinder interpretation or rather reformulation of the text. But this is not a generous rewriting that produces a text that, unlike Husserl's actual text, conforms to Husserl's intentions. What Derrida gives is actually no more than an accurate *paraphrase* of Husserl's text. It is this immediately evidenced ability to give an accurate rendition of the sense of Husserl's sentence that indicates that Derrida's misreading was no accident. So for the moment it remains far from clear that only indication is truly a sign for Husserl.

We are still looking for the significance of the turn to solitary life. We have seen that Derrida describes it as a "reduction," and now he puts that word's connotations to work. "The reduction to the monologue is really a putting of empirical worldly existence between brackets" (*SP*, 47/43); it is an epochē. Derrida has carefully prepared the way for this assertion (see *SP*, 22–23/22, 28/27, 32/30, 45/41), but the language of bracketing makes little sense in this context.

The bracketing of the epochē is an essentially *reflective* operation. It is not a question of objects in the world being bracketed in an operation of straightforward experience. It is rather our consciousness of the world, our belief in the world and the world *as* believed, that is put in brackets by a reflective thematization of this experience as experience of the world. In the *Cartesian Meditations* Husserl describes this situation using the (dangerous) metaphor of a "splitting of the ego" (*Hua* I, 73/35). It is the reflective ego that is the "disinterested spectator" of its own engaged life in the world, bracketing that life, that is, refusing to participate in its belief. The point of such a suspension is not to get rid of that belief, but precisely to study it as such.

Interior monologue is in no sense parallel to the epochē. The imagining of words that are "as if uttered" is a neutralized experience, which is to say that it does not posit the reality of its objects, the imagined words. But it remains a straightforward experience, directed toward its objects, the imagined words, and is anything but a reflective experience directed toward experiencing. The neutralization of belief is not a bracketing of belief. There is a relation between neutralization and bracketing, and Husserl was tempted to describe it as a close one. But he later distanced himself from this (*Hua* III.1, 248/258; *Hua* III.2, 510).

In addition, interior monologue in no sense involves a bracketing of "empirical worldly existence." In such a monologue I can discourse about the world, the existing world, and I can deal with it as existing. In no sense can one speak here of "reducing the relative existence of the transcendent world" (*SP*, 49/44).

Note two curiosities in Derrida's discussion: he writes that in monologue (meaning *interior* monologue, without real utterances), "nonexistent signs *show* significations (*Bedeutung*en) that are ideal (and thus nonexistent)" (*SP*, 48/43). If we take ideal meanings as objects, as Derrida does throughout, then it makes no sense for Husserl to say that they do not exist. In the Second Investigation Husserl makes this very clear: "Ideal objects, on the other hand, exist genuinely [*existieren wahrhaft*]" (*LI* II.1, 124/I, 352). The ideal is not to be confused with the fictive. This leads to the second curiosity. Derrida writes that in interior monologue "if we need the *imagination* of the word, we can do without the *imagined word* [*du mot imaginé*]" (*SP*, 48/44). Now, it is true that the word that we imagine does not exist; it is precisely an imaginary word. But in inner monologue as Husserl describes it, we do not do without the imagined word, for it is precisely the imagined word that is expressive. Derrida quotes Husserl's statement that in solitary discourse "we are in general content with imagined rather than with actual words [*mit vorgestellten, anstatt mit wirklichen Worten*, which Derrida translates as *nous nous contentons en effet normalement de mots représentés*]'' (*LI* II.1, 36/I, 279). One wonders what sense it makes to say that we can do without the *mot imaginé* while making use of the *mots représentés*.

But Derrida's conclusion follows, if at all, mainly from his discussion of imagination, and that discussion is deeply flawed by the fact that he systematically ignores the radical changes in Husserl's account of imagination between the *Investigations* and the *Ideas*. ''In the interior monologue, a word is thus only represented [*représenté*]'' (*SP*, 48/43). Represented in what sense? Does something stand for something else here? In the account in the *Investigations*, there are indeed immanent image-contents (*Phantasieinhalte*), phantasmas, which are ''representing contents'' (*LI* II.1, 503–4/II, 655, translation altered). Husserl refers to them as ''the complex of representing contents of the phantasy image [*Phantasiebildlichkeit*]'' (*LI* II.1, 504/II, 656, translation altered). Derrida is careful to distinguish Husserl's phenomenological analysis of imagination from classical psychology. According to the latter, what we find in imagination is a real mental image. In the *Investigations* Husserl still assumes the existence of phantasmas as the counterparts of sensations. But already in the *Investigations* Husserl is aware that being an image is not an internal characteristic (not a ''real predicate'') of the object that functions as an image. By the same token, the ''inner 'image' '' of imagination, that which is concretely imagined, is intentionally constituted and is not an immanent [*reelles*] moment of the imagining (*LI* II.1, 422, 502/II, 593, 654). Yet Husserl still posits the phantasmas as immanent, nonintentional components of consciousness. This is rejected in the *Ideas*, where Husserl writes that ''the phantasma is not a mere, pale sensation-Datum but instead, in accord with its essence, phantasy *of* the corresponding sensation-Datum'' (*Hua* III.1, 253/263). Thus the noetic-noematic structure of imagining is stressed.

Despite his numerous references to the *Ideas*, Derrida confuses the two analyses in the final paragraph of chapter 3 when he tries to find the essential components of the analysis of the *Ideas* already in the *Investigations*. The most essential thing is that ''phenomenal experience does not belong to reality (*Realität*)'' (*SP* 51/47). It quickly becomes clear that *le vécu phénoménal* refers to the noema. This sets up the real confusions that come at the very end when Derrida quotes from §8 of the First Investigation: ''[In imagination a] spoken or printed word floats before us, though in reality it has no existence. After all, we won't confuse imaginative presentations [*Phantasievorstellungen*], still less the image-contents [*Phantasieinhalte*] they rest on, with their imagined objects [*phantasierten Gegenständen*]'' (*LI* II.1, 36/I, 279, translation altered).[9] Derrida follows this with a sentence that can only be called bizarre: ''Not only, then, does the imagination of the word, which is not the word imagined, not exist, but the *content* (the noema) of this imagination exists *even less* than the act" (*SP*, 52/ 47).

Derrida had prepared the way for this claim in the Introduction, where he spoke of "acts of repetition, themselves ideal" (*SP*, 8/10). Now he imports the *Ideas* into this text from the *Investigations*, garbling both in the process. In the context of the *Investigations*, "image-contents" clearly refers to the phantasmas, to immanent counterparts of sensory contents. As immanent parts of consciousness, they are as real as anything else in consciousness, and they cannot be taken to be simply identical with noemata. In addition, there is absolutely no reason to assert that "the imagination of the word . . . [does] not exist." The whole point of the passage from the *Investigations* is that the *imagined word*—unlike the imaginative presentations and their immanent image-contents—does not exist.

Chapter 5
"Wanting-to-Say and Representation"

Chapter 4 of *Speech and Phenomena* follows Husserl's attempt to isolate pure expression, free from all indicative functions, in the monologue of solitary discourse. According to Husserl, even when I talk to myself there is no genuine communication and thus no indication: I merely imagine or represent myself as speaking and communicating. This is Derrida's opportunity to investigate the role of representation in language. "Representation" has a variety of senses, and Derrida argues that through all the registers of its meaning, the "fundamental distinction between reality and representation" cannot be drawn, since in language it is impossible to distinguish them. Thus to "merely imagine" oneself speaking is really to speak, and all real speech involves representative moments. "Effective language," which involves indication, involves imaginary moments, and imaginary speech involves effective moments, and along with them indication.

Husserl can protect expressive purity only if it can be located in a simple present prior to all repetition, but Husserl's own analysis shows that presentation itself depends on re-presentation. Presence as the very form of transcendental life, as the form within which repetition is possible, bears within itself the essential possibility of my absence: the sign, with its repetition, is the very relationship with death itself, as the sign is essentially that which can be present to others beyond my presence, beyond my life. Here Derrida develops what one might call a "semiotic *cogito*": the reflexivity of the "I think" is the representation of oneself as speaking. "Speech represents itself; it *is* its representation. Even better, speech is *the* representation of itself" (*SP*, 64/57). Thus, self-presence turns out to be a representational structure, and this puts into question Husserl's claim that there is no role for the indicative intimating function within soliloquy.

Soliloquy

Derrida begins chapter 4 with an accurate summary of the reasons for Husserl's turn to "solitary mental life": the point is to show that the expressive function is distinct from the indicative function, or more specifically, that the expressive function as such is not essentially dependent on the intimating function. To this end, Husserl develops two arguments: (1) In inner speech I do not manifest anything to myself, I at most represent or imagine myself doing so. (2) In monologue I do not intimate or manifest anything to myself because "such indication would there be quite purposeless" (*LI* II.1, 36–37/I, 280). "The existence of mental acts does not have to be indicated (let us recall that in general only an existence can be indicated) because it is immediately present to the subject in the present moment" (*SP*, 53–54/48).

Thus (1) I cannot intimate anything to myself in inner speech, and (2) I cannot do so because there would be no point in it, since what intimation would achieve is always already achieved prior to the indicative function. Derrida quotes the crucial argument:

> One of course *speaks*, in a certain sense, even in solitary discourse, and it is certainly possible to think of oneself as speaking, and even as speaking to oneself, as, e.g., when someone says to himself: "You have gone wrong, you can't go on like that." But in the genuine sense of communication, there is no speech in such cases, nor does one tell oneself anything: one merely represents oneself [*man stellt sich vor; on se représente*] as speaking and communicating. In a monologue words can perform no function of indicating the existence [*Dasein*] of mental acts, since such indication would there be quite purposeless [*ganz zwecklos wäre*]. For the acts in question are themselves lived through [*erlebt*] by us at that very moment [*im selben Augenblick*]. (*LI* II.1, 37/I, 280, translation altered)

This argument turns on the distinction between representing or imagining oneself as speaking and really speaking. The argument also turns on the distinction between having the existence of mental acts represented to one, in the sense of intimation, and experiencing or living through those acts themselves. These distinctions bring in two different dimensions of representation: on the one hand, I represent or imagine myself speaking; on the other hand, an utterance represents or intimates the speaker's (always another person's) mental acts to me.

Now, notice that I can also imagine another person saying, to me, to someone else, to him- or herself, that I have gone wrong. If I imagine this as communication, then the imagined utterances are imagined as exercising an intimating function, though of course they do not really do so. I don't *discover* via a functioning intimation that the person I am imagining thinks that I have gone wrong, though I may imagine myself doing so, nor do the imagined utterances lead me to discover that I am imagining them as thinking that I have gone wrong. I can also imagine myself telling another person, "You have gone wrong." In this case, my imagined utterances are imagined as exercising an intimating function, and the other is imagined as coming to see me as someone who is thinking certain thoughts. A third possibility is also of interest here. I may think to myself that another person has gone wrong, and I may do so while paying careful attention to just what it is that I think is the case, perhaps thinking that it is not so much that the person has "gone wrong" as that he or she has "strayed from the path just a bit." In this case, I am not "speaking to myself" in Husserl's sense of addressing myself ("You have gone wrong"), and there need be no imagined communication (I need not even consider telling the person what I think).

There is a sense in which I can "discover what I think" in this process, as when I realize that it is not so much that the other person has "gone wrong" as that she has merely "strayed from the path a bit," that "gone wrong" wasn't what I had really discovered about her action. Husserl's point is that *this* discovery is not a result of the intimating function of the imagined words in the inner monologue in which I figure out just what it is that I should think about her actions. I don't conclude that I must think that she has strayed from the path *because* the imagined words "strayed from the path" appear in my inner monologue. To formulate my thoughts in the imagined words simply *is* to think those thoughts, simply is to view the person in that light. For intimation to play a functional role in this process, I would have to formulate the explicit judgment "X has gone wrong" and then discover via the intimating function that I am thinking that X has gone wrong. Without the intimating function, I not only would not know that I am thinking that X has gone wrong, I would not know or think that X has gone wrong, in which case *there would be nothing for the intimating function to indicate*. If I must first think something in order for the signs to intimate that thinking to me, and if that intimation is a condition for my thinking something, thought is impossible.

Speech and Discourse

Before we follow Derrida's text, we might ask whether the entire discussion is not based on a misinterpretation. Derrida asks whether Husserl can succeed in applying "the fundamental distinction between reality and representation to language" (*SP*, 54/49), and his entire discussion is dominated by the assumption that this is what Husserl is doing. A closer reading of the final paragraph of §8 of the First Investigation, however, suggests that Husserl is doing nothing of the sort. He is applying the distinction between representation and reality to a specific *function* of language, namely, the communicative function, not to language in general. The crucial passage is:

> One of course speaks [*spricht*], in a certain sense, even in solitary discourse [*einsamen Rede*], and it is certainly possible to think of oneself as speaking and even as speaking to oneself. . . . But in the genuine sense of communication, there is no speech in such cases, nor does one tell oneself anything: one merely conceives of oneself as speaking and communicating. (*LI* II.1, 36/I, 279–80, translation altered)

I have changed the translation of *einsamen Rede* from "soliloquy," which is hardly false, to "solitary discourse" (adopting the translation Derrida uses in the French) in order to highlight the distinction between *speech* and *discourse* that this passage requires. One imagines or represents oneself as speaking and communicating: the speaking is a speaking-to, be it to others or to oneself. But this occurs within a solitary discourse that is not an imaginary discourse. The words may be imaginary, but their expressive function is not. I may imagine the words, but I do not merely imagine that the imagined words have a certain meaning. This effectively undercuts Derrida's entire reading.

Vorstellung and Representation

Derrida takes Husserl's appeal to the representation or imagination of oneself as speaking as the occasion to raise a general question concerning "the status of *representation* [*représentation*] in language." Can "the fundamental distinction between reality and representation" be applied to language (*SP*, 54/49)? The term "representation" has a wide variety of meanings, three of which are at issue here:

> These affirmations raise some very diverse questions, all concerned with the status of *representation* in language. Of representation in the general sense of *Vorstellung*, but also in the sense of re-presentation as the repetition or reproduction of presentation, as *Vergegenwärtigung* which modifies a *Präsentation* or *Gegenwärtigung*; and finally in the sense of what takes the place of, what occupies the place of, another *Vorstellung* (*Repräsentation*, *Repräsentant*, *Stellvertreter*). (*SP*, 54/49, translation altered)

This torrent of German words requires some comment. *Vorstellung* is derived from the verb *vorstellen*, which in turn is a compound of *vor* (before, in front of) and *stellen* (to put, to place), thus meaning "to place something before." *Vor-*

stellung has long been a key term in philosophical writing (see Knüfer) and has traditionally been translated as "representation," which is unsatisfactory outside the context of representational theories of cognition. It has been used to translate "idea" in the Cartesian-Lockean sense, "representation" and "conception" in Mill, and "perception" in Hume (see Cairns 1973, 131). In normal usage it can have a range of meanings covering "conception," "idea," "notion," "imagination," "presentation," "representation," "thought," and so on. (I have ignored meanings not directly relevant to this context.) Thus the term can bear a bewildering variety of meanings. Indeed, the ambiguities are such that Husserl devotes two sections at the end of the Fifth Investigation to distinguishing the most important senses of *Vorstellung* and *Vorstellungsinhalt* ("content of *Vorstellung*") (see *LI* II.1, 501–6/II, 652–59). In §44 he distinguishes no less than thirteen different senses of *Vorstellung*, a performance that Gustav Bergmann has called "as richly satisfying as a Bach concerto" (Bergmann, 219 n. 28). Derrida's failure even to mention this section is, to say the least, curious. He refers only to the translators' notes in the French editions of the *Logical Investigations* and the *Lectures on the Phenomenology of Internal Time-Consciousness*. The translators of the *Investigations* are primarily concerned to distinguish between *Vorstellung* and *Repräsentation*, using *représentation* and *représentation représentative* for this purpose (*LI*, French translation, 276–77).

What is "representation in the general sense of *Vorstellung*"? Given the diversity of meanings of *Vorstellung*, reading this phrase as meaning "representation in the general sense of *Vorstellung*, as opposed to any other sense of 'representation' having nothing to do with *Vorstellung*" is hardly enlightening. If we read it as referring to the *general* sense of *Vorstellung* as opposed to some more specific sense of the word, however, we may make some progress. In the catalogue of meanings of *Vorstellung* at the end of the Fifth Investigation, the most general meaning would seem to be the fourth, namely, "*Vorstellung* as *objectivating act*," which would include acts of belief as well as acts of merely considering something without believing or disbelieving, accepting or rejecting, and so on (*LI* II.1, 500/II, 652).[1] In this most general sense, *Vorstellung* is the act in which something, some content, is placed before the mind, the act in which we become aware of something in some mode of consciousness. In the *Ideas* Husserl writes, "Any acts whatever—even emotional and volitional acts—are 'objectivating' " (*Hua* III.1, 272/282). *Vorstellung* would thus include perception, predication, memory, imagination, and the mere entertainment of a thought. Cairns suggests "(mental) objectivation" for the broadest Husserlian sense of *Vorstellung*, and "(objectivating or objective) phantasy; objectivation in memory or in phantasy" for the narrower senses that distinguish presentation from representation and thus exclude perception (Cairns 1973, 131).

There is, however, another possibility for understanding what Derrida might mean by *Vorstellung* here. Derrida's second sense of "representation" will be developed in terms of the distinction between presentation (*Präsentation, Gegenwärtigung) and* re-presentation (*Re-präsentation*) in the sense of repetition and reproduction, as presentiation (*Vergegenwärtigung*). This would suggest that "representation" in the sense of *Vorstellung* might be identified with "presentation" in the sense of having something actually present to consciousness as it itself as opposed to being merely imagined or remembered, that is, re-presented. This suggestion will find some confirmation later, when Derrida speaks of "presentation as *Vorstellung* and re-presentation as *Vergegenwärtigung* (*SP*, 58/52), and of the ideal object's being "pre-sent [*pré-sent*] . . . (*Vor-stellung* being the general form of presence as proximity to a viewing)" (*SP*, 59/53).

Finally, there is one more possible interpretation of *Vorstellung* as Derrida uses it here. A glance over the early chapters of *Speech and Phenomena* shows that the word *Vorstellung* appears for the first time in chapter 3, with Husserl's introduction of "imagined [*vorgestellt*] words" (*SP*, 47/43). In the following pages of that chapter it reappears, generally as *Phantasievorstellung* (*SP*, 49/44 and 52/47). In addition, Derrida has just quoted at the beginning of chapter 4 the text in which Husserl speaks of imagined discourse: "one merely imagines oneself [*man stellt sich vor*]" (*SP*, 54/49). Thus it is possible and would indeed be quite natural to read Derrida as meaning imagination when he writes "representation . . . understood in the general sense of *Vorstellung*." This would fit with some of his later usages, as when he speaks of "the difference between real presence and presence in representation as *Vorstellung*" (*SP*, 57/52), the latter meaning imagination. However, this reading would present us with the problem of distinguishing this meaning of representation from the second meaning, representation as *Vergegenwärtigung*. We might try to introduce some clarity by distinguishing imagination in the sense of phantasy as representation in the sense of *Vorstellung* from the re-production of the past in memory, but Derrida has already observed that imagination is a form of *Vergegenwärtigung* (*SP* 50/45 n. 4). Thus we will have to be guided by the context when we encounter the term *Vorstellung*.

Derrida's second sense of *représentation* is also a meaning of *Vorstellung*, a more specific meaning than the general meaning sketched above. It is also the most relevant sense of *Vorstellung* or "representation" in the context of Husserl's example of imagining oneself communicating with oneself (*man stellt sich vor*, "one conceives, represents, imagines oneself," *on se représente*), which Derrida has just quoted. This would be Husserl's sixth meaning, which distinguishes *Vorstellung* in the sense of imagination (in a broad sense that covers memory and phantasy) from perception (*LI* II.1, 501/II, 654). Here one would contrast the perception of something, the making present of the thing itself, with *Vorstellung* as the imagination (or memory) of something that is not itself brought to intuitive presence in the act. In §17 of the *Lectures on the Phenomenology of Internal Time-Consciousness*, Husserl distinguishes between perception, in which the present itself is given, and memory, in which the remembered present "is not 'perceived,' i.e., itself given, but rather presentiated [*vergegenwärtigt*]. It objectivates a now [*Es stellt ein Jetzt vor*] that is not given" (*Hua* X, 41). In perception, the thing perceived is itself given or present. In presentiation (*Vergegenwärtigung*) or re-presentation (*Re-Präsentation*), the object itself is not present "before our eyes," but merely presentiated. Husserl thus contrasts a presentative (*präsentativ*) consciousness with a representative (*repräsentativ*) consciousness, covering both memory and imagination in the narrower sense. *Vergegenwärtigung* is structurally a "reproductive modification" of perception (*Hua* III.1, 233/244).

Finally, Derrida's third sense of "representation" is also a sense of *Vorstellung*, namely, the eighth meaning of the Fifth Investigation. A picture "represents" something, is in a sense its "representative" (*Repräsentant*) or "proxy" (*Stellvertreter*). Similarly, a sign such as an algebraic symbol can stand for something. Here Husserl prefers to use the term *Repräsentation* for the representation of an object by another object, but the sign, be it an image or a name (*Nennzeichen*), is the *Vorstellung* of what it stands for or signifies (*LI* II.1, 503/II, 655). It is unclear why Derrida writes that representation in this sense is that which takes the place of "another *Vorstellung*." He might possibly be using the word in this context in Husserl's tenth meaning. *Vorstellung* can mean the object of *Vorstellung* in the broadest sense of any objectivating act whatsoever (*LI* II.1, 504/II, 656), so *Vorstellung* in the tenth sense refers to the object of *Vorstellung* in the fourth sense. Thus Derrida's third sense would be "representation" understood as what takes the place of an object of (possible) conscious consideration.

Language and Representation

Now, according to Derrida, the key to Husserl's first argument is the application of the distinction between reality and representation to language (a distinction that would correspond to that between *Vorstellung* as presentation and representation as *Vergegenwärtigung* or imagination). This application occurs in two closely related ways. In the first case, we can speak of the sign either as encountered in perception as really existing (that is, as presented) or as being merely imagined (and thus represented in this sense). In the second case, we can speak of communication either as being real (and thus based on the perception of real signs) or as being merely imagined (and note that this can occur even when I really utter the words). In *this* sense (and this is only one sense), "inward language" (Derrida's expression) is "pure representation (*Vorstellung*)" in the sense of something imagined (this would be Husserl's tenth sense of *Vorstellung* [*LI* II.1, 504/II, 656]): we imagine the communication and we imagine the words. Derrida asks whether this distinction can apply to language.

Why might it not apply? In the first place, writes Derrida, "from the start we would have to suppose that representation (in every sense of the term) is neither essential to nor constitutive of communication, the 'effective' practice of language, but is only an accident eventually occurring in the practice of discourse" (*SP*, 55/49). This claim makes use of the distinction between reality, which is presented in perception, and that which is merely imagined, which is represented: real language is presented, imagined language is represented. But given Derrida's parenthetical "representation (in every sense of the word)," one wonders whether any univocal distinction is being made here. Moreover, this is a very curious claim, as Husserl insists that in communication there is an indicative function at work, namely, the intimating function, and this is a representative dimension of the sign in communication. This indicative function falls under Husserl's eighth sense of *Vorstellung* — *Vorstellung* as representative or proxy (*LI* II.1, 502/II, 654–55) — which is Derrida's third sense. And Husserl also insists that words *always*, whether in communication or in soliloquy, function as signs, "pointing" away from themselves to their meanings (*LI* II.1, 35–36/I, 279). It is thus hard to imagine what it would mean to say that "representation (in every sense of the term) is neither essential to nor constitutive of communication, the 'effective' practice of language."

Whatever Derrida's sentence might mean, its function is to set up the statement of a thesis: "There is every reason to believe that representation and reality are not merely added together here and there in language, for the simple reason that it is impossible in principle to rigorously distinguish them. . . . language in general — and language alone — *is* this" (*SP*, 55/49–50). (This claim concerns the "effective" use of words, regardless of whether they are used communicatively or not. "Effectiveness" signifies the physical side of meaning, and Derrida claimes that this entire stratum "belongs to indication" (*SP*, 36/34), and thus to representation. Just a few lines before the statement we are presently concerned with, he writes "communication, the 'effective' practice of language" [*SP*, 55/49]. It is a bit unclear just what the claimed relationship between effectiveness and indication is supposed to mean, but if the indicative dimension of signs involves intimation and thus communication, both statements would seem to conflict with Derrida's present claim that empirical signs can be used noncommunicatively [*SP*, 55/50].) The basis of this claim is the fact that any use of signs involves "a structure of repetition whose basic element can only be representative" (*SP*, 55/50).

Derrida is recalling here one side of the double ideality at work in expression. When we speak of a certain expression (Husserl's example is "quadratic remainder"), we are not referring to "the sound-pattern uttered here and now" or the particular lines of ink on the page; we mean, as Husserl puts it, "the expression *in specie*," the species of the individual sounds and marks that count as the same expression (*LI* II.1, 42-43/I, 284).[2] Something counts as a sign only because we can recognize "the same sign" across a series of instances. A more contemporary terminology would speak here of types and tokens. A series of utterances by different persons at different times can all be recognized as different tokens of one and the same type. And although the tokens may be similar to one another, this is not always the case: the sounds are not similar to the written signs, and we may be hard put to hear the similarity between the sounds uttered by different persons, though they are uttering "the same words." Thus repeatability is essential to what it is to be a sign. The sign has an ideal identity.

The conclusion Derrida draws from this is dramatic:

> This identity is necessarily ideal. It thus necessarily implies representation: as *Vorstellung*, the locus of ideality in general, as *Vergegenwärtigung*, the possibility of reproductive repetition in general, and as *Repräsentation*, insofar as each signifying event is a substitute (for the signified as well as for the ideal form of the signifier). (*SP*, 56/50)

At least the conclusion *seems* dramatic, since it was set up by Derrida's strange claim that for Husserl representation must be inessential to communication. Now representation is popping up all over the place, in every appearance of language, effective or not, communicative or not, for the ideality of the sign is just as much at work in soliloquy and imagined speech as in effective communication. Let us take a closer look at these dimensions of representation.

In the first place, we have "*Vorstellung*, the locus of ideality in general." Now, *Vorstellung* in the broadest sense of the Fifth Investigation is not just the locus of ideality in general; it is the locus of everything that can in any sense be present to or considered by consciousness. Thus my apprehension of the sign uttered by another person is a *Vorstellung* of the sign, and my imagination of my own fictitious utterances is likewise a *Vorstellung*, both in the general sense and in the more specific sense of an act of imagination. In both cases, my consciousness of the ideal sign is a *Vorstellung*. But *Vorstellung* could also, as we have seen, mean "presentation" in this context—the presence to consciousness of the ideal sign as well as the ideal meaning. What seems to be of importance to Derrida is the fact that such presentation, such presence to consciousness of the ideal sign or meaning itself, is necessarily a *re-cognition* of the sign as a sign. Such a recognition involves in principle capacities of repetition: to recognize this sequence of sounds as being the realization or instantiation of a certain expression is to be able to recognize other sequences of sounds as realizing identically the same expression.

Second, we have *Vergegenwärtigung*, reproductive repetition. Now, although our discussion of *Vorstellung* as the locus of ideality did indeed bring us to the necessity of repetition, it is not at all clear that the repetition whose essential possibility is constitutive of the ideal identity of the sign involves "reproductive repetition" in the sense of *Vergegenwärtigung*, presentation. *Vergegenwärtigung* involves the objectivation of something as being itself absent (past, merely imaginary, and so on), whereas the repetition and re-cognition of an expression does not, at least not at first glance. The identity of a type, however, is meaningful only with reference to an indefinite multiplicity of possible tokens, so one might argue that the possible repetition of the same (type) over a multiplicity of tokens requires the *possibility* of the presentiation of past (remembered) and indeed merely possible (imagined) tokens of the same type. This would be plausible, but Derrida has presented no such argument. (Such an argument would be a free phantasy variation in Husserl's sense, here in the sense of a demonstration that the exercise of recognitional capacities involves the essential possibility, the capacity, of presentiation.)

Finally, we have *Repräsentation* in the sense of a substitute — for the signified (presumably the ideal meaning) and for the ideal expression itself. It is true that for Husserl the relationship between expression and meaning is representative: the sign "points to" (in the sense of *Hinzeigen*) its meaning. But does the sound really "substitute for" the ideal expression? It instantiates or realizes that expression *in specie*, but is it a substitute for it? Indeed, the very term "substitute" is odd here, as it might suggest that one can always return from the substitute to the real thing. This would of course be water on Husserl's mill, as it would suggest that while the linguistic sign as "substitute" might be required for communication and pragmatically indispensable for the growth of scientific knowledge, it is in principle dispensable for thought. This would not, of course, get rid of the structure of repetition, although it would show that the repetition-structure of the sign is inessential. But objective truth involves the possibility of returning to identically the same thought content in repeated acts of cognition: ideality is always a function of possible repetition. Can it be shown that *all* such repetition involves signs?

Now, in spite of their unclarities, Derrida's claims all admit of a Husserlian reading; indeed, only that reading seems to make sense of them. They appear to challenge Husserl only because of Derrida's claim that effective language must not, for Husserl or for a Husserlian position, involve representation in any sense of the term. Thus when Derrida flirts with the objection that what he has just outlined is basically Husserlian, we needn't take the deconstructive intent of the remark too seriously. But then things seem to get serious: "But according to Husserl's description, it is only expression [*l'expression*] and not signification in general [*signification en général*] that belongs to the order of representation as *Vorstellung*" (*SP*, 56/50). What does *Vorstellung* mean in this context? In view of Husserl's presentation in the early paragraphs of the First Investigation, *Vorstellung* would here have to mean imagination. Prior to Husserl's discussion of solitary speech, the word appears in only one sentence. In a discussion of the meaning of names, Husserl speaks of "the sense or 'content' of [their] nominal presentation [*nominale Vorstellung*: Cairns suggests translating this as "naming objectivation" (Cairns 1973, 87)]" (*LI* II.1, 32/I, 276, translation altered) — a use that doesn't help us in the present context. Furthermore, only expressions continue to exercise their expressive function in imaginary discourse; imaginary indications could at most be imagined to exercise an indicative function. So it makes sense to say that only expression, and not signification in general (which would include indications), can *function* in imagination, as opposed to being imagined to function.

Derrida now moves to close his trap: "However, we have just suggested that the latter [namely, *Vorstellung*]—and its other representative modifications—is implied by any sign whatsoever" (*SP*, 56/50). But in what sense has it been shown, or even suggested, that *Vorstellung* belongs to any sign? As we have seen, the most that Derrida can justifiably claim is that the recognition of any sign involves the possibility of repetition and thus the possibility of presentation. But it is difficult to see why this point should count against Husserl's claim that only imagined expressions continue to exercise their expressive function, whereas imagined indications do not actually indicate.

But the trap has another side: "On the other hand, and more importantly, as soon as we admit that speech belongs essentially to the order of representation, the distinction between 'effective' speech and the representation of speech becomes suspect, whether the speech is purely 'expressive' or engaged in 'communication' " (*SP*, 56/50–51). Since *all* signs involve repetition, and repetition involves imagination, " 'effective' language is just as imaginary as imaginary speech and . . . imaginary speech is just as effective as effective speech" (*SP*, 56/51). No (real) tokens without types and a system of repetition; therefore, effective language is imaginary. No types without (real) tokens, without a language that has been learned and spoken; therefore, imaginary language is effective. The imagination of the words, as a *Vergegenwärtigung*, is a modification of the perception of words, and thus presupposes perception: the imaginary presupposes the effective. This thesis is to be understood not in the sense of empirical psychology, but rather as a structural analysis of the very sense of imagining itself (cf. *Hua* III.1, §111). Derrida has not really made this argument, though he has the materials for doing so when he speaks of "the *Vergegenwärtigung* which modifies a *Präsentation* or *Gegenwärtigung*" (*SP*, 54/49). In addition, he has suggested that even the imagination of a sign involves "the *possibility* of reproductive repetition" (*SP*, 56/50, emphasis added) and the representative structure in which a sign, even an imagined sign, points to its meaning. But this argument is much too weak to establish the desired conclusion. It might, however, be thought to be effective against an assertion of the possibility of pure presence, of a *Vorstellung* not indebted to anything outside itself, a pure making-present of that which it presents. And this is in fact Derrida's goal.

John Caputo interprets Derrida's thesis as follows:

Derrida argues that the distinction between "real" communication, in the intersubjective sphere, and "imaginary" communication, in the monological sphere, is just one more metaphysical apparatus which comes undone. Real communication is not really real, effective communication. It is an illusion to think that in communication one makes naked contact, that mind is joined to mind in perfect immediacy. On the contrary, "real" communication is a work of signs and mediation and hence beset with confusion and exposed to misunderstanding and failure to communicate. It is caught up as much in the medium of "representations" (and hence likeness, image, the imaginary) as is the so-called imaginary dialogue within inner life. "Real" communication can be every bit as fictitious as "inner soliloquy" can be a work of productive clarification. (Caputo, 132–33)

The problem with this interpretation is that there is absolutely nothing here with which Husserl would quarrel. Of course solitary speech can be a work of productive clarification, be it about the world, other persons, or myself. Husserl's only point is that the clarification is not mediated by the intimating function of the sign. And Husserl never denies that genuine communication is a chancy affair, subject to ambiguity, confusion, and misunderstanding. But then so is thought itself, and Husserl knew that.

The crucial difference that Derrida sees Husserl trying to save as he draws his essential distinctions is the difference between "simple presence and repetition" (SP, 56/51). The pure imagination of the sign that isolates the purely expressive function should be a simple presence, presence of the expression and presence of the meaning. Such a presence requires that Husserl "reduce or derive the sign, and with it all powers of repetition" (SP, 57/51), since repetition would bring in not just *Vorstellung* as the locus of ideality, the locus of presence, but also reproduction and thus something that stands for something else: the sign function becomes essential. Thus Derrida's claim is that in moving to save presence and to reduce the sign, Husserl is "living *in* the effect—the assured, consolidated, constituted effect of repetition and representation, of the difference which removes presence" (SP, 57/51). The presence whose purity is to be defended is itself an effect of something other than pure presence, of repetition and representation, of the difference between that which represents and that which is represented, between two sign events that are the same sign. This difference "removes presence" while producing it, for the presence it produces can never be pure or simple.

This result amounts to "the very obliteration of the sign" (SP, 57/51). This is not an obliteration of the sign in the manner of classical philosophy, which generally viewed the sign as having a merely derivative and instrumental function in communication, as standing for a meaning given independently of the sign in the self-presence of conscious life. It is rather an obliteration of precisely this classical concept of the sign itself—the sign as mere representative of something given independently of its representation. Along with it go traditional metaphysical concepts such as representation as the modification of a primordial presentation, repetition as the repeating of something originally given in a simple (non-repetitive) present, and difference as founded upon an original identity. If presentation is always re-presentation (as cognition is always re-cognition), if repetition is the condition for the present, if difference is the source of identity, then phenomenology's principle of principles, which asserts the absolute validity of presence, is put into question, for now we see that this presence moves within a finite and contingent system of representation and is thus conditioned by absence.

It is this argument that might explain the apparently contradictory uses of *Vorstellung* in the following paragraph. On the one hand, Derrida speaks of "the difference between real presence and presence in representation as *Vorstellung*" (*SP*, 57/52). On the other hand, he speaks of the difference between "presentation as *Vorstellung* and re-presentation as *Vergegenwärtigung*" (*SP*, 58/52). The point here is that presentation involves representation, since it necessarily involves repetition. All *Vorstellung* in the most general sense, which includes *Vorstellung* as presentation in contrast to representation, involves repetition and thus re-production. We thus encounter a familiar structure of Derrida's deconstructive dialectical logic: re-presentation is the genus of presentation (*Präsentation*, *Gegenwärtigung*) and representation (*Vergegenwärtigung*). The distinction between presentation and representation can, and indeed must, be made, but it cannot be given a metaphysical form, that is, a form that begins with presentation as primordial or simple presence and views representation as a modification of this simple presence. It is this latter metaphysical strategy that Derrida sees at work in Husserl, and seeks to deconstruct. "The presence-of-the-present is derived from repetition and not the reverse" (*SP*, 58/52). This result, which Derrida views as a reversal of Husserl's own intentions, has thus far been derived from Husserl's own account of ideality and repetition, but it is to find its deeper justification in Husserl's descriptions of temporality and the relation to the other.

Ideality and Representation

For the moment, Derrida dwells on the concept of ideality, which is found in the three dimensions of the ideality of the sign, the ideality of the meaning, and the ideality of the object itself in certain cases. Ideality "does not exist in the world" (*SP*, 58/52); its being is that of "nonreality, nonexistence" (*SP*, 59/53 n. 3). Here one has to be careful, as Husserl insists that "ideal objects . . . exist genuinely [*existieren wahrhaft*]" (*LI* II.1, 124/I, 352), though they are not real. (Curiously enough, Derrida quotes from this paragraph of the Second Investigation, but takes no notice of this sentence.) Taking ideal objects to be real is the error of what is traditionally understood as Platonic realism. Husserl's working criterion for reality is temporality, so both physical objects and conscious acts are real, but ideal signs as such, ideal meanings, and ideal objects such as numbers are not real, though they exist. The sense of that existence would have to be the object of phenomenological investigation. Given this, in what sense would it be true that "being is determined by Husserl as ideality, that is, as repetition" (*SP*, 58/52)? To be sure, anything that can meaningfully be said to exist must in principle be presentable *as* existing, as a noematic phenomenon, and the noematic sense, the object *as* it is given, necessarily involves structures of repetition. But this does not mean that being is equated with ideality. For example, the ideal objects of ideal geometry are not *equated* with the real that is studied by applied geometry using the tools of ideal geometry (see *Hua* VI, 30–31/32–33).

Derrida is interested here in the relationship between ideality and *Vorstellung* as the locus of ideality: "Now . . . this determination of being as ideality is paradoxically one with the determination of being as presence" (*SP*, 59/53). This identity is paradoxical because in the *Logical Investigations* ideality is defined in terms of nontemporality (see *LI* II.1, 123/I, 351). (Later Husserl will revise this, understanding irreality as "supertemporality [*Überzeitlichkeit*]" or "*omnitemporality* [*Allzeitlichkeit*], which, *nevertheless, is a mode of temporality*" [Husserl 1938, 313/261].) But if an ideal object is to be an "ob-ject," that is, a thing thrown before or present to the mind (cf. the German *Gegen-stand*), and thus pre-sent to *Vor-stellung* as the placing of something before the mind, this must occur in the living present of consciousness, the very locus of repeatability. Even the presence to consciousness of the nontemporal is referred to the present of consciousness.

This brings the discussion to Husserl's "principle of principles," namely, "*that every originary presentive intuition [originär gebende Anschauung] is a legitimizing source of cognition*, that *everything originarily* (so to speak, in its 'personal actuality') *offered* to us *in 'intuition' is to be accepted simply as what it is presented as being*, but also *only within the limits in which it is presented there*" (*Hua* III.1, 51/44). Here the normative value of presence, of originary intuition, is tied to the present as "the universal form of all experience (*Erlebnis*)." Life, the life of consciousness, takes place in the present; life *is* the present: "The present alone is and ever will be" (*SP*, 60/53). Without the presence of the present, the self-constitution of consciousness as present to itself in the present, there could be no presence of atemporal ideal objects, and thus no truth (or falsity) at all. Everything that in any sense can be said to be must be able to come to presence in this present and will itself be either present or a modification of such being-present (past as a past-present, future as a future-present, merely imaginary as a possible present, and so on). The possibility of presence (with its most fundamental form, the presence of the present) is the condition of possibility of meaning, validity, and truth; it is that which opens up what would otherwise be a pure immediacy (such as Hegel's sense-certainty) to intersubjec-tivity and objectivity.

But, and here Derrida's deconstructive movement sets in, "to think of pres-ence as the universal form of transcendental life is to open myself to the knowl-edge that in my absence, beyond my empirical existence, before my birth and after my death, *the present is*" (*SP*, 60/54). We must pause a moment to consider the sense of this statement. Derrida argued earlier that phenomenology is a phi-losophy of life "because at its center death is recognized as but an empirical and extrinsic signification, a worldly accident" (*SP*, 9/10), one that cannot under-mine the integrity of the act of living that is the source of sense. This life was then determined as self-presence, and the externality, the visibility, of the effec-tive sign was said to be "literally the death of that self-presence" (*SP*, 37/35). Finally, indication, which requires the reality of the sign, was said to be "the process of death at work in signs" (*SP*, 44/40), the deadly contamination of the purity of expression. Now we find that presence to intuition in the present, as the universal form of all experience, bears within itself the differentiation into pres-ence to me and presence to others, indeed, yields the possibility of the not-being of my presence. "The relationship with *my* death (my disappearance in general) thus lurks in this determination of being as presence, ideality, the absolute pos-sibility of repetition" (*SP*, 60/54). Death ceases to be accidental and empirical, as it is a structure of the eidos ego itself.

As Paul Ricoeur has noted, the late Husserl of the *Cartesian Meditations* would deny the premises of this argument. Since the *ego cogito* is for Husserl a personal function (and not a consciousness in general), the transcendentally re-duced eidos ego will not, in the first instance, cover "the self-function in gen-eral," that is, all human beings or all conscious beings. It is the eidos of myself and not that of "anybody." "I have no access to the plural by way of the uni-versal" (Ricoeur, 92). Applying this to the eidetic structure of my living present, we can conclude only that this is the eidetic structure of my own transcendental life. An investigation of the sense "other transcendental life" remains open (and is taken up in the Fifth Meditation).

Moreover, in a text from 1922–23, Husserl develops a demonstration of the "immortality" of the transcendental ego on the basis of the temporal structure of consciousness. The demonstration has two steps, one oriented toward the future, and one toward the past: (1) Given that the present is always a fulfilled present, that is, the fulfillment of past protentions, Husserl argues that the "continuation of the present [*Fortwähren der Gegenwart*]" is necessary. "It is unthinkable that everything would cease and then there would be nothing," for the very thought "then there would be nothing" is a consciousness in the mode of a "then there is [*Dann-sein*]." Thus, "living-on and the ego who lives on are immortal—*nota bene* the pure transcendental ego, not the empirical world-ego, which most cer-tainly can die." (2) Because every present appears as the fulfillment of past protentions, and thus necessarily has its horizon of retentions, "no now is conceivable that does not already have retentions." Thus transcendental life and the transcendental ego cannot be born: "I was eternally." In short: "Just as ceasing is conceivable only in the process, whereas the ceasing of the process itself is inconceivable, beginning is conceivable only in process, whereas the beginning of the process is not conceivable" (*Hua* XI, 377–78).

This is a curious argument, and deserves a more exhaustive critical commentary than can be given here. One might argue, for example, that given the functional nature of the distinction between the mundane and the transcendental ego, to call the transcendental ego immortal is to make a straightforward category mistake, to take the categories proper to one functional context over into another context. But more to the point of the argument itself, what Husserl has actually demonstrated is that there cannot be a "last present" in the sense of a present *experienced as being* the last present, a present that has no protentional horizon of a future. If, as we will see in the next chapter, every present is a living into a future, we cannot experience the ceasing of conscious life as a ceasing, but that by no means proves that conscious life cannot cease or that I cannot give meaning to the possibility of its cessation. Similarly, the second step of the argument proves that I can never experience a moment as being the first moment, that is, a moment that has no horizon of a past that just-was, a moment that is not in some way experienced as being the fulfillment of the protentions of that just-past consciousness. But does it follow that "I was eternally"?

Regardless of how we evaluate Husserl's argument, Derrida is trying to establish that death has in some sense a transcendental function and is not merely an empirical accident (accident from the point of view of the transcendental). But Husserl's argument raises the question whether the very categories of birth and death, mortality and immortality, are at all applicable to transcendental "life." Repetition, the structure of sense (*Sinn*) in the broadest sense, yields the essential possibility that what is presented to me *as* this or that can be presented to another consciousness as the same, though within perspectival variations. One might say that Derrida has offered a transcendental deduction of the intersubjectivity of experience (though as we have seen, Husserl would deny the demonstration) and the perspectival nature of such experience. Such a demonstration would be a demonstration of the impossibility of the reduction to ownness of the Fifth Meditation, for even experience in the sphere of ownness requires the identity of noematic sense as experience unfolds temporally.

Assuming that Derrida's argument is compelling, what does it show? It claims to show that there is an otherness that is constitutive of my experience, that the world is always already a world for others. The sense "other ego" cannot come to modify the sense of the world for me, for it is always already constitutive of the sense of the world. Like sense-data, which are essentially the product of an abstraction and not the building blocks of experience, the world-for-me would be an abstraction and not a stratum that can be found in experience, isolated by *Abbau*, (unbuilding or deconstruction [cf. Evans 1990a]), and so on. Does it therefore follow that "*I am* originally means *I am mortal*" or that "*I am immortal* is an impossible proposition" (*SP*, 61–62/54)? It clearly shows that "I am God" is an impossible proposition, for God would be that being to whom all meaning is present. Since experience is perspectival, Derrida can legitimately claim that "the linguistic statement 'I am he who am' is the admission of a mortal" (*SP*, 61/54).

Derrida's error in drawing too strong a conclusion from his demonstration is simply the counterpart to his misleadingly strong reading of Descartes: "The move which leads from the *I am* to the determination of my being as *res cogitans* (thus, as an immortality) is a move by which the origin of presence and ideality is concealed in the very presence and ideality it makes possible" (*SP*, 61/54–55). This is misleading because the interpretation of the being of the subject of thought as *res cogitans* does not, for Descartes, immediately imply immortality, but at most the possibility of immortality. Indeed, at the very end of his Sixth Meditation Descartes has still not proven the immortality of the soul; he has merely shown that the soul *can* be immortal if God so chooses. He has not even argued that given God's goodness (something questionable on Cartesian grounds themselves), God *will have* chosen to make us immortal. Just as Descartes could claim to prove only the possibility, not the reality, of immortality, Derrida can at most claim to have shown that the *I am* bears within itself the possibility of its own death.

Ideality and the Neutrality Modification

The interpretation of the "I am" in terms of presence, of *res cogitans*, and thus of immortality is of a piece with another confusion: "The effacement (or derivation) of signs is thereby confused with the reduction of the imagination" (*SP*, 61/55). The word "derivation" seems to be the key to a first step toward making sense of this claim. Just as the representative function of signs presupposes presentation, on Husserl's analysis, so the representation in both memory and imagination is structurally derivative from perception. Imagination, in turn, is structurally a neutrality modification of memory. (Husserl's analysis of imagination is in no sense a "reduction," and here again Derrida's use of the term yields no determinate meaning.)

The following paragraph deals with imagination, and what seems to be at stake is the relationship between "the power of pure repetition that opens up ideality and the power which liberates the imaginative reproduction of empirical perception." Derrida's claim is that these two powers "cannot be foreign to each other; nor can their products" (*SP*, 62/55). Ideality would thus be a function not of pure presentation, but rather of representation.

The image is not positional;[3] it is the modification of a positional presentiation (with the iterability that makes it possible). This is important for Derrida because "[the image] retains a primary reference to a primordial presentation, that is, to a perception and positing of existence, to a belief in general" (SP, 62/55). Both neutralizing presentation and the neutralizing modification taken universally (see Hua III.1, §112) are modifications of belief. The former is the modification of memory in the broadest sense, the latter of positing in general. Derrida seems to be arguing that the very fictiveness of the image is the result of the fact that it is not a "pure neutralization" (SP, 62/55), that it refers back to presentation. The image would thus stand in contrast to pure ideality: "This is why pure ideality, reached through neutralization, is not fictitious" (SP, 62/55).

Now, in what sense is pure ideality reached through neutralization? Derrida refers to chapter 2 of the Second Investigation. In §8 Husserl distinguishes the being of ideal objects from the "being-thought-of [Gedachtsein] which characterizes the fictitious" (LI II.1, 124/I, 352). The fictitious can be, and in reading a novel is, the correlate of a neutralization (compare Husserl's analysis of picture consciousness in Hua III.1, §111). But what does ideality have to do with neutrality? Consciousness of an ideal object or state of affairs by no means requires neutrality. Husserl notes in the Lectures on the Phenomenology of Internal Time-Consciousness that in the case of ideal objects, we cannot draw the distinction between presentation and presentation. The act of judging about a mathematical object is located in a present, but the mathematical state of affairs itself is not temporal, and the judging is neither the presencing of a present (Gegenwärtigung) nor a presentation (Vergegenwärtigung); the mathematical state of affairs does not appear as either present or presentiated (Hua X, 96). One can merely consider the state of affairs in a neutrality modification, but this is not presentiation. Why would such a neutrality modification attain "pure ideality" in a sense that is withheld from the positing judging of the state of affairs? Why are repetition and neutrality connected with each other here? Is it merely because of the asserted relationship between pure repetition and imaginative reproduction? But the passage in the Lectures just referred to shows that the modalities of belief are not identical with the (temporally) present and the nonpresent [Gegenwärtig-Nichtgegenwärtig] (see Hua X, 97).

The relationship between the power of pure repetition and the power of imaginative reproduction leads Derrida to find the First Investigation "disconcerting": (1) For Husserl, expressions in which we find only the expressive function are imaginary. (2) Within the inner sphere disengaged by this fiction, we find a fictitious communicative use of language. Thus within the inner sphere we have a distinction between an effective use of language (purely expressive and non-communicative) and a fictitious use (communicative). (3) In communication, which requires "pure idealities" (SP, 63/56), we can distinguish between the fictitious and the effective, the ideal and the real. If we begin with ideal meanings in effective inner discourse, communicative effectiveness will come in the form of a real body, an empirically real token. (4) Within soliloquy, there can be speech that is "*effectively* representative" (expressive and purely theoretical language as opposed to practical discourse), while other speech "would remain purely *fictitious* (those fictions located in fiction would be the acts of indicative communication between the self and the self, between the self taken as other and the self taken as self, etc.)" (*SP*, 63/56).

Now, some aspects of these four points, which taken together are said to be "disconcerting," are worth pointing out. In (2) and (4) there is said to be an effective (as opposed to fictitious) use of inner language, namely, as expression, whereas in (1) language in its expressive purity is purely imaginary, fictitious. But (1) is simply false. Husserl does not identify purely expressive or solitary speech with imagined speech. The latter is a special case of the former. With regard to (4), it makes no sense to say that the imagined self-address in soliloquy is "purely fictitious" speech, since whether such speech is actually uttered or not, although the communication is imagined, the real or imagined signs do indeed exercise an expressive function: they express a meaning. A purely fictitious speech would presumably be one in which I imagine that certain (real or imagined) words have a meaning (which I may not know), when in fact they are meaningless. The distinction Husserl needs in the context of §8 of the First Investigation is the distinction between genuine and merely imagined communication, not "the general distinction between the fictitious and effective usages of the sign" (*SP*, 63/56).

When Derrida asserts that "the sign is originally wrought by fiction" (*SP*, 63/56), he relies on the fact that the ideal sign is a function of possible repetitions: no type without (possible) tokens. But to say that this "threatens" the distinction between the fictitious and effective usages of the sign (*SP*, 63/56) does not make much sense. Whether the distinction is between fictitious and effective meaning functions or between the expressive and the effectively communicative use of language, Derrida has offered no reason to think that this distinction has been threatened.

One might strengthen the thesis, as we have seen Derrida do: no type without *real* tokens. Derrida also asserts the other side: no real *sign* without the presentiation of tokens. The imaginary presupposes the real, the real presupposes the imaginary. This would be the content of Derrida's claim that the very distinction between the fictitious and effective usages is threatened. Note too that "fictitious usage" is ambiguous. It can refer to imaginary tokens, but it can also refer to an imagined intimating function of real tokens; and in either case, as Derrida has just admitted, there can be a dimension of real, effective representation or expression. Indeed, one could go further and claim that it is impossible really to imagine the expressive function. Either we imagine tokens of genuine linguistic types, in which case the imagined tokens really do express their meaning; or we utter, hear, or imagine sounds that we imagine to realize linguistic types, in which case we have only imagined that they are tokens. I can of course hear sounds that I know to be linguistic tokens in a language I cannot understand, but this is not the same thing as imagining them to be tokens.

When Derrida develops his thesis into the claim that there is no sure criterion for distinguishing "an outward language [*langage*] from an inward language or, in the hypothesis of an inward language, an effective language from a fictitious language" (*SP*, 63/56), he seems to shift dramatically what is at stake. We are now apparently confronted with what since Wittgenstein has become known as a private language. Up to now we have been dealing with an inward *use* of language, with solitary speech; now we confront the question of an inward *language*. I have just suggested that an "inward" language in the sense of a purely imagined language doesn't make sense. Is Husserl committed to a private language, a language that I speak, as effectively as possible, only in the solitary life of my soul? Derrida thinks so: "Such a distinction, however, is indispensable to Husserl for proving that indication is exterior to expression, with all that this entails" (*SP*, 63/56). There is, however, absolutely no reason for making this assertion in the context of the *Logical Investigations*. The language I speak in solitary speech is the same language I speak to others, and there is no reason to think that this intersubjective horizon is not essential to any use at all of that language.

There is only one text known to me that would even seem to give aid and comfort to Derrida's claim here, and that is the Fifth Cartesian Meditation. As we have seen, the reduction to the sphere of ownness violates the noetic/noematic correlation by attempting to disregard or abstract from the constitutional effects of intentionality relating to other subjects while including in the sphere of ownness these intentional acts in which we are conscious of other subjects. Thus the world appearing to my ownness loses its cultural predicates (cf. *Hua* I, 127/95), while "my whole world-experiencing life and therefore . . . my actual and possible experience *of* what is other, is wholly unaffected by screening off what is other" (*Hua* I, 129/98). This means that my linguistic competence, like all my habitualities (*Hua* I, 134/104) belongs to the sphere of ownness: language is by definition part of the sphere of ownness. This would seem to be a radical form of private language.

However, two things should be kept in mind here. In the first place, the reduction to ownness is not an *Abbau*, an unbuilding or deconstruction of conscious life along the lines Husserl developed in the early to mid 1920s. Such an *Abbau* might allow the question of a private language to be posed. The reduction to ownness as elaborated in the *Cartesian Meditations*, however, does not even allow the problem to be raised as a problem, and this impossibility results from the violation of one of the most basic principles of Husserl's transcendental phenomenology. In the second place, the sphere of ownness is an artificial product, and cannot be said to be "private" in any normal sense of the term. It is thus not at all clear that it would be legitimate to talk of an "inward language" even if we were to accept the concept of ownness itself. Be that as it may, Derrida does not appeal to the reduction to ownness in this context. He had earlier functionally equated imagined speech with the reduction to ownness, but we have seen that this equation simply does not hold up.

Derrida's transition to consideration of the second argument concerning the lack of communication in inward speech is much more interesting. The sign is a structure of repetition in which real or imagined tokens realize one and the same sign, and "what we have just said concerning the sign holds, by the same token, for the act of the speaking subject" (*SP*, 63/57). What holds for the uttered or imagined word holds for the act of imagining that word: the act is "originally wrought by fiction." If an act of imagination is to be an act of imagining a specific word, an act of imagining a token of a certain type, then it must be part of a system of repetition in which I can imagine another token of the *same* type. Similarly, if I can imagine a word that expresses a certain meaning, I must be able to think that meaning in other acts, and this in a twofold sense. I must be able to imagine other tokens expressing the same meaning (repetition of the tokens of a type, repetition of words expressing the same meaning), and I must be able to think that meaning itself. To be able to imagine oneself or another person thinking something, one must be able to think that meaning oneself; it *is* in a sense to think that meaning. Consciousness itself would then involve the tokening of types: to be an act of consciousness *is* to be a token of a type. This is a radical extension and modification of Husserl's own theory. Husserl could write, "To be a sign . . . is no real predicate" (*LI* II.1, 424/II, 595). There is no real or substantive moment in the sign-event that exemplifies the expression *in specie*. Being a sign is rather a functional predicate, but this functionality has its origin in consciousness, which *takes* the sound as a token of a type and the type as expressing a meaning. The arbitrariness of the sign is possible only because it is an arbitrariness *for consciousness*. For the Husserl of the *Logical Investigations*, however, being the act of thinking "The sky is blue" *is* a real predicate; to the ideal meaning as species there correspond really immanent (*reell*) moments of the act of meaning:

> The manifold singulars for the ideal unity Meaning are naturally the corresponding act-moments of meaning, the *meaning-intentions*. Meaning is related to varied acts of meaning . . . just as Redness *in specie* is to the slips of paper which lie here, and which all 'have' the same redness. Each slip has, in addition to other constitutive aspects . . . its own individual redness, i.e. its instance of this colour-species, though [the species] neither exists in the slip nor anywhere else in the whole world, and particularly not 'in our thought', in so far as this latter is part of the domain of real being, the sphere of temporality. (*LI* II.1, 100–101/I, 330)

Husserl's "second argument" against the reality of communication in inward speech hinges on the claim that such communication would make no sense, that there would be no point to it. What is at issue is the conditions of effective communication: Husserl assumes that in the case of communication, the distinction between the effective and the fictitious can be drawn. "Between effective communication and the representation of the self as speaking subject, Husserl must suppose a difference such that the representation of the self can only be added on to the act of communication contingently and from the outside" (*SP*, 64/57).

What does this mean? The issue concerns the self that imagines, the self of "effective experience," and the self that is imagined: "Husserl seems to allow that the subject as he is in his effective experience and the subject as he represents himself to be can be simply external to each other" (*SP*, 64/57). If we start with an act of effective communication, "You, Tom, have done wrong," we can modify it to "You have done wrong," where the "you" addressed is the speaker himself. This case should be compared with that of "I have done wrong," in which the speaker makes a statement about him- or herself that may express a genuine discovery of judgment, but in which there is no imagined communication in Husserl's sense. In the case of imagined communication, the communicative moment is embodied in a "you" and not in an "I." Now, here we might say that we have the structure of an act of communication that is modified by a representation of the self ("you").

Why is this considered important? "But the primordial structure of repetition that we just evoked for signs must govern all acts of signification. The subject cannot speak without giving himself a representation of his speaking, and this is no accident" (*SP*, 64/57). What does "signification" (*signification*) mean here? Not *bedeuten*, not wanting-to-say, not *vouloir-dire*. Signification is the general term covering both expression and indication. The next sentence speaks of "speaking," so presumably "acts of signification" refers to *vouloir-dire*.

Now Derrida is moving between the representation of oneself as imagining oneself communicating, on the one hand, and self-representation in the sense of one's immediate awareness of oneself as speaking, on the other (Sartre's pre-reflexive *cogito*). The former involves the latter in two senses: on the one hand, to imagine is to be aware of oneself as imagining; on the other hand, one's imagined speaking involves an imagined awareness of oneself as speaking. Derrida's move here is to claim that this representation of oneself as speaking is itself speech: "Speech represents itself; it *is* its representation. Even better, speech is *the* representation of itself" (*SP*, 64/57). Speech is re-presented to itself as the condition of its being speech. To speak is to speak to and about oneself. There is not a self, present to itself, that is then re-presented in speech: this "self" is such only in being re-presented in speech.

Husserl, in contrast, distinguishes the self-presence of consciousness to itself from the re-presentation of the self in imagination, taking these two to be "simply external to each other" (*SP*, 64/57). Real, as opposed to imagined, consciousness is "simple," is present to itself "in an absolute proximity." This is why language is secondary, inessential, and merely instrumental for consciousness as such: "Language and its representation is added on to a consciousness that is simple and simply present to itself, or in any event to an experience which could reflect its own presence in silence" (*SP*, 65/58). For Husserl, the act of imagining oneself speaking is not itself a speaking, and its presence to itself is not mediated by signs, by re-presentation. Derrida quotes from the *Ideas*: "Any mental process [*Erlebnis*] whatever (any so to speak actually living one) is a mental process 'presently existing [*gegenwärtig seiendes*].' Belonging to its essence is the possibility of reflection on [that experience], in which [reflection] it is necessarily characterized as certainly and presently *existing*" (*Hua* III.1, 251/261, translation altered).[4] But the self-presence in question here is a function of an explicit reflection on the lived experience, a reflection that, while always essentially possible, may or may not occur. This cannot be the original self-presence characteristic of *all* experience. The question would be how any mental process whatever is constituted *as* "presently existing" for itself, prior to all reflection. It is only here that we can discover the extent to which this presence is "simple" or an "absolute proximity." Derrida's basic point here is that signs, being essentially re-presentative, are foreign to this self-presence. For Husserl, the latter is the source of the former. Genuine indication is useless in solitary speech because experience is present to itself prior to all reflection and thus does not need the indirect mediation of the intimating function: genuine intimation would be redundant, therefore it can only be imagined.

Thus Husserl's argument presupposes a self-presence prior to the mediacy introduced by the intimating function of signs. This self-presence must, on Derrida's reading, be simple: "The self-presence of experience must be produced in the present taken as a now," where the now is an instant (*SP*, 66/59). As Husserl writes: "In a monologue words can perform no function of indicating the existence of mental acts, since such indication would there be quite purposeless. For the acts in question are themselves experienced by us at that very moment [*im selben Augenblick*]" (*LI* II.1, 36–37/I, 280). In Derrida's reading: "The present of self-presence would be as indivisible as the *blink of an eye* [*clin d'oeil*]" (*SP*, 66/59).

Clin d'oeil means "wink," and in the phrase *en un clin d'oeil*, it can also be translated as "in the twinkling of an eye." The latter meaning connects more directly with the root meaning of *Augen-blick*: the *glance* or *look*—not the blink—of an eye. Derrida has thus chosen a translation diametrically opposed to the direction Heidegger takes in *Being and Time*, where he speaks of the "Augen*blick*" (Heidegger 1927, 328/376, Heidegger's emphasis). Macquarrie and Robinson translate this as "moment of *vision*." This *Augenblick* is the present (*Gegenwart*) of authentic temporality, and must, on Heidegger's analysis, be sharply distinguished from the "now" (*Jetzt*) (Heidegger 1927, 338/387). This amounts to an implicit critique of Husserl's explication of the present in terms of the now, and Derrida's translation of *Husserl's* term *Augenblick* by *clin d'oeil* is a move to make this critique explicit.

This suggests that a specific strategy is at work: If Husserl's use of the term *Augenblick* involves an essential reference to a "now" in the sense of an instantaneous moment, it should be possible to show that Husserl is committed to metaphysical presuppositions that his own analyses cannot sustain. Derrida will argue in chapter 5 that the *Augenblick*, the moment or instant, is never instantaneous, that there is "duration to the blink [*clin d'oeil*], and it closes the eye [*elle ferme l'oeil*]" (*SP*, 73/65). This is just what one would expect if *Augenblick* means "blink of an eye." But the "glance of an eye" is not so clearly instantaneous. Derrida's whole argument depends on his interpretation of the "moment" (*Augenblick*) as instantaneous, the point of simple self-presence, absolute self-proximity. His reading of *Augenblick* as "blink of an eye" is part and parcel of that interpretation. Does it do justice to Husserl?

Chapter 6
"Signs and the Blink of an Eye"

The title of chapter 5 means, in the first instance, "Signs and the Moment," the moment in which the self is present to itself in absolute proximity. But Derrida will try to show that this moment is the *blink* of an eye, not its glance, as the German term *Augenblick* would suggest. It is the instantaneous moment of the blink, which closes the eye, not the glance, which opens up a field of vision. This moment of the blink, of absence, will turn out to be the condition of possibility of presence itself, the very "origin" of presence. Everything depends on the instantaneousness of the instant in Husserl's analysis—both in the sense of Husserl's actual analysis of the present and in the sense that such an analysis is required by the exclusion of indication from solitary speech and imagined self-communication. "The force of this demonstration presupposes the instant as a point, the identity of experience instantaneously present to itself. Self-presence must be produced in the undivided unity of a temporal present so as to have nothing to reveal to itself by the agency of signs" (*SP*, 67/60).

The concept of the instantaneous present is decisive, for

> a certain concept of the "now," of the present as punctuality of the
> instant, discretely but decisively sanctions the whole system of
> "essential distinctions." If the punctuality of the instant is a myth, a
> spatial or mechanical metaphor, an inherited metaphysical concept, or
> all that at once, and if the present of self-presence is not *simple*, if it is
> constituted in a primordial and irreducible synthesis, then the whole of
> Husserl's argumentation is threatened by its very principle. (*SP*, 68/61)

Derrida's general strategy is thus clear: the structure of repetition and absence that in chapter 4 was found to permeate ideality, then presence, and then consciousness itself will now be searched out within the structures of time-consciousness — working solely within the Husserlian analyses themselves. Derrida's chapter 5 should thus provide a critical check on and confirmation of the results of chapter 4.

The Punctual Now

Derrida quickly points out that his interpretation might seem untenable: "Undoubtedly, no now can be isolated as a pure instant, a pure punctuality. Not only does Husserl recognize this . . . but his whole description is incomparably well adapted to the original modifications of this irreducible spreading-out" (*SP*, 68–69/61). On the one hand, Husserl insists that "it belongs to the essence of lived experiences that they must be extended in this fashion, that a punctual phase can never be for itself" (*Hua* X, 47/70, quoted at *SP*, 68–69/61). Such a "being for itself" would require that the punctual present fail to appear within the horizon of just-past and just-to-come moments, and Husserl rejects this possibility. On the other hand, this does not, for Derrida, undermine the sense of the concept of the instant. Indeed, it is the present as a point that is the "source-point" for the temporal field within which the present essentially appears (cf. *Hua* X, 28/48–49, quoted at *SP*, 69/62). And as Husserl himself writes, "the current *Now* is necessarily and remains something punctual, a *persisting form for ever new material*" (*Hua* III.1, 183/195, translation altered; quoted at *SP*, 69–70/62).

It remains to be seen, however, whether Derrida's interpretation of the moment and his understanding of the punctuality of the present are adequate to Husserl's analyses. In the *Lectures on the Phenomenology of Internal Time-Consciousness*, Husserl does speak of "a punctual phase," but he quickly notes that this is to be understood only as an "ideal limit." Such an ideal limit cannot be phenomenologically given, and the concept of such a punctual present is a limiting concept. The "pure now" is "only an ideal limit, something abstract, which cannot be anything for itself" (*Hua* X, 39–40). From the *Philosophy of Arithmetic* of 1890 (see *Hua* XII, 246–50) to the discussion of limiting shapes in the *Crisis* (see *Hua* VI, §9a), ideal limits are the result of an idealizing activity and are never simply encountered as such. Here the activity that produces the concept of the punctual now is that of the phenomenologist's "dividing" the continuum of the temporal field (*Hua* X, 40). The question is, does it make sense to speak of self-presence in terms of such limiting concepts? Is there a limiting concept of self-presence in the punctual present? Or is it only meaningful to speak of self-presence in terms of the concrete unity of just-past/present/just-to-come, of the temporal *field* that Husserl later names the "living present" (*lebendige*

Gegenwart) (cf. Held, 19)? (Derrida mentions this concept twice [*SP*, 5/6, 77/69], but does not thematize or make any real use of it.)

Derrida attempts to bolster his interpretation by a reference to the "motif of the punctual now as the 'primal form' (*Urform*) of consciousness (*Ideas I*)" (*SP*, 71/63). Unfortunately, he gives no page reference for this quotation from the *Ideas*, which makes it rather difficult to check. However, a look at the paragraphs discussing time-consciousness shows that the phrase appears once, in §83, where Husserl speaks of "this primal form [*Urform*] of consciousness" (*Hua* III.1, 185/197). The context makes it clear that this phrase does *not* refer to the punctual now, but rather to the "stream-form" (*Stromform*) of the stream of consciousness, in which every now of lived experience has its horizons of before and after (*Hua* III.1, 196/184). Husserl does speak of the now as "something punctual, a persisting form for ever new material" and of "the originary form of now" (*Hua* III.1, 183–84/195–96), but this "form" is immediately integrated into the three dimensions of earlier, later, and simultaneity, with the emphasis falling on the *stream* of consciousness.

Derrida, however, has no doubts here: the "moment" (*Augenblick*) of the *Investigations* is this punctual phase. Moreover, this punctual now "is *evidence* itself, conscious thought itself, it governs every possible concept of truth and sense" (*SP*, 70/62). Now Derrida's strategy is clear: if the concept of the punctual present is made the key to the phenomenological concept of evidence and thus to the concept of truth (cf. *LI* II.2, 115–27/II, 760–70), a deconstruction of the former will be ipso facto a deconstruction of the latter concepts.

Official Doctrine versus Concrete Description: The Simple Self-Identity of the Now

The theme of the punctual now is not the only motif of the *Lectures*:

> Despite this motif of the punctual now as "primal form" (*Urform*) of consciousness (Ideas I), the body of the description in *The Phenomenology of Internal Time-Consciousness* and elsewhere prohibits our speaking of a simple self-identity of the present. In this way not only is what could be called the metaphysical assurance par excellence shaken, but, closer to our concerns, the "*im selben Augenblick*" argument in the *Investigations* is undermined. (*SP*, 71/63–64)

Note that it is not a matter of playing the *Investigations* off against the later text of the *Lectures*. It is rather a matter of two different motifs at work in the *Lectures* themselves: an officially stated doctrine and the concrete analyses that tend to undermine that doctrine. In contrast to the "official" doctrine of the punctual present as source-point, the analysis of the *Lectures* "demonstrates and confirms throughout the irreducibility [*l'irréductibilité*] of re-presentation (*Vergegenwärti-*

gung, Repräsentation) to presentative perception (*Gegenwärtigen, Präsentieren*), secondary and reproductive memory to retention, imagination to the primordial impression, the re-produced now to the perceived or retained actual now, etc." (*SP*, 72/64).

The term "irreducible" is not well chosen here. Husserl never attempted to reduce, for example, memory to perception. Derrida's thesis should rather be that the analyses show the impossibility of considering representation as a *modification* of presentation, and so on. Husserl writes that

> every lived experience has its parallel in the different forms of reproductions that can be regarded as ideally 'operative' *transformations* of the original mental process: each has its 'precisely corresponding' and yet thoroughly *modified* [emphases added] counterpart in a recollection, . . . anticipation, . . . mere phantasy. . . . Conversely, starting from any mental process already characterized as such a modification, which then *in itself* is always characterized as that [modification], we are led back to certain primal mental processes, to '*impressions*' that *absolutely originary* mental processes exhibit in the phenomenological sense. (*Hua* III.1, 167/179, translation altered).

In this context Derrida is particularly interested in the relations between presentation and representation, presence and nonpresence. In the analysis of the hearing of a melody, the term "perception" can be used in several different ways. On the one hand, I am perceiving the currently sounding tone, whereas the past tones are not currently perceived. In a slightly different sense, I am perceiving the entire melody, from the perspective of the tone perceived in the first sense. One perceives[1] the melody by hearing it played (*Hua* X, 38). But with regard to the temporally extended individual tone, we can say both that the tone is perceived as long as it sounds (*Hua* X, 39) and that at any given moment in this perception "only the point of the duration that is characterized as now is truly properly perceived [*voll eigentlich wahrgenommen*]" (*Hua* X, 26; see also 39–40). These portions of the extended tone that are past are not perceived in this strict sense, but rather retended as being just-past.

The interesting thing here is that in saying that I perceive the currently sounding tone (as opposed to the now-phase of that tone), we are saying that the just-past phases of that tone are perceived. Husserl regards this as entirely appropriate: "Indeed, do we not perceive the passing, are we not . . . directly aware of the just-having-been, of the 'just past' in its itself-givenness, in the mode of being-itself-given?" The concept of perception being used here is that of "the act that originally constitutes the object," in contrast to acts of presentation or representation, which do not place the object itself before our eyes (*Hua* X, 39,41). This is the background for the passage quoted by Derrida: "if we call perception *the act in which all 'origination' lies, which constitutes originarily*, then *primary remembrance* [that is, retention] *is perception*. For only in *primary remembrance do we see what is past*; only in it is the past constituted, i.e., *not in a representative but in a presentative way"* (*Hua* X, 41). In retention we have a direct intuition of the past as past, just as the phase of primal impression is a direct intuition of the present, the now. Memory, on the other hand, is not a direct intuition or perception of the past, but rather its re-presentation, re-membering as becoming mindful again (*re-* plus *memor* [mindful]). Thus, depending on the concept of perception used, we have

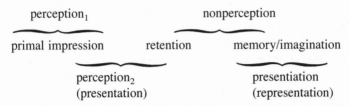

perception₁   nonperception

primal impression   retention   memory/imagination

perception₂   presentation
(presentation)   (representation)

But Derrida will try to show that this neat set of distinctions is unstable. On the one hand, Husserl writes in §17 of the *Lectures* that "there is no mention here [that is, as concerns perception][2] of a continuous mediation [*Vermittlung*; *d'une conciliation continue*] of perception with its opposite" (*Hua* X, 41, quoted at *SP*, 72/64–65, translation altered), a mediation that would be required for perception₁. This is what one would expect of the "official" position that the now is a simple self-identity, self-sufficient in its own present. Being past is something that happens to the present now; it is derivative, a modification of the original. And yet, Derrida asks, "did not the preceding section quite explicitly entertain this very possibility [of a continuous mediation of perception with its opposite]?" (*SP*, 72/65). He quotes from §16 of the *Lectures*:

If we now relate what has been said about perception to the *differences of the givenness* with which temporal objects make their appearance, then the *antithesis of perception* is primary remembrance, which appears here, and *primary expectation* (retention and protention), whereby *perception and non-perception continually* pass over into one another [*ineinander übergehen*]. (*Hua* X, 39)

This is followed by another quotation from the same paragraph in which perception in the sense of the impression that constitutes the "pure now" is contrasted with every other phase, the latter being called memory. The impressional phase is an ideal limit, abstract. "Moreover, it is also true that even this ideal now is not something *toto caelo* different from the not-now but continually mediates itself [*sich vermittelt*; *en commerce continuel avec lui*] with it. The continual transition [*Übergang*] from perception to primary remembrance conforms to this mediation" (*Hua* X, 40).

Derrida's conclusion is dramatic:

As soon as we admit this continuity of the now and the not-now, perception and nonperception, in the zone of primordiality common to primordial impression and primordial retention, we admit the other into the self-identity of the *Augenblick*; nonpresence and nonevidence are admitted into the *blink of the instant*. There is a duration to the blink, and it closes the eye. (*SP*, 73/65)

Thus, we seem to have an official doctrine, the expression of a metaphysics of presence, which asserts the simple self-identity of the now. But when Husserl turns to concrete analysis, the rigor and honesty of his descriptions lead to results that contradict that official doctrine. This assertion requires examination.

In the first place, Derrida finds Husserl both denying and affirming a continuous mediation between perception and nonperception. However, a glance at the context of the denial ("there is no mention here of a continuous mediation of perception with its opposite") shows that Husserl is talking about presentation, re-presentation (*Vergegenwärtigung, Re-Präsentation*), and not about perception at all.[3] In such presentation of an event, there would indeed be a continuous mediation, not between perception and nonperception, but between that which is, for example, remembered as having been present and that which is remembered as having been past. Thus there is a mediation between remembered perception and remembered nonperception. In imagination there would be a continuous mediation of "as if" perception and "as if" nonperception (cf. *Hua* I, §25), all within the nonperception of imaginative consciousness. Husserl's denial of a continuous mediation concerns presentation, whereas the two texts Derrida quotes as affirming a continuous mediation between perception and nonperception concern perception, not presentation. They are not even discussing the same thing as the first text and prove absolutely nothing in this context. The texts that affirm a mediation are working with perception$_1$, the impressional phase of consciousness. The only reason to be surprised at finding a continual mediation of perception$_1$ and nonperception, impression and retention, would be the assumption that the punctual now that is the correlate of the impressional phase is, in a functional sense, for itself — that is, that its functioning as impressional phase does not require temporal horizons. Derrida makes just this assumption, for on his reading the punctual now of the *Augenblick* is the moment of pure self-presence and "simple self-identity" (*SP*, 73/66). This is not to take the punctual now as an abstract moment, an ideal limit that cannot exist for itself, but to reify it.

In 1891–92 and again in 1894, Husserl read William James, who wrote that the present is like "a saddle-back, with a certain breadth of its own on which we sit perched, and from which we look in two directions into time" (James, vol. 1, 609), and Rudolf Bernet suggests that Husserl's discovery of the "extension" (*Ausdehnung*) of the present was influenced by this reading (Bernet 1985, xxii).

As early as 1901, Husserl wrote, "The now is . . . as little a fictive mathematical temporal point as is the 'tone before,' the first, second tone before or after. Rather, each has, as can be seen, its perceptible [*sichtbare*] extension. . . . That which is 'given' to perception is necessarily something temporally extended, not a mere temporal point" (*Hua* X, 168). "The point of clearest vision is not a point, but rather a small field, and the point now is also a small field" (*Hua* X, 176). The discovery of this field is disturbing only if one is committed to the punctual "blink" of the eye rather than the glance whose correlate is a field.

What is the sense of the "continuity" that Derrida finds so devastating for Husserl's program of presence and self-presence? A punctual now cannot be anything for itself because it is precisely a "passing over" into another present; the now is a becoming not-now. Even if Husserl were committed to the now as a proper moment—and in an early text dealing with Brentano, Husserl uses the phrase "now-moment as a moment proper [*Jetzt-Moment als einem eigenen Moment*]" (*Hua* X, 172)—he would still have to recognize the manner in which a now becomes past. The mere phenomenon of the *Übergang* cannot be the key to Derrida's argument: the fact that the now is always becoming not-now does not seem to "admit the other into the self-identity of the *Augenblick*." But with a bit of digging, we can easily reconstruct an argument. Husserl insists that every now has horizons of before and after (*Hua* III.1, §82) that are retended and protended. But retention has a double intentionality: not only is the past phase of the tone retended, the perception or primal impression of that tone is also retended. That primal impression itself was essentially accompanied by a protention of the coming moment, that is, the moment that is now. Thus *any* present encountered as now is such in a synthesis of fulfillment of the protentions of the preceding now (cf. *Hua* X, 116f.). It belongs to the very essence of the now that it be a transformation of a previous now and a fulfillment of the protentions that constituted the temporal horizon of the future of that previous now. A pure, isolated punctual now cannot even be imagined, and with it goes any possibility of a "simple self-identity." The primary phenomenon is duration (cf. the discussion in *Hua* IX, 378).

Derrida's conclusion shows evidence of a certain strain: "The difference between retention and reproduction, between primary and secondary memory, is not the radical difference Husserl wanted between perception and nonperception; it is rather a difference between two modifications of perception" (*SP*, 73/65). This is true for Husserl, but only if we take "perception" in the sense of perception$_1$, that is, in the sense of the abstract phase of primal impression. But if we take perception to be the act in which something is originally constituted, the act that, as it were, places something before our eyes as it itself, then retention belongs to perception, perception$_2$. It is the act in which the past is intuitively present, the act in which we perceive or "see" the past. Husserl's "radical difference" is maintained if one attends to the sense of the distinction being drawn. And the claim that this analysis "radically destroys any possibility of a simple self-identity" (*SP*, 73/66), while true enough, cannot be turned against Husserl.

Derrida concludes this portion of his argument with a quotation:

> If, in comparison [to the constituted unities], we turn to the *constituting* phenomena, we find a flow [*Fluss; flux*], and every phase of this flow is a continuity of adumbration [*Abschattungskontinuität; continuité de dégradés*]. But in principle no phase of this flow is to be spread out [*auszubreiten*] in a continuous succession, which would be to think the flow as transformed in such a manner that this phase is [temporally] spread out in identity with itself. (*Hua* X, 74, quoted at *SP*, 74/66)

Derrida does not comment on this passage, but a number of things need to be said about it. In the first place, the context of the passage is important. Husserl is discussing what he calls "the absolute time-constituting flow of consciousness" (*Hua* X, 73), and he attributes to this level of consciousness properties that make it incomparable to any other level of consciousness

Husserl had great difficulties with the phenomenon of consciousness's awareness of itself, its presence to itself. Though Derrida does not discuss the topic,[4] the *Lectures* develop the doctrine of an absolute level of consciousness, a strictly speaking nontemporal level at which the temporality of consciousness is itself constituted. This is the level at which, for example, perceptual acts are experienced or lived through, the level of the awareness of those acts, a level that, according to Husserl, can and must be structurally distinguished from the level of immanent acts. Making sense of Husserl's texts requires a clear understanding of what this level is supposed to be and what its constitutive function is.[5]

Now, when the passage Derrida quotes is read in the context of the account of the absolute time-constituting flow of consciousness, it begins to become intelligible. A phase of the absolute flow is a "continuity of adumbration" in the sense of being a continuity of adumbrating consciousness, but that phase is not temporally "spread out" in the sense of a succession in which a phase is first future, then present, then past, in identity with itself as the self-same phase in a series of temporal adumbrations. The impressional phase of absolute consciousness "*belongs* to a now, namely, to the one it *constitutes*" (*Hua* X, 75), but it cannot be said to *be* now. This lack of identity with itself is the lack of any sense of being an object, any sense of being temporal, and not the lack of the "simple self-identity" Derrida has been attributing to Husserl's "official" doctrine. Husserl's denial of the former has no direct connection with the latter. There is an indirect connection, however, because if we do accept the theory of absolute time-constituting consciousness, it follows that every now is the correlate of a phase of absolute consciousness that necessarily contains impressional, retentional, and protentional moments. Thus the constituted now is essentially the now that results from a just-past now having become just-past: the now is continuously mediated with the just-past.

The Necessity of Retention and the Necessity of Signs

Derrida ends the second section of chapter 5 with a thesis: "The fact that nonpresence and otherness are internal to presence strikes at the very root of the argument for the uselessness of signs in the self-relation." This must now be shown, and Derrida notes that "doubtless Husserl would refuse to assimilate the necessity of retention and the necessity of signs, for it is only the latter which (like the image) belong to the genus of representation and symbolism" (*SP*, 74/66). Now, the first part of this statement is surely correct, but the latter part, in assimilating representation in general and symbolism, may well stack the deck. In terms of the three senses of "representation" delineated in chapter 4 of *Speech and Phenomena*, Derrida's strategy amounts to the following. We have already seen that there is no pure immediacy of presentation for Husserl in the sense of a making-present that is not caught up in and indebted to the structures of retention and protention, in the sense of presence in and of a simple present. If Derrida can show that retention and protention involve representation in the third sense of *Repräsentation*, in which something functions as a substitute for something else, then he will have established his thesis. (Will he thereby also have established his earlier thesis that expression is *essentially* interwoven with indication, namely, with intimation?)

For Derrida, what is in question here is nothing less than phenomenology's "principle of principles." But in what sense is it in question? In a footnote Derrida observes that Husserl not only called retention the perception of the past, but took the evidence of retention to be absolutely certain. He quotes a passage from §78 of the *Ideas*, which speaks of "the *absolute legitimacy of retention of something immanent*" (*Hua* III.1, 168, quoted at *SP*, 74/67 n. 5). Husserl elaborates on this somewhat in the *Lectures*. There he argues that not only the immanent[6] now phase, but also the succession, alteration, or change of immanent data is "absolutely certain," and this seems to be a correlate of saying that in retention "I see [*erschaue*] . . . that which is past" (*Hua* X, 34; see also 49). There is a strong Cartesian bias at work in this emphasis on the absolutely certain, and Derrida is surely correct to point this out. He argues that Husserl is trying to maintain two irreconcilable positions:

(*a*) The living now is constituted as the absolute perceptual source only in a state of continuity with retention taken as nonperception. . . .

(*b*) The source of certitude in general is the primordial character of the living now; it is necessary therefore to keep retention in the sphere of primordial certitude and to shift the frontier between the primordial and the nonprimordial. The frontier must pass not between the pure present and the nonpresent, i.e., between the actuality and inactuality of a living now, but rather between two forms of the re-turn or re-stitution of the present: re-tention and re-presentation. (*SP*, 75/67)

But in what sense are these two "irreconcilable"? In §§16–17 of the *Lectures*, Husserl carefully distinguishes various senses of "perception," and the sense of perception that is contrasted with retention (the perception that Husserl later in §16 calls "impression") is not the sense of perception that is contrasted with re-production or memory.

In what sense are these two positions irreconcilable? Although retention and the re-presentation of memory are indeed distinct phenomena, "we should be able to say *a priori* that their common root—the possibility of re-petition in its most general form, that is, the constitution of a trace[7] in the most universal sense—is a possibility which not only must inhabit the pure actuality of the now but must constitute it through the very movement of difference it introduces" (*SP*, 75/67). This statement is best approached, I think, in terms of the question "What makes the present retendable?" What is it about the presence of what is present in a primal impression that makes it retendable? The answer would have to be that the present is not pure event, pure immediacy, the "this-there" of Hegelian sense-certainty. Rather, what is present is such *as* this or *as* that. It is this "as" structure that makes something not only presentable, but also protendable and retendable. The same "something as something" that was protended is now presented and will be retended. Husserl analyzes this under the headings of the "horizon-structure of experience" and the "typical preacquaintedness of every individual object of experience" (Husserl 1938, §8, translation altered). "Particular apperceptions make us conscious of particular real things, but these apperceptions are inevitably provided with a stock of sense which, although it does not become thematized, extends beyond the apperceptions" (Husserl 1938, 29–30/34). "*Unfamiliarity* is at the same time always *a mode of familiarity*" (Husserl 1938, 34/37). Thus a strict Humean immediacy or presence is inconsistent with the results of phenomenological analysis. What makes retention and protention, as well as presentation and indeed self-reflection (cf. *SP*, 76/67–68), possible is the intentional structure of consciousness of something as something. We have already seen Husserl denying that there can be a first moment, and only such a moment could be the kind of simple presence or self-presence that Derrida imputes to him. It is always a structure of sense, a system of typifications that allow a preacquaintedness with whatever becomes present to consciousness, that makes presence possible. Derrida calls the effect of such structures in concrete consciousness a "trace," and in this sense he is right that "such a trace is . . . more 'primordial' than what is phenomenologically primordial" (*SP*,

76/67), more primordial than presence itself. But this is itself a result of phenomenological analysis.

As we saw in chapter 5, Husserl encountered these structures in the early 1920s, concluding that the transcendental ego is immortal and that "I was eternally." We suggested there that Husserl's statements amount to category mistakes, an application of the categories of the mundane to the transcendental. (Derrida makes much the same suggestion in his own terms when he writes that "what we are calling time must be given a different name—for 'time' has always designated a movement conceived in terms of the present, and can mean nothing else" [SP, 77/68].) If the transcendental is understood functionally, then we can see that Husserl's statement amounts to the claim that a functional nexus is immortal. The category mistake is possible because the functional nexus is operative only in the form of a consciousness, which makes it possible to speak of myself as transcendental ego. But the ego that exercises a transcendental function does so as an always already mundanized ego, and it is only the mundane ego that can be said to be mortal or immortal. The transcendental function as such has at most the eternity of a principle of validity.

Thus if the "trace" is identified with this structure of "preacquaintedness," which is the condition of possibility of *every* modality of consciousness (impression, retention, protention, memory, imagination, self-reflection, and so on), Derrida is right to say that it is "older than presence and procures for it its openness" (SP, 76/68). (In a sense, Husserl tries to avoid the "older than" by concluding that the very structure of consciousness implies the "I was eternal," for that posits a prior presence ad infinitum. This is similar to the argument for *anamnēsis* and immortality in Plato's *Meno* [81a–86c], but there Socrates distances himself from the conclusion.) And Derrida is correct to conclude that this structure "prevent[s] us from speaking about a simple self-identity '*im selben Augenblick*' " (SP, 76/68), but only if we interpret *Augenblick* in the sense of a simple punctual instant—and as we have seen, Husserl makes no such assumption. Thus Derrida's second question, "Does this not compromise the usage Husserl wants to make of the concept of 'solitary mental life,' and consequently of the rigorous separation of indication from expression?" must be answered with a "not necessarily," at the very least.

The answer might seem to be more properly a simple "no," but it remains possible that Derrida will establish that indication plays a constitutive role in this temporalization of consciousness. He suggests that he is already well on the way to establishing this conclusion, for he asks, "Do indication and the several concepts on whose basis we have thus far tried to think it through (the concepts of existence, nature, mediation, the empirical, etc.) not have an ineradicable origin in the movement of transcendental temporalization?" (SP, 76/68). This question seems a bit weak for Derrida's purposes, however. Given his thesis that signs play an essential role in retention and in self-relation, surely he means to suggest that indication *is* this movement of temporalization. Everything will depend on the way Derrida develops his concept of " 'time'," which is "to be conceived anew on the basis now of difference within auto-affection" (*SP*, 77/68). What he has done thus far is to argue against the concept of the punctual present, against the concept of a simple self-presence in the punctual present. This is quite consistent with Husserlian description and thought, but it may yet turn out that the living present (as opposed to the punctual present, the "living now" of the *Ideas*) is constituted by that which Husserl tries to exclude from certain forms of consciousness. "Does not this 'dialectic' [of "identifying identity and nonidentity within the 'sameness' of the *im selben Augenblick*"] . . . open up living to difference, and constitute, in the pure immanence of experience, the *divergence* involved in indicative communication and even in signification in general?" (*SP*, 77/69). The first part of this question is given an affirmative answer by Husserl himself: living can be defined only in terms of the living present of retention-impression-protention; all else is a mere abstraction. But it remains to be shown that this implies indicative communication.

Presence and the Principle of Principles

As we noted earlier, Derrida claims that Husserl's "principle of principles" stands or falls with the concept of the self-identity of the now as point and source-point. He mentions the principle several times in *Speech and Phenomena* (*SP*, 59/53, 67/60, 69/62 n. 3), quoting Husserl's statement of it once, but he does not seem to think that it requires much discussion.

The principle of principles is stated in §24 of the *Ideas*. The context is Husserl's discussion of the distinction between fact and essence (§§1–17) and the "naturalistic misinterpretations" of essences (§§18–26). Against the empiricist restriction of acts in which things are given as they themselves — what Husserl calls "originally presentive intuition" (*originär[8] gebende Intuition*) — to the experience of real individual objects (*Hua* III.1, §§2, 19), Husserl argues that "*immediate 'seeing'*, not merely sensuous, experiential seeing, but *seeing in the universal sense as originally presentive consciousness of any kind whatever*, is the ultimate legitimizing source of all rational assertions" (*Hua* III.1, 43/36). Originality or originarity is defined in terms of the distinction between perception and other modes of givenness (such as recollection, expectation, imagination, and nonfulfilled thought): "The experience that is presentive of something *originarily* is perception. . . . We have originary experience of concrete physical things in 'external perception,' but no longer in memory or forward-regarding expectation" (*Hua* III.1, 11/5–6). Husserl insists that once original intuition has been defined in this broad manner, we cannot deny that we have an originally presentive intuition of ideal objects such as meanings and numbers. Here too we encounter the distinction between an empty meaning-intention and a fulfillment of that meaning-intention.

This leads to the statement of the principle of principles:

> Enough now of absurd theories. No conceivable theory can make us err with respect to the *principle of all principles: that every originary presentive intuition is a legitimizing source of cognition*, that *everything originarily* (so to speak, in its "personal" actuality) *offered* to us *in "intuition" is to be accepted simply as what it is presented as being*, but also *only within the limits in which it is presented there*. (*Hua* III.1, 51/44)

This principle operates on two distinct levels. On the one hand, systematic investigation in any given field of knowledge requires an orientation to the original presentive intuition of the objects in question, and this intuition is "of such a character as prescribed by the *sense* of the judgments, or correlatively by the *proper essence of the predicatively formed judgment-complex*" (*Hua* III.1, 42/36). But this statement itself is the result of original intuition, an intuition reflectively concerned with the distinction between empty and fulfilled intentions, the modes of original intuition, and so on.

One clause in the statement of the principle of principles should be given special attention: "but also only within the limits in which it is presented there." Intuition is the source of legitimacy in cognition, but that does not mean that intuition is necessarily incorrigible. Husserl insists on this point:

> Not to assign any value to "I see it" as an answer to the question, "Why?" would be a countersense—as, yet again, we see. Moreover, as may be added here to prevent possible misinterpretations, that does not exclude the possibility that, under some circumstance, one seeing conflicts with another and likewise that one *legitimate* assertion conflicts with another. For that does not perchance imply that seeing is not a legitimizing basis. . . . It does say, however, that perhaps in a certain category of intuitions . . . seeing is, according to its essence, "imperfect," that of essential necessity it can become strengthened or weakened, that consequently an assertion having an immediate, and therefore genuine, legitimizing ground in experience nevertheless may have to be abandoned in the further course of experience because of a counter-legitimacy outweighing and annulling it. (*Hua* III.1, 43/37, translation altered)

This corrigibility gives rise to one of the major tasks of phenomenology, namely, the critique of evidence (*Hua* XVII, 294/288). All evidence is in need of critique so that we may come to an understanding of the kind of evidence it is and of the limits of that evidence. And the evidence of the reflecting phenomenologist is no exception. Here Husserl recognized the task of a "critique of transcendental self-experience" (*Hua* I, 67/29, translation altered; cf. 178/151–52), a phenomenology of phenomenology,[9] and it was in the course of an attempt to carry out aspects of this phenomenology of phenomenology that he was forced to begin revising his own earlier claims that there is a core of adequate evidence in phenomenological reflection.[10]

Given this background, our response to Derrida's references to the principle of principles can be brief. In the first place, intuition is not the "source of sense" (*SP*, 60/53) but rather the source of the legitimacy of sense. Second, Husserl's statement that intuition can be undermined by intuition clearly shows that the principle of principles itself does not assert or require "the self-identity of the now as point, as a 'source-point' " (*SP*, 69/61). Husserl does speak of primordial presence, but nothing in this text from the *Ideas* suggests Derrida's statement "In phenomenology, the idea of primordial presence and in general of 'beginning,' 'absolute beginning' or *principium*, always refers back to this 'source-point' [namely, to the self-identity of the now as point]" (*SP*, 69/61–62).

Chapter 7
"The Voice that Keeps Silence"

In chapter 6 of *Speech and Phenomena* most of the threads that have been prepared in the previous chapters flow together in a dense tapestry in which each thread is intricately intertwined with all the others. Keeping the various strands clear is a difficult but crucial job.

As we have seen, Husserl attempts to delimit expression in two directions. In the first place, he distinguishes expression from indication, arguing that while the two functions are interwoven in communication, we find the expressive function without the indicative function in soliloquy. In the second place, he distinguishes logical meaning as expression from the preexpressive stratum of sense.

In soliloquy we have the "phenomenological voice," which speaks a false discourse to a fictive other in a false language. As Derrida points out, however, the examples Husserl uses come from the practical as opposed to the cognitive order ("You have gone wrong, you can't go on like that"), and Derrida finds this "revelatory" of the Husserlian project in two ways.

The examples must be practical because they must show two things: (1) that there is no indication at work in them, that they are fictitious communication; and (2) that they are "false language," that they do not give the subject any knowledge of herself. These two are intimately interrelated. For Husserl, there is no real communication in soliloquy, and this means that interior speech cannot give the "speaker" knowledge of herself. If the examples were cognitive, they would have to take the form of a "telling oneself that *S* is *p*" and would thus indeed give the subject knowledge of herself. Therefore, the examples must be practical, that is, nontheoretical, noncognitive. But this strategy cannot succeed, for Husserl determines language in general, including both indication and expression, on the model of theoretical language, of a cognitive relation to an object. His treatment of both indication and expression as *Zeigen* has an essential unity, so that to exclude one function is to exclude the other. Thus the speech in his examples must be "false discourse." But since expression has been determined in terms of a cognitive relation to an object, this means that the examples, against Husserl's express intentions, are not examples of expression at all. The baby has been thrown out with the bath water.

Thus Husserl is caught in a pincers movement of his own making. If the expressive function is to be protected in its purity, we must turn to the voice: the sense of the being of that which is essentially an object is determined by the uncontaminated unity of voice and sense. But this sense of being requires that the voice be heard/understood (*s'entendre*). In this hearing/understanding, in which the voice affects itself, two essential moments come together: the preservation of the objectness of the object in the purity of meaning and the proximity of the voice to itself. Objectivity and subjectivity — the outside of the ob-ject and the inside of thought, of the sub-ject — mutually imply each other. But by the same token, the contamination of the one will be the contamination of the other.

Indeed, this dignity of the voice is merely apparent. Here the voice is consciousness, but since self-presence as hearing/understanding oneself is an auto-affection, the self-presence of consciousness is divided by difference. Consciousness is present to itself only by virtue of the inner diremption into speaker/hearer: this difference produces the subject. Thus the attempt to find self-presence in the *Augenblick* fails when we turn to soliloquy.

But what of the phenomenological silence of the preexpressive stratum of experience? Surely here we can find a pure self-presence prior even to the voice itself. The study of Husserl's phenomenology of internal time-consciousness, however, shows that autoaffection is at work at the most primitive levels of temporalization: a now is a now only by means of self-affection, a movement in which retention is constitutive of the presence of the present itself. Thus, prior even to the "phenomenological voice" itself, we find a "protowriting" of the retentional trace. Sense is itself always already expressive. The search for an "inside" fails, for autoaffection means that consciousness is always already a "going-forth" into the world.

Thus both moves fail: the search for a purity of self-presence in the voice and the search for a preexpressive stratum of sense. In both sites we find the movement of difference already at work. This primordiality of difference is the interweaving of indication and expression, of sense and expression. What Husserl views as an additional function under specific conditions turns out to be essential: it makes up for an essential deficiency and is thus required.

Self-Presence and the Voice

The search for the "inside" that would be the origin of the exteriorization of expression has two stages. In the first we move from the "outside" voice of communication to the "inner life" of soliloquy, free of indicative functions. In the second we move from the expressiveness of logical meaning to the prevocal silence of preexpressive sense. In each case, Derrida sees Husserl searching for pure self-presence in the unity of the moment, the *Augenblick*, first in the purity of expression of the "phenomenological voice" that is uncontaminated by indication and then in the source of that expression in a preexpressive silence. This silence can be found only if we exclude or reduce both the outer voice of communication, with its indicative dimension, and the inner voice of soliloquy, where words, though imaginary, continue to play their role and thus to bring in repetition and absence. This silence would be the ultimate inside, the source of all ex-pression. Derrida will focus on each of these exclusions in turn, claiming that each demonstrates its own impossibility. At the same time, the privilege of the voice that he has claimed for phenomenological analysis ever since the Introduction should finally be clarified at the very moment that it is undermined.

Now, it should be noted that this stress on the inside is Derrida's, not Husserl's. Derrida refers to Husserl's "all too summary description of 'inner life' " (*SP*, 78/70), but his quotation marks are scare quotes, not the sign of a quotation (this is also true of the term " 'simplified' " at *SP*, 79/71). Husserl does not speak of "inner life" in §8, and as we have seen, soliloquy can be uttered and can concern the world. And rather than discussing the full range of soliloquy, Derrida focuses on the representation of oneself as talking to oneself.

Husserl's example of a merely represented speaking and communicating is an example of self-address: "You have gone wrong, you can't go on like that." This is an example, not of solitary speech in general, but rather of the special case in which one not only "speaks, in a certain sense, even in soliloquy," but in addition thinks "of oneself as speaking, and even as speaking to oneself" (*LI* II.1, 36/I, 279–80). There is a three-stage specification here. First we have soliloquy, which need not be addressed to anyone—as when I muse, "That simply doesn't follow." Then we have the special case in which I think of myself as speaking— as when I muse, out loud or silently, "That simply doesn't follow, M. Derrida." Finally, we have the additional specification that I think of myself as speaking to myself, and this is where Husserl gives his example. Derrida thinks that the fact that this example comes from the practical as opposed to the cognitive order is telling.

In claiming that Husserl has to choose his examples from the practical sphere, Derrida has several things in mind. (1) He is assuming a very strong distinction between the practical and the cognitive. He is claiming that, in spite of appearances, "You have gone wrong" is "nontheoretical, nonlogical, and noncognitive," that it does not formulate anything that could be called "knowledge" of oneself (*SP*, 81/72) Nowhere does he attempt to show that Husserl accepts such a position, or that, regardless of Husserl's position, it is correct. (2) He is assuming that Husserl says or is committed to saying that in such examples not only is there no speech "in the genuine sense of communication" (*LI* II.1, 36/I, 280), but the "feigned communication" is "false languages" (*faux langages*), "false discourse" (*discours faux*), and "completely fictitious signification" (*signification parfaitement fictif* (*SP*, 78/70, 79/71, 81/72). This is precisely what Husserl does not claim. (3) Derrida confronts the examples from the practical sphere with the fact that Husserl "always determined the model of language in general— indicative   as   well   as   expressive—on   the   basis   of   *theōrein*" (*SP*, 79/71). But there is no discussion of what this means in Husserl's analyses. (4) He is assuming that since there is no real communication and thus no indication in such examples, the words cannot even formulate any knowledge concerning the speaker. Only on this assumption does it make sense to move from the correct statement that the proposition "does not give the subject any knowledge of himself" (where "give" must be taken in the sense of "communicate") to the false claim that therefore the proposition is "nontheoretical, nonlogical, and noncognitive" (*SP*, 81/72). These issues clearly require more discussion.

It is true enough that in the Sixth Investigation Husserl argues that questions, orders, wishes, and so on are equivalent to judgments about the acts of asking, commanding, wishing, and so on (see *LI*, Sixth Investigation, §§66–70, esp. §69). For example, "Is *S p*?" "in essence says the same" as "I should like to know . . . " (*LI* II.2, 213/II, 844). Thus performatives are interpreted in terms of constatives, the practical in terms of the theoretical. Two comments are in order here. In the first place, it remains to be seen whether this position is the necessary result of fundamental principles of phenomenology, and only in this case could it be used against Husserl in the broad manner required by Derrida's argument. In fact, early Munich phenomenologists such as Johannes Daubert, Alexander Pfänder, and Adolf Reinach challenged Husserl on precisely this issue (cf. Schuhmann 1988; 1985; 1987). So we are faced with a controversial issue within phenomenology itself, and Derrida's investigation is not set up to take such things into account. In the second place, Husserl's account works *against* Derrida's claims. If in the course of an inner pep talk one "says," "Would that you would think things through more carefully in the future," on Husserl's account this would be equivalent to "I wish that . . . ," which is a judgment, and judgments for Husserl can be true or false. Derrida's distinction between the practical and the "cognitive" or "logical" is not what is at issue in Husserl's examples. A careful reading of Husserl's text indicates that there is no reason such "speech" should not be theoretical or cognitive.

Derrida's strategy seems to be to construct a parallel: Just as

(1) Merely imagined indicative signs do not function indicatively; they are merely imagined to do so.

and

(2) Merely imagined communicative signs do not function communicatively; they are merely imagined to do so.

so also

(3) Merely imagined expressive signs do not function expressively; they are merely imagined to do so.

Which would allow Derrida to draw his conclusion:

(4) "Thus we confirm the unity of *Zeigen* before its diffraction into indication and expression."

But the third statement is, for Husserl, false, so the conclusion does not follow. Only to the extent that speech pretends to be genuine communication is it merely represented or imagined speech. If we take this restriction to communication to be a stipulative definition of "speech," then we will have to speak of discourse, as opposed to speech, in solitary life, and it is clear that even the imagined words of such discourse still exercise an expressive function for Husserl. Husserl writes, "But in the genuine, communicative sense [*im eigentlichen, kommunikativen Sinne*] one does not speak in such cases, one does not pass on anything to oneself [*man teilt sich nichts mit*]: one merely imagines oneself as speaking and communicating" (*LI* II.1 36/I, 280, translation altered). But he turns right around and speaks of "monological discourse" (*monologischen Rede*) in the next sentence. And he has no difficulty writing "One of course speaks, in a certain sense, even in soliloquy" (*LI* II.1, 36/I, 279). There is nothing about "false languages," "false discourse," or "fictitious signification" here. Finally, Husserl does not recognize — and Derrida gives us no reason to recognize — an essential connection between the exclusion of communication and the exclusion of knowledge. I can formulate knowledge about myself (or, for that matter, about others) in soliloquy. Indeed, I can surely discover new things about myself in soliloquy. But I cannot, Husserl argues, in the true sense communicate such knowledge, once discovered, to myself.

There remains one last point in this regard. Derrida asserts that not only expression but also indication is defined as an essentially theoretical function of "aiming at an object" (*SP*, 80/71). This may be, but it is not at all clear that for this reason expression may be "contaminated" by indication. We have encountered this claim before, and it is no more convincing now than it was then. But now it seems to open the way for an argument or demonstration. "Signs

(*Zeichen*) always refer to *Zeigen*, to the space, visibility, field, and compass of what is ob-jected and pro-jected" (*SP*, 80/72), of things set over against the subject (*Gegen-stand*). This picks up on Derrida's claim that indication always moves between existents, one existing thing indicating the existence of another thing. "Space" here indicates an order of difference, of "being outside itself" (*SP*, 94/84 n. 9) and thus of exteriority. It is contrasted with time, the order in which (for Husserl) such difference is excluded, in which a pure self-presence without difference is possible in the unity of the moment: Derrida assumes that the move to soliloquy is a move from field, space, and exteriority to immanence and interiority, to pure self-presence in time, in the present. And while Derrida is suggesting that *no* sign will be able to conserve that presence, on his reading of Husserl this conservation is the task of speech, the voice, and especially the inner or "phenomenological" voice, purified of all indication and thus of all space, all difference.

True presence is thus to be possible only in speech: "It is here that it is necessary *to speak*" (*SP*, 82/74, translation altered). Being as presence is a function of "the unity of the *phōnē* and sense."[1] The very sense of being as presence has its origin in the immediate presence of meaning in the voice, "the unity of thought and voice in logos" (*SP*, 82–83/74). It is thus clear that if this immediate presence of meaning is "deconstructed," the sense of being as presence will be similarly deconstructed. And it is only in *listening* to the spoken word that we can *understand* its peculiar prerogative: "It is here that it is necessary to hear/ understand (oneself) [C'est ici qu'il faut s'entendre]" (*SP*, 83/74, translation altered).[2] Here we can see how the "it is necessary to speak" and the "it is necessary to listen/understand" fit together. Derrida does not use the more normal *écouter* (to listen), nor does he use the nonreflexive *entendre* (to hear; to understand). Thus in the first place it is necessary to speak, since thought moves in speech. But in the second place it is necessary to hear/understand oneself speak, since there is an essential self-presence or reflexivity in all thought/speech.

On Derrida's reading we find the origin of the sense of the object's being as presence and the subject's being as self-presence in this self-presence of speech to itself. An "object" is "a thing thrown before or presented to the mind or thought" (the prefix "ob-" carries the meanings "in the direction of, towards, facing; against, in opposition"), and "presence" is formed from the prefix "pre-," meaning "before, in front, in advance," and "-ence," which forms an abstract substantive (Oxford English Dictionary). Thus Derrida writes that expression "must protect, respect, and restore the *presence* of sense, *both as the object's being before us*, open to view, and *as a proximity to self in interiority*. The *pre* of the *present ob*ject now-before us is an *against* (*Gegen*wart, *Gegen*-stand) both in the sense of the 'up-against' [*tout-contre*] of proximity and as the *opposition* [*l'encontre*] of the op-posed" (*SP*, 84–85/75). Present to me in the present: this is what logical meaning must protect—the object present to me, my presence to myself. To be pre-sent is to be set over against (ob-ject, *Gegen-stand*, *Gegen-wart*): both proximity and opposition.

Here Derrida recurs to *Ideas* §124: logical meaning is expression of the pre-expressive stratum, a mirroring. Expression is "the specifically 'logical' medium" (*Hua* III.1, 287/296), a "unique intentional medium . . . which, according to its essence, has the distinction, so to speak, of mirroring every other intentionality according to form and content, depicting it in its own colors and hence imprinting on it its own form of 'conceptuality' " (*Hua* III.1, 286/295, translation altered). This meaning is what it is only by reference to possible reiteration, repetition. What Derrida calls the "phenomenological voice" (*SP*, 84/75), the "voice that keeps silence," *is* this repetition. The voice "points to" (*hinzeigen*) its meaning: the voice is part of the system of *Zeigen*. Repetition and ideality are a function of the *phōnē*.

Derrida considers the objection that the ideal form of any signifier is nonreal, is not in the world. Why should the voice be privileged? But even the imaginative presentation of a written sign "involves a spatial reference in its very 'phenomenon,' in the phenomenological (nonworldly) sphere of experience in which it is given." It is the imagination of a worldly phenomenon. Speech, however, according to the account Derrida is attributing to Husserl, is different: "Apparently there is nothing like this in the phenomenon of speech" (*SP*, 85/76) (the "apparently" attributes this position to Husserl). The lived experience of seeing oneself (even imagining seeing oneself) involves an intrinsic spatial reference, whereas the experience of hearing oneself does not. In hearing/understanding the inner voice, "the subject does not have to pass forth beyond himself to be immediately affected by his expressive activity" (*SP*, 85/76). This is Derrida's semiotic *cogito*, which was introduced in chapter 4: "The subject cannot speak without giving himself a representation of his speaking, and this is no accident" (*SP*, 64/57). Now it turns out that for Derrida's Husserl, it is not enough to see the reflexivity of the *cogito* in speech; speech *is* the *cogito*. "No consciousness is possible without the voice" (*SP*, 89/79). Consciousness is present to itself in this purely inner, silent hearing/understanding of the phenomenological voice, in this self-affection of the self by the self.

Now Derrida draws some preliminary conclusions:

> We can understand why the hypothesis of the "monologue" could have sanctioned the distinction between indication and expression only by presupposing an essential tie between expression and *phōnē*. Between the phonic element (in the phenomenological sense and not that of a real sound)[3] and expression, taken as the logical character of a signifier that is *animated* in view of the ideal presence of a *Bedeutung* (itself related to an object), there must be a necessary bond. Husserl is unable to bracket what in glossamatics is called the "substance of expression" without menacing his whole enterprise. (*SP*, 85–86/76–77).

Before we look at Derrida's demonstration that this peculiar dignity of the voice is merely apparent, a few things should be noted. Although Derrida appeals to §124 of the *Ideas* (*SP*, 82/73), as we noted earlier, Husserl is not talking about signs when he speaks of logical meaning as an expression. Such meaning and expression is the precondition for there being verbal signs: "The verbal sound can be called an expression only because the meaning belonging to it expresses; expressing inheres in [the meaning] originaliter" (*Hua* III.1, 286/295, translation altered). The "medium" is an "intentional medium," not a linguistic medium. This is made clear in *Ideas*, §94, which in entitled "Noesis and Noema in the Realm of Judgment." In discussing the noema of the act of judging, the "judged as judged," or the "judgment," Husserl suggests that "here, for the sake of simplicity, [we] disregard the higher stratum pertaining to *verbal 'expression'* " (*Hua* III.1, 216/227–28, emphasis added). Thus neither judging nor judgment is linguistic. The "intentional medium" of logical meaning as an expression is not linguistic. Husserl even emphasizes this: the process of judging "does not require the slightest bit of 'expression,' either expression in the sense of verbal sound or anything like a verbal signifying, which is also capable of being present independently of the verbal sound (as when the sound is 'forgotten')" (*Hua* III.1, 285/295, translation altered). Yet the logical meaning, the judgment, that is constituted in this act is "an expression" — an explication or conceptual articulation of the preexpressive perceptual sense. All of this makes it clear that for Husserl the voice, be it the "phenomenological voice" or not, is not the original medium of meaning, is not the locus of presence that Derrida claims it is.

So when Derrida speaks of a "necessary bond" between expression and the phenomenological voice, this is precisely what Husserl has *not* asserted. But is this bond implied by Husserl's position, even if it is contradicted by his explicit claims? Derrida suggests that it is: "Deaf and dumb go hand in hand. He who is deaf can engage in colloquy only by shaping his acts in the form of words, whose telos requires that they be heard by him who utters them" (*SP*, 87–88/78). This statement expresses a prejudice concerning the profoundly deaf, a prejudice that could properly be called phonologistic. It is this prejudice that led to the insistence that the deaf learn to speak rather than learning sign language. This prejudice is now rather widely recognized as such, and deaf persons who are raised with American Sign Language as their "mother tongue" (!) *think* in ASL. There is no *telos* of vocality here, and nothing in Husserl's position requires that he claim that there is such a *telos*. The prejudice is all Derrida's. Husserl's example of soliloquy is indeed one of an imagined speaking to oneself, but there is no reason his example could not have concerned an imagined self-communication in ASL. When Derrida sets out to show that "the phenomenological value of the voice, its transcendent dignity . . . is only apparent," he is arguing against an imaginary opponent.

Language and the Epochē

Speech has a unique status on Derrida's account: "Considered from a purely phenomenological point of view, within the reduction, the process of speech has the originality of representing itself already as pure phenomenon, as having already suspended the natural attitude and the existential thesis of the world" (*SP*, 88/78). In what sense is this the case? In his earlier *Edmund Husserl's 'Origin of Geometry': An Introduction*, Derrida cites André de Muralt as the source of this interpretation: "André de Muralt notes very precisely that the '*reduction is implicitly carried out*—simply performed and not yet made explicit—as soon as language is considered on its own account' " (Derrida 1978a, 67–68, quoting Muralt, 128)[4]. It is clear from the context that Muralt is talking about the phenomenological reduction. But Derrida carefully notes against Muralt that when we are speaking of language what is at issue is the eidetic, not the phenomenological, reduction:

> Here we are concerned with the eidetic reduction. But, paradoxically, for this reason it seems more difficult to say that 'a thought which moves solely on the level of language is necessarily in the attitude of the *phenomenological reduction*; it is set squarely in the eidetic world of significations or pure lived experiences.' (Derrida 1978a, 68, quoting Muralt, 128, Derrida's emphasis)

Derrida agrees with the latter part of Muralt's statement, but properly distances himself from the first part. In *Speech and Phenomena* he seems to have joined Muralt completely, though he offers no reason for this shift.

Now, it must be granted that the ability to speak in the full sense necessarily involves the ability to consider what one has said and thought purely as something asserted or thought. Husserl characterizes this as a noematic reflection in which, instead of thematizing things and making judgments about them, we thematize "the supposed objectivities *as supposed*" (*Hua* XVII, 122). As we no longer posit the being of the supposed object, this involves a neutrality modification, but not a phenomenological reduction. In the *Ideas* Husserl describes the neutrality modification as a "putting-something-out-of-action, 'parenthesizing-' it, 'leaving-something-undecided,' " and so on, and he goes on to say that such modifying "parentheses" are "closely akin to that of which we have spoken so much before" (*Hua* III.1, 248/258–59), namely, the phenomenological reduction. But in his personal copy of the *Ideas* he wrote "*nein*" in the margin next to this sentence. Husserl's reason for rejecting his own claim is, I think, that the reduction is a reflective operation, performed as one reflects on conscious life. It is related to, but not identical with, the normal neutrality modification. Thus the most one might claim would be that the ability to speak and think involves the capacity in principle to perform the reduction. But this is a far cry from claiming that speech has "already suspended the natural attitude and the existential thesis of the world." Nothing in Husserl supports such a claim.

Derrida's reason for asserting it is that in speaking, even in speaking out loud, the speaking subject's self-presence does not pass through the world, is not a function of a true hearing. "The subject can hear or speak to himself and be affected by the signifier he produces, without passing through an external detour, the world, the sphere of what is not 'his own' " (*SP*, 88/78). But as we have noted, soliloquy has nothing to do with Husserl's later "reduction to the sphere of ownness." Soliloquy concerns *imagined* words, and the field of that imagination—in the sense both of the imagining and of the imagined words—is an intersubjective field.

Writing and the Merely Apparent Dignity of the Voice

On the one hand, Husserl thinks that all language (and, more importantly, all meaning, linguistic or not) is founded upon a prelinguistic and preexpressive stratum of sense. Derrida speaks of "reducing" language (*SP*, 90/80), but this is rather an example of Husserl's method of *Abbau*, un-building or de-constructing (cf. Evans 1990a). On the other hand, Husserl emphasizes the crucial role writing plays in the development of sciences such as geometry, which deal with ideal objects. But according to Derrida, this writing is phonetic writing, writing oriented toward the primacy of the spoken word, and phonetic writing is indicative of the spoken, expressive word (*SP*, 90/80–81). Derrida suggested in chapter 2 of *Speech and Phenomena* that "writing is *indicative* in its own sphere" (*SP*, 29/27 n. 1), but here as there we find no argument for this claim. Derrida's strongest reason for claiming such indicative status for writing is found in his statement that "writing is a body that expresses something only if we actually pronounce the verbal expression that animates it, if its space is temporalized," and this requires an act of meaning, *bedeuten*, that is, "an act of wanting-to-say" (*SP*, 91/81). Reading is speaking.

Husserl does not seem to accept this thesis. In the *Crisis* he writes that "written signs . . . as linguistic signs . . . awaken, as do linguistic sounds, their familiar significations" (*Hua* VI, 371/361). Husserl neither here nor elsewhere asserts a metaphysical primacy of the voice. But this secondary, indicative status of the written is crucial to Derrida's argument, for his claim is that in Husserl's own analyses "the possibility of writing dwelt within speech" (*SP*, 92/82). If the movement of thought is a hearing/understanding oneself speak, the essential moment of autoaffection introduces difference into the supposed unity of self-presence. Whereas Husserl could argue that the second person in the imaginative self-address of soliloquy is "a fiction," as Derrida puts it (*SP*, 78/70), here the structure of difference, of speaking/hearing, is essential. And Derrida draws a strong conclusion from this: "Taking auto-affection as the exercise of the voice, auto-affection supposes that a pure difference comes to divide self-presence. . . . As soon as it is admitted that auto-affection is the condition for self-presence, no pure transcendental reduction is possible. . . . We come closest to [this difference] in the movement of differance" (*SP*, 92/82). *Différance* brings together the "spatial" order of difference, of "being outside itself" in the sense of a field of differentiations, and the "temporal" order of deferring. On Derrida's reading, both dimensions turn out to be at work at the very heart of self-presence, and this *différance* is constitutive of the subject.

Now, granting for the moment Derrida's claim that difference is primordial, why would it follow that "no pure transcendental reduction is possible"? This makes sense only on the assumption that the reduction is a search for an "inside" that bans all exteriority and difference, an inside that is pure self-presence indebted to no difference at all, whether "spatial" or temporal. But this is not the sense of the transcendental reduction. Husserl repeatedly speaks of the "*field* of transcendental experience' (*Hua* I, 69/31, emphasis added; *Hua* VIII, 69f.; cf. Landgrebe, §3). Intentional life is shot through with "co-awareness," "potentiality," and "horizon intentionalities" (*Hua* I, 75/37, 81/44, 83/45). If the primordiality of difference makes such transcendental reflection impossible, this will have to be shown.

In the 1920s, Husserl did attempt to work out an "apodictic reduction" within the framework of the transcendental reduction. But in the course of his lectures on "First Philosophy" in 1923–24 Husserl subjected the Cartesian presuppositions of this project to a critique, which has been analyzed in an exemplary manner by Ludwig Landgrebe. As Landgrebe puts it, Husserl discovered that "transcendental subjectivity is not exhausted by the 'present actuality' [*Aktuosität*] of consciousness and that all constituted 'sense' and 'meaning' cannot be traced back to this aspect of consciousness' (Landgrebe, 152/90). This recapitulates on the level of a phenomenology of phenomenology the results of Husserl's investigations of internal time-consciousness. In both cases, it turns out that there is no such thing as an immediate self-presence in a pure present, that horizons are necessarily constitutive of any present. These horizons include both the temporal horizons of past and future and the (in Derrida's broad sense) "spatial" horizon of the world. The pure ego "conceals within itself unsuspected and deeply hidden mediacies of *intentional implications*, without whose unravelling pure life remains completely unintelligible" (*Hua* VIII, 123). It is the Cartesian motif in Husserl's thought that makes Derrida's claims seem plausible, but this motif was effectively criticized by Husserl himself, and the "shipwreck" of the Cartesian path to the phenomenological reduction, which Landgrebe argues is in a specific sense the "shipwreck of transcendental subjectivism" (Landgrebe, 136/68), is not the shipwreck of transcendental phenomenology. It rather opens the way for Husserl's later turn to the life-world and to historical becoming in the *Crisis*.

Self-Presence and the Preexpressive

Derrida follows Husserl's last remaining possibility of avoiding the conclusion that difference is primordial. Perhaps, after all, difference enters the life of consciousness with the voice and its autoaffection. This would leave the preexpressive as the realm of pure self-present identity. But this too will turn out to be a dead end on Derrida's reading.

Derrida argues that the concept of autoaffection is necessary because "even before being expressed, sense is through and through temporal" (SP, 93/83), and autoaffection turns up again at the very heart of temporalization in Husserl's own analysis. The primordial impression that for Husserl is the source-point for all temporalization is itself autoaffection. Derrida's argument for this centers on a text from Husserl's lectures on time-consciousness:

> The primal impression is the absolute beginning of this generation—the primal source, that from which all others are continuously generated. In itself, however, it is not generated; it does not come into existence as that which is generated but through *genesis spontanea*: it is *original generation*. It does not grow up (it has no seed): it is primal creation. (*Hua* X, 100/131, Derrida's emphasis, quoted at *SP*, 93–94/83–84, translation altered)[5]

In this text Husserl analyzes primal impression and retention as a continuum, namely, as a "rectilinear [*orthoidal*] multiplicity limited on one side" (*Hua* X, 99/129, translation altered). Every point on this continuum, with one exception, is characterized as a systematic modification of another point, and in this respect Husserl compares the continuum to a continuity of intensities beginning with zero. Thus we find modification, modification of modification, and so on, "*ad infinitum* and infinitesimally" (*Hua* X, 100/130). Every point can be viewed as the modification of another point, with the exception of the primal impression, which in terms of this continuum is the absolute beginning, that is, is not a modification of anything else in this series.

This last phrase is important, for if the continuum is defined in these terms, Husserl is quite right to say that the primal impression is "spontaneous generation," which is to say that it is not generated within the continuum as a modification. But by the same token, it becomes clear that this is a very limited context. Specifically, the entire dimension of protentions is left out. As we have seen, Husserl later came to realize that the present and thus primal impression is essentially the fulfillment of past protentions. And once protentions are added to the continuum, there is a sense, which would require precise analysis, in which the primal impression is generated: it is a modification of and a fulfillment (in a broad sense that includes degrees of fulfillment) of a protention.

Now, it is clear that the generation that Husserl analyzes here, namely, the structure of modification, modification of modification, and so on, can be called autoaffection: the modification is a structure of consciousness produced by consciousness itself. Within Husserl's framework in the text in question, the one exception would seem to be the primal impression. Husserl first tries to distinguish primal impression, as something which is "not generated," from all retentional modifications by saying that it comes to be through "*genesis spontanea*," and then improves this to "it is primal creation" (*Hua* X, 100/131). Derrida argues, however, that it is precisely the primal impression that is generated by autoaffection:

> The process by which the living now, produced by spontaneous generation, must, in order to be a now and to be retained in another now, affect itself without recourse to anything empirical but with a new primordial actuality in which it would become a non-now, a past now— this process is indeed a pure auto-affection in which the same is the same only in being affected by the other, only by becoming the other of the same. (*SP*, 95/85)

This autoaffection seems to have two aspects. In the first place, the living now must affect itself with a new living now, the former thereby becoming a non-now. But this is precisely what Husserl denies, namely, that the new now is generated as a modification of an element of the continuum. In the second place, the primal impression is affected by another primal impression, this affection generating the modification of the former primal impression into a retentional modification. Derrida describes this as the process whereby "the primordial impression is here affected by nothing other than itself, by the absolute 'novelty' of another primordial impression which is another now" (*SP*, 95/85).

Derrida's own description, which equates "nothing other than itself" with "another primordial impression which is another now," betrays a misplaced concreteness. The "nothing other than itself" must move on the generic level, or rather on the level of form. Here we can speak of the unchanging form of appearing temporality, with changing contents filling the form of past-present-future. But the "another now" must be a particular primal impression. (Note that as is often the case, the structure of primal impression/retention is not distinguished from the structure of the now/past constituted in the former.)

Derrida emphasizes the frankly metaphorical character of Husserl's descriptions, quoting Husserl's famous "For all of this, names are lacking" (*Hua* X, 75/100, quoted at *SP*, 94/84 n. 9). But it is not at all clear that Husserl is using metaphors in his description of absolute consciousness. Husserl argues rather that it makes no sense to say that the time-constituting phenomena are themselves now or have been previously:

> To be sure, one can and must say that a certain continuity of
> appearance, namely, one which is a phase of the temporally constituting
> flux, *belongs* to a now, namely, to that which it *constitutes*. . . . But is
> not the flux a succession? Does it not, after all, have a now, a current
> phase, and a continuity of pasts of which we are now conscious in
> retentions? We cannot say anything other than: This flux is something
> which we name thus *in conformity with what is constituted*, but it is
> nothing temporally 'Objective'. (*Hua* X, 75/100, quoted at *SP*, 94/84 n.
> 9, translation altered)

Does this mean that such descriptions are metaphorical? Husserl says only that
the description of absolute consciousness as a "flow" or "flux" is an image.
(One might wonder whether this image does not function as a model. Observe
how in §35 Husserl begins with the concept of a flow and then systematically
notes the points of disanalogy with what is normally called a flow, namely, a constituted flow.) But saying that the phases "belong to" the now that they constitute seems to be anything but a metaphor. On Husserl's account, this would seem
to be the specifically adequate description of absolute consciousness itself. Note
too that when Husserl speaks of the continuum of primal impression and retention, he writes that "whereas with other continua the talk of generation was only
figurative, what we have here is an authentic way of speaking" (*Hua* X,
100/130, translation altered). To say that "every language fails to describe this
pure movement other than by metaphor" (*SP*, 94/84) is thus to distort Husserl's
claims.

When Derrida writes, "But we have been always already adrift in ontic metaphor; temporalization here is the root of a metaphor that can only be primordial" (*SP*, 95/85), the strategic thrust is unmistakable. We noted earlier the un-
dramatic appearance of the phrase "indicative or metaphorical" (*SP*, 6/8, 9/10)
in the Introduction to *Speech and Phenomena*. The importance of this equation is
clear once we realize that when Husserl distinguishes indication from expression,
metaphor will fall on the side of indication if we blindly accept Derrida's phrase.
And Derrida is now quick to make use of that suggestion: "The word 'time' itself, as it has always been understood in the history of metaphysics, is a metaphor which *at the same time* both indicates and dissimulates the 'movement' of
this auto-affection" (*SP*, 95/85).

All of this concerns what Husserl calls "absolute consciousness" or "absolute subjectivity." Derrida writes:

> It is not by chance that he still designates this unnameable as an
> "absolute subjectivity," that is, as a being conceived on the basis of
> presence as substance, *ousia*, *hypokeimenon*: a self-identical being in
> self-presence which forms the substance of a subject. . . . *All this is
> present, and we can name it, the proof being that its being as absolute*

subjectivity is not questioned. What is unnameable, according to Husserl, are only the "absolute properties" of this subject; the subject therefore is indeed designated in terms of the classical metaphysical schema which distinguishes substance (present being) from its attributes. (*SP*, 94/84 n. 9)

Now in the first place, Husserl does not call anything "unnameable," he merely says that we do not have already formulated names for this dimension; and we have just looked at other texts that make it clear that Husserl thinks that we can give an authentic account of the structures of absolute consciousness. In addition, falling back into a classical metaphysics of presence as substance, and so on, seems to be precisely what Husserl is not doing here. Absolute consciousness is fundamentally a presencing of inner objects, and the issue of its own self-presence is raised only subsequently. When it is raised, it seems to be given two answers: (1) It is answered in terms of the double intentionality of retention (*Hua* X, §39). But even here one must recall the warnings given in §35: in this flow, and even in the unity of the ultimate constituting flow of consciousness, "any Object which changes is lacking here, and inasmuch as in every process 'something' proceeds, it is not a question here of a process. There is nothing here which changes, and therefore it makes no sense to speak here of something that endures" (*Hua* X, 74/99, translation altered). (2) In a text written in about 1911, Husserl toys with the suggestion that absolute consciousness is itself constituted in a "last consciousness." As Husserl sees, this model produces the problem of "a necessarily 'unconscious' consciousness" (*Hua* X, 382), a non-self-present presencing (see Evans 1990b for a discussion of this attempt). In neither answer do we have anything that can be called "substance, *ousia, hypokeimenon*" in any classical sense, in the sense of a self-identical being in self-presence. There is nothing here that could be self-identical.

Ultimately, Derrida's claim for self-affection hinges on the claim that the presentness of the present is dependent on, affected by, the horizon of the past, and that for this reason primal impression itself must be seen as a modification of retention. In this sense even the primal impression would be "generated" in Husserl's sense: there would be no unmodified zero point, no pure origin of all modification. Derrida speaks of this dependence of the present on the horizon of the past as "a retentional trace" that is constitutive of the present itself: "It is always already a trace" (*SP*, 95/85). As the trace is nothing other than re-petition (see *SP*, 75/67), this means that the very presentness of the present consists in repetition. This is to make good on Derrida's earlier claim that "the possibility of writing dwelt within speech" (*SP*, 92/82), for the trace is a "protowriting" (*SP*, 95/85) inscribed in the text of the present. This concept is developed further in Derrida's essay "*Différance*," where he writes:

Différance is what makes the movement of signification possible only if each element that is said to be "present," appearing on the stage of presence, is related to something other than itself, thereby keeping within itself the mark of a past element and already letting itself be hollowed out by the mark of its relation to a future element. This trace . . . constitutes what is called the present by this very relation to what it is not, to what it absolutely is not; that is, not even to a past or future considered as a modified present. . . . The use of language or the employment of any code that implies a play of forms . . . also presupposes a retention and protention of differences, a spacing and temporalizing, a play of traces. This play must be a sort of inscription prior to writing, a protowriting without a present origin, without an *archē*. (Derrida 1973b, 142, 146, translation altered)

For traditional accounts, writing is fundamentally the sign of a sign (*OG*, 45/29), and Derrida has suggested earlier that writing is indicative. Thus the present is indicative of a past, and indication turns out to be constitutive of the very presentness of the present. The project of eliminating this indicative moment would be the effacement of consciousness itself.

For Derrida this shows that for structural reasons one cannot speak of a preexpressive stratum of sense. If sense is a trace, if sense is such only by an immanent relation to other sense, rather than being simply present as it itself in the moment, then it brings with it an entire structure, and this structure can no longer be distinguished from the order of meaning, the expressive order. Sense is fundamentally a structure, an "order of 'signification' " (*SP*, 96/85); because any given sense is an "openness upon exteriority in general, upon the sphere of what is not 'one's own,' " etc., *the temporalization of sense is, from the outset, a spacing*" (*SP*, 96/86). Not only is the so-called preexpressive stratum always already expression, the self-present moment required for the autoaffection of the "phenomenological voice" turns out to bear within itself reference to an outside.

In evaluating this argument two things must be kept in mind, aside from the points already made. In the first place, all of this operates within Husserl's framework of absolute consciousness. When Derrida writes that "this determination of 'absolute subjectivity' would also have to be crossed out [*raturée*] as soon as we conceive the present on the basis of difference, and not the reverse. The concept of *subjectivity* belongs *a priori and in general* to the order of the *constituted*" (*SP*, 94/84 n. 9), I have a certain sympathy for this view. But I do not think Derrida goes far enough. I would argue that the entire conceptual apparatus of absolute time-constituting consciousness should not be merely crossed out, which for Derrida means to cross out the word and retain it as crossed out (cf. *OG*, 37–38/23; Spivak, xiv; Heidegger 1978, 31/83). That is not at all what is required. We need to reject the entire theory as a myth, not to deconstruct it (cf. Evans 1990b). The subject does belong to the order of the constituted, but for

Husserl this means that we must take seriously the concept of self-constitution. This would indeed involve "conceiving the present on the basis of difference," but it is by no means clear that it leads to *différance*. Indeed, at least a start toward making the needed revisions can be found in Husserl's own work. And note that the concept of absolute time-constituting consciousness is a concept developed within transcendental phenomenology, within the reduction. It is not to be equated with the transcendental field itself.

This leads to the second point. Derrida's analyses have a powerfully deconstructive force only if we assume that Husserl's enterprise is essentially wedded to the concept of "an inside that is closed in upon itself" (*SP*, 96/86). The transcendental field, however, is not an inside, but rather a field that "rightly understood, contains within itself, 'constitutes' within itself, all worldly transcendencies" (*Hua* III.1, 107/113). In addition, we have seen that Derrida's interpretation of Husserl's concept of the "moment" [*Augenblick*] in the *Logical Investigations* and of the now-phase in the manuscripts on time-consciousness is indefensible. If one drops Derrida's often rather overheated rhetoric and weeds out the misinterpretations, one can find his analyses in Husserl's own work.

Moreover, Derrida claims on the basis of the discovery of difference at the very heart of presence as self-presence that "phenomenological reduction is a scene, a theater stage [*scène*]" (*SP*, 96/86). In one sense, this is just what Husserl himself claims in saying that there is a "field" of transcendental experience. Husserl did pursue the Cartesian project of finding a moment of adequate givenness in this field, but that project collapsed in the course of his lectures on "First Philosophy." Everything that appears in this field does so with its "as this" or "as that," and this "as" involves horizons, an "outside." The things themselves appear, but always constituted "as." The concept of constitution is radicalized, not deconstructed as Derrida would have it (*SP*, 94/85 n. 9). But Derrida has something different in mind here. On his stage there appear, not the things themselves, but rather representatives, actors. These representatives are, as it were, pure representatives, pure actors, nothing but functionality; they are the pure play of roles. But here the rhetoric must be stripped away. Just as Derrida has protested against readers who took his famous "There is nothing outside the text" too literally (though they certainly seemed to have good reason to read it as they did), so here too we must take care. Once the misconceptions of Husserl's enterprise have been stripped away, is the defensible moment in Derrida's concept of the stage really that different from Husserl's field?

Finally, when Derrida claims in the final paragraph of chapter 6 that just as the so-called preexpressive is already expressive, so too expression is already indicative, this is not argued, but merely suggested by analogy. Only on the assumption that expression has its origin in a pure and immediate self-presence and that the metaphors required to describe this self-presence reimport indication into that presence would the conclusion seem to follow. But Derrida provides no convincing reason to accept either assumption.

The concept of the "primordial 'supplement' " that Derrida introduces in the final paragraph (*SP*, 97/87) requires little comment from a Husserlian point of view.[6] It is basically the concept of foundation that Husserl introduces in the Third Investigation, "On the Theory of Wholes and Parts." In §14 Husserl writes: "The indefinite expression: A_0 *requires supplementation by, is founded upon a certain moment*, plainly means the same as the expression: 'A_0 is non-independent' " (*LI* II.1, 261/463). Such relationships are established by means of what Husserl calls free phantasy variation, in which one aspect of a whole is varied in order to see whether other aspects are systematically dependent on the presence or absence of that *aspect*. A relevant example would be a variation that shows that primal impression is founded upon other moments, such as retention and protention, which together make up the whole of the living present. When two moments are mutually founded upon each other, it makes no sense to call the one the absolute origin of the other. It is not clear, however, that it makes sense to say of the primordial 'supplement' that "their *addition* comes to *make up for* a deficiency" (*SP*, 97/87). If a moment is founded upon another moment, it makes little sense to speak of adding the latter to the former, for the discovery is precisely that the one always already requires the other. Derrida's description seems to make sense only if we assume the necessity of a Humean immediacy, an absolute, nonmediated (which is to say also nonintentional) presence. But in that case, what the supplement is added to is a fiction.

Chapter 8
"The Supplement of Origin"

The final chapter of *Speech and Phenomena* contains a complex argument. In the first place, Derrida argues that expression not only (as Husserl sees) does not require fulfillment in order to exercise its meaning function, but essentially involves a lack of fulfillment.[1] The very structure of Husserl's pure grammar shows that meaning excludes intuition, the presence of the object meant. This would be true even for words such as "I," which means that the meaningfulness of my own utterances requires my own absence or death. Since writing is defined as those signs that function even in the absence of the subject, it is clear that writing, which in metaphysical accounts is always secondary to the immediacy of the voice, dwells within speech, as Derrida asserted in the previous chapter. Finally, Derrida's analysis of Husserl's account of "essentially occasional expressions" shows that, against Husserl's express view, the word "I" is never fulfilled when it is used: nonfulfillment is required by the very structure of the sign itself.

Signs and Supplements

The "primordial 'supplement'" is, for Derrida, nothing other than *différance*, Derrida's neologism incorporating the senses of deferral and difference. We saw in chapter 7 that the basic structure of the supplement is modeled on Husserl's account of moments as dependent parts in the Third Investigation, and there is a sense in which we can find such a supplement in Husserl's own writing. Husserl insists that all experience is structured in terms of a more or less indeterminate "inner horizon" (*Innenhorizont*) as well as an "outer horizon (*Außenhorizont*] of

129

co-objects" (Husserl 1938, 28/32–33, translation altered). Both of these result from the fact that all experience and all cognition "takes place against the background of the world" (Husserl 1938, 26/31; see also *Hua* III.1, 91/94, 189/200). Later, Gurwitsch and, following him, Maurice Merleau-Ponty use Gestalt-theoretical concepts (see Gurwitsch 1966, 175–286) in arguing that the figure-ground structure and along with it the theme-margin structure are fundamental to the field of consciousness itself (see Gurwitsch 1964, 320f.). Presence is constituted in terms of context rather than context being built up out of pregiven, present elements, and this lends itself to a description in terms of difference (a strong emphasis on the concept of difference is generally a sign of Heidegger's or Saussure's influence). And as we have seen, Husserl's early discovery that the present is a field, along with his deepened sense of the implications of this discovery in the 1920s, is an analogue to the temporal dimension that Derrida describes as a deferring.

But Derrida would at most regard these as formal analogies that hide the radicality of *différance*. In *différance*, deferring is delay, which does not so much constitute presence or the present as defer it in principle, thus "simulating" presence (cf. *SP*, 15/15). And differing is "the active work of difference" that does not so much constitute identity as constantly displace it. "The supplementary difference vicariously stands in for presence due to its primordial self-deficiency." And as it involves a "function of substitutive supplementation [*suppléance*] in general, the 'in the place of' (*für etwas*) structure which belongs to every sign in general" (*SP*, 98/88), the movement of *différance* is the work of signs, and the very self-presence of consciousness is an "in the place of." The self is a result of *différance*: "The *for-itself* would be an *in-the-place-of-itself*: put *for itself*, instead of itself. The strange structure of the supplement appears here: by delayed reaction, a possibility produces that to which it is said to be added on" (*SP*, 99/89). The example Derrida uses to show this structure of supplementation is the indicative sign, which is "substituted for" the more highly valued expression, replacing it in communication: "In real communicative speech, expression gives way to [*céde la place à*] indication because, we saw, the sense aimed at by the other and, more generally, his experience are not presented to me in person and never can be. This is why Husserl says that, in such cases, expression functions 'as indication [*comme indice*]' " (*SP*, 99/89, translation altered).[2]

This requires some comment. In the first place, it is not at all clear why Derrida sees a substitution at work here. In communication, the expressive sign is not replaced by another type of sign; rather, the sign that has an expressive function also exercises an indicative function. Derrida seems to ignore his earlier recognition that the distinction between indication and expression is functional, not substantial (*SP*, 20/20).[3] In the second place, in what sense can one say that the "sense aimed at by the other" cannot be present to me? Uttered words intimate or manifest indicatively the lived experiences of the speaker, but they express the speaker's meaning, and it is precisely Husserl's claim that this meaning can indeed be communicated.

Meaning and Intuition

This sets up the key question of Derrida's final chapter: "It now remains to be seen — and this is most important — in which respect expression itself implies, in its very structure, a nonplenitude" (*SP*, 99/89). As we have seen, for Husserl expression and meaning involve reference to an object, but this reference need not be fulfilled by the actual presence of the object as intended. Derrida refers to this as a "last exclusion — or reduction — to which Husserl invites us" (*SP*, 100/90).

Husserl does not and would not call this an exclusion or reduction in any sense related to the phenomenological epochē. When he writes that "the relation to an actually given objective correlate, which fulfils the meaning-intention, is *not* essential to an expression" (*LI* II.1, 50/I, 290), this is not an exclusion or reduction performed by the phenomenologist, but the result of a free phantasy variation. It could only be called an eidetic reduction. Derrida seems to realize this when he writes that "it belongs to the original structure of expression to be able to dispense with the full presence of the object aimed at by intuition [*l'intuition*]" (*SP*, 100/90), though it would have made more sense to write *l'intention* rather than *l'intuition*. The importance of this recognition on Husserl's part is that it shows that it is meaning that makes certain forms of givenness possible, rather than meaning being straightforwardly derived from and thus reduced to preexpressive sense (cf. Evans 1984, 108–11). Husserl does not commit himself to any form of phenomenalism here. And as Derrida notes, it is this recognition that enables Husserl to differentiate levels in the a priori structure of meanings, distinguishing nonsense (*Sinnlosigkeit, Unsinn*) from logical countersense (*Widersinnigkeit*).

Against the background of a brief sketch of the general sense of Husserl's pure logical grammar — one that not only does not fall into the errors we found in Derrida's Introduction (*SP*, 7/8) but correctly interprets that grammar in precisely the opposite way — Derrida makes a startling suggestion:

> Following the logic and necessity of these distinctions, we might be tempted to maintain not only that meaning does not imply the intuition of the object but that it essentially excludes it. What is structurally original about meaning would be the *Gegenstandslosigkeit*, the absence of any object given to intuition. . . . This is to say that the language that speaks in the presence of its object effaces its own originality or lets it melt away. . . . Are not two possibilities excluded from the start, namely, that the unity of intuition and intention can ever be homogeneous at all and that meaning can be fused into intuition without disappearing? (*SP*, 102–3/92)

Now, I find the "temptation" in question anything but obvious, and the suggestion (even against the background of Husserl's analyses) anything but immediately plausible. I do have one proposal as to how Derrida might arrive at this suggestion given the preceding discussion. As Derrida notes, many theories of linguistic meaning current in the late nineteenth century identified meaning with mental images. On such a model, language can at most be a medium for communication, one that ideally would be transparent when brought back to the images themselves. It would efface itself before the images immanent to the mind. Since such images provide a form of fulfillment to the meaning-intention, this might suggest the following inference: relation to the object is either essential, in which case linguistic meaning effaces itself in the face of the object, or it is nonessential, in which case a fulfilled relation to the object is impossible. Alternatively: either *all* well-formed expressions necessarily have genuine reference, in which case expressions are either true and fulfilled or meaningless, or expressions can be meaningful even when realized reference is a priori excluded, in which case reference can never be realized or fulfilled.

Be this as it may, we must turn to Derrida's example for clarification of the sense of his suggestion. If I say, "I see a particular person by the window" while in fact seeing that person, Husserl's analysis would require a distinction between the content and the object. The content is the ideal meaning of my utterance, which can be understood by a hearer even if he or she does not see the person in question. But as the meaning is essentially graspable even in the absence of the object, this should, Derrida argues, be true of the speaker as well. "My nonperception, my nonintuition, my *hic et nunc* absence are said [*sont dits*] by that very thing that I say, by *that* which I say and *because* I say it" (*SP*, 104/93, translation altered). This is a very strong statement, rich in deliberate paradox: as speaker I say, "I see . . . ," but what I say, namely, "I see . . . ," is structurally constrained to say that I do not see. "The absence of intuition—and therefore of the subject of the intuition—is not only *tolerated* by speech; it is *required* by the general structure of signification, when considered *in itself*" (*SP*, 104/93). When Husserl gives an example in the First Investigation, he writes, "If I sincerely say—we shall always presume sincerity— . . . " (*LI* II.1, 43/I, 284), but on Derrida's analysis, such sincerity is structurally impossible: this amounts to the deconstruction of sincerity.

But the air of paradox is alleviated considerably when we read on and see that Derrida does not really mean what he seemed to be saying:

It [the absence of intuition and of the subject of intuition] is radically requisite: the total absence of the subject and object of a statement—the death of the writer and/or the disappearance of the objects he was able to describe—does not prevent a text from "wanting to say" something. On the contrary, this possibility gives birth to wanting-to-say as such, gives it out to be heard [*entendre*] and read. (*SP*, 104/93, translation altered)

This casts a very different light on things. What is "radically requisite" is not the absence of intuition and of the subject of intuition but rather that such absence does not prevent the text from meaning something, from wanting to say something. A more judicious formulation of the paradoxical statement quoted above would be, "My possible nonperception, my possible nonintuition, my possible *hic et nunc* absence are presupposed by that very thing that I say . . . "

Now, if one defines writing as "signs which function despite the total absence of the subject because of (beyond) his death" (*SP*, 104/93), then it is clear that any structure of repetition is writing in this sense. Any utterance can be repeated, can be quoted, in the absence of the speaker—this is a straightforward consequence of the ideality of the sign—and it will be meaningful in such repetition. The question is why writing in this very broad sense "is involved in the very movement of signification in general and, in particular, in what is called 'living' speech" (*SP*, 104/93, translation altered). This question is to be answered by an examination of Husserl's treatment of the pronoun "I."

The Logic of "I"

For Husserl, "I" is an essentially occasional expression, that is, an expression whose meaning is a function of the occasion of its use, in contrast to objective expressions, whose meaning is not a function of the circumstances of their utterance (see *LI*, First Investigation, §26). Derrida defines objective expressions as "absolutely pure expressions, free from all indicative contamination" (*SP*, 105/94). This allusion to expressions as they function in soliloquy is surely no accident, but is "contamination" really the issue here? And if so, is it the same contamination as that which Derrida saw at work between expression and indication? Husserl does speak of indication in analyzing occasional expressions: he speaks of an "indicating function" and of "indicating and indicated meaning" (*LI* II.1, 83/I, 316). And when he later admits that we are "infinitely removed" from the ideal that objective truths in themselves be expressed by means of objective meanings, this seems to confirm Derrida's earlier promise that "indicative adherences, sometimes of another kind, continually reappear further on, and getting rid of them will be an infinite task" (*SP*, 28/27). Now Derrida finds a "massive return of indication into expression" (*SP*, 105/94), and the scope that Husserl himself gives to this return—expressions concerning oneself, perceptions, beliefs, doubts, wishes, fears, commands—shows just how important it is.[4] Wherever we find expressions such as "I," "here," and "now," "the meaning (*Bedeutung*) of these expressions is carried off into indication whenever it animates real intended speech for someone else" (*SP*, 105/94). Given Derrida's emphasis on the rhetoric of threat, it is clear that he assumes that such a result would be most unwelcome for Husserl.

Derrida chooses the essentially occasional expression "I" for closer attention. There are two issues here. First, as an expression, "I" should express an ideal meaning that is independent of any "realized" relation to an object (cf. *LI* II.1, 37–38/I, 280–82). Second, the expressive function of "I" should not essentially involve indication. Husserl is committed to these principles, but Derrida finds that his concrete analysis of "I" contradicts both of them. In the first place, Husserl states that in solitary speech (where we should find expressions freed from interwovenness with the indicative function of intimating or manifesting the intentional life of the speaker), "the meaning of 'I' is essentially realized [*vollzieht sich . . . wesentlich*; *se réalise essentiellement*] in the immediate idea [*unmittelbare Vorstellung*] of one's own personality" (*LI* II.1, 82/I, 316, quoted at *SP*, 106/94 n. 5). In the second place, the word "I" "has the character of a universally operative *indication*" of the fact that "each speaker has his own I-presentation [*Ichvorstellung*] and thus his own individual concept of I" (*LI* II.1, 82/I, 316, quoted at *SP*, 106/94–95 n. 5, translation altered, emphasis added). Fulfillment seems essential to the speaker's meaningful use of "I," and the word seems to function indicatively.

Husserl thus seems to be caught between conflicting demands that he places on his own account. When he takes account of the role of occasional expressions, Husserl must write:

> What its meaning [*Bedeutung*—that of the word "I"] is at the moment can be gleaned only from the living utterance and from the intuitive circumstances which surround it. If we read this word without knowing who wrote it, it is perhaps not meaningless (*bedeutungslos*) but is at least estranged from its normal meaning (*Bedeutung*). (*LI* II.1, 82/I, 315, quoted at *SP* 107/96)

But if one recalls Husserl's insistence on distinguishing between the mere meaning-intention and the realized relation to an object in §9 of the First Investigation, it would seem that Husserl's position should be just the opposite. The word "I" is ideal, the same in a multiplicity of contexts and even in my own absence or death. And the ideality of meaning is never dependent on the givenness of the object referred to: understanding—even in the case of our own utterances—cannot require that we know who is speaking. Husserl's account of meaning was built on the refusal to identify meaningfulness with the realized relation to an object, but he now claims that the word "I" has its "normal meaning" only when its meaning is "realized." And whereas Husserl had insisted on the ideality of meaning, he now claims that "I" has "an ever new meaning" depending on who utters it (*LI* II.1, 82/I, 315, translation altered). Derrida thus feels compelled to object that "*Husserl's premises should sanction our saying exactly the contrary.* Just as I need not perceive in order to understand a state-ment about perception, so there is no need to intuit the object *I* in order to un-derstand the word *I*. The possibility of this nonintuition constitutes the *Bedeutung* as such, the *normal Bedeutung* as such" (*SP*, 107/96). The "normal meaning" of the expression is constituted by the possibility of nonintuition.

This interpretation requires several comments. In the first place, the transla-tion of *vollzieht sich* by "is realized" in the English and *se réalise* in the French translations, while not false, can easily mislead the unwary reader. Husserl uses the word *realisiert* in §9 of the First Investigation—for example, in the phrase "in the realized relation of the expression to its object" (*LI* II.1, 38/I, 281, quoted at *SP*, 103/92 n. 3). In such contexts it always refers to the fulfillment of the meaning-intention. To use the same word in §26 to translate *vollzieht sich* is to suggest that these are simply two ways of saying the same thing.[5] This is pre-cisely the way Derrida reads the passage: "But Husserl seems to think that this *Bedeutung*, as a relationship with the object (*I, here, now*), is 'realized' *for the one who is speaking*" (*SP*, 105–6/94). And indeed there would seem to be good reason to make this assumption. After all, how is the "immediate presentation of one's own personality" to be understood other than as immediate self-presence, essential fulfillment?

A closer look at the broader context, however, shows that this cannot be the correct reading. The two crucial sentences, which Derrida quotes in a footnote, read:

> In solitary speech the meaning of 'I' is essentially realized in the
> immediate idea of one's own personality, and thus the meaning of the
> word in communicated speech also lies in it. Each speaker has his own
> I-presentation (and with it his individual concept of *I*) and this is why
> the word's meaning differs from person to person. (*LI* II.1, 82/I, 316,
> quoted at *SP*, 106/94–95 n. 5)

Several things become apparent when these two sentences are read carefully. In the first place, even if for Husserl the meaning of the word "I" is always fulfilled for the speaker (when the word is used in what Husserl takes to be the normal manner), this does not mean that we can translate the passage as "In solitary speech the meaning of 'I' is essentially fulfilled in the immediate idea of one's own personality . . . " If this were the proper meaning of Husserl's statement— that is, if the immediate idea were a fulfilling sense—the second part of the sen-tence, "which is also the meaning of the word in communicated speech," would make no sense. Husserl is clearly stating that the meaning of the word "I" "lies in" the immediate idea of the speaker's personality, and this is true for both the speaker and the hearer. Only in the first case is the meaning also, for Husserl, necessarily fulfilled. The hearer may know who is speaking or writing without having intuitive fulfillment of this individual presentation. Thus nothing that

Husserl says here contradicts his claim that there is an essential distinction between meaning and the fulfilled relation to an object.[6]

It is particularly noteworthy that Derrida gives no details of Husserl's analysis of occasional expressions. Husserl argues that in the "normal" use of the word "I" we find two meanings at work:

> The one, relating to the word's general function, is so connected with the word that its indicating function can be exercised once something is actually presented: this indicative function is, in its turn, exercised *for* the other, singular presentation, and, by subsumption, makes the latter's object known as what is here and now meant. The former meaning can be called the *indicating* meaning, the latter the *indicated meaning*. (*LI* II.1, 83/I, 316)

The "normal meaning" of the word requires both of these elements. Now, both of these meanings are ideal. The first constitutes the word's "general function" or the word's "universal *semantic function* [*Bedeutungsfunktion*]," namely, "to designate whoever is speaking" (*LI* II.1, 82/I, 315–16). This enables us to understand the expression even if we do not know who uttered or wrote it, and here it is clear that meaningfulness is not dependent on a realized relation to an object. In concrete use, or rather in successful communication, this general function guides the hearer's or reader's understanding to the indicated meaning, namely, to the singular presentation (*Vorstellung*) of a specific individual. This would concern "nominal presentation in the purely logical sense" (*LI* II.1, 505/II, 656). This meaning is again ideal—a multiplicity of auditors can understand the same indicated meaning. In addition, this understanding need not be intuitive. Husserl does make statements that seem to imply stricter demands: he says that "what its meaning is at the moment, can be gleaned only from the living utterance and from the *intuitive circumstances* which surround it" and that "through such indication the hearer achieves understanding of the meaning, he takes the person who confronts him *intuitively*, not merely as the speaker, but also as the immediate object of this speaker's speech" (*LI* II.1, 82–83/I, 315–16, emphasis added). But these statements are oriented to the face-to-face situation, and when we turn to other communicative situations it becomes clear that intuition is not the crucial thing. Thus "if we read the word without knowing who wrote it, it is perhaps not meaningless, but is at least estranged from its normal sense" (*LI* II.1, 82/I, 315). A properly oriented reader, one who knows who the (absent) writer is, can understand the indicated meaning quite adequately in the absence of the writer. The possibility of nonintuition, indeed of not knowing at all who the writer is, is built into the situation, and there is a level of understanding appropriate to it.

Once these details of Husserl's analysis are brought in, it becomes obvious that Derrida's claim—namely, that Husserl's own premises sanction precisely the opposite conclusion from the one Husserl actually draws—is dead wrong. Further, it becomes an easy task to make Husserlian sense of Derrida's rather hyperbolic conclusions. Thus when Derrida writes, "When the word *I* appears, the ideality of its *Bedeutung* . . . puts us in what Husserl describes as an abnormal situation—just as if *I* were written by someone unknown" (*SP*, 107/96), it is clear that he is taking into account only the indicating meaning.[7] When he writes that "the signifying value [*la valeur signifiante*] of the *I* does not depend on the life of the speaking subject" (*SP*, 107/96, translation altered), he is again taking into account merely the general function of the word "I," and not the specific indicated meaning of this token of "I" now at issue. Similar things can be said about claims such as "my death is structurally necessary to the pronouncing of the *I*" and "whether or not life as self-presence accompanies the uttering of the *I*, is quite indifferent with regard to the function of meaning" (*SP*, 107–8/96): both claims neglect the fact that a marginal awareness of my own conscious life—which is not the immediate self-presence in an instantaneous present that Derrida reads into Husserl—is a condition for the full use of the "I." And Husserl's claim that the indicated meaning is part of the "normal meaning" is anything but arbitrary: all he is doing is taking the case of normal communication (and not even necessarily face-to-face communication) as a point of departure.

Robert Scholes has written that "we have here one of the weakest points in Derrida's theory of language" (Scholes 1988, 290). Its plausibility—and it has been considered plausible (see Harvey, 66–67; Llewelyn, 24)—depends on simply ignoring texts that do not fit into the desired interpretation. And this is a curious suppression, for anyone who takes the time to read the section under discussion will run into the missing passages.

There is one other point to be made here. Derrida is very open about the fact that he is reading early texts in light of later texts, an approach sanctioned by the thesis of continuity, though subject to the cautions noted earlier. But here Derrida is taking an early text to be representative without paying any attention to Husserl's own criticisms of the position under discussion. In the Foreword to the second edition of the *Logical Investigations* Husserl writes, "The manner in which it deals with occasional meanings (to which, however, in strictness, all empirical predications belong) is a tour de force—the enforced consequence of the imperfect conception of the essence of 'truth in itself' in the Prolegomena" (*LI* I, xiv/I, 48). As the problem with the conception of truth in itself was that it was "too one-sidedly oriented to *vérités de raison*" (*LI* I, xiii/I, 47), this would mean that the issue of "objective reason" (*LI* II.1, 90/I, 321) requires reexamination.

And indeed, Husserl undertook such a reexamination, above all in *Formal and Transcendental Logic* and in the *Crisis*. In *Formal and Transcendental Logic* this reexamination leads to a brief reconsideration of occasional expressions. Husserl relates the intersubjective truth or falsity of occasional judgments to an intersubjective "typical specific likeness among situations" that is a function of "the constituting horizon-intentionality" (*Hua* VII, 207/199). In a footnote Husserl notes that in the *Logical Investigations* he had not yet worked out the theory of horizon-intentionality and thus could not deal adequately with occasional judgments and their meaning (*Hua* VII, 297n./199n.). Thus, rather than recurring to an "I-presentation" (*Ichvorstellung*), that is, to a singular presentation as the indicated meaning, Husserl now analyzes occasional expressions in terms of the consciousness of horizons. In the case of the occasional expression "I," this analysis would refer us to the marginal awareness that any conscious act has of itself, an awareness rooted in the structures of time-consciousness.[8]

None of these critical reconsiderations attract Derrida's attention, and the reason is fairly obvious. He must concentrate on what Husserl calls the general meaning function because this enables him to identify the "autonomy of meaning" with writing (*SP*, 108/97). Writing was characterized earlier as "the common name for signs which function despite the total absence of the subject because of (beyond) his death" (*SP*, 104/93), and the general meaning function, like ideality in general, is never dependent on any specific existent, be it a specific subject, a specific object, or a specific token. Writing in this sense is not an addition to speech but rather the fundamental structure of speech itself, and as writing was earlier said to be indicative even in Husserl's own terms (*SP*, 29/27 n. 1), Derrida can conclude that indication, far from being the "contamination" that it is for Husserl, "dictates" expression (*SP*, 108/97). But as we have noted, Derrida never attempts to demonstrate that writing is intrinsically indicative.

On Derrida's reading, the "*decision* which subordinates a reflection on the sign to a logic" (*SP*, 6/7) makes it impossible for Husserl to draw the proper conclusions from his own analyses. In the face of a presupposed *telos*, Husserl has to sacrifice his own best insights: "Husserl describes, and in one and the same movement effaces, the emancipation of speech as nonknowing" (*SP*, 109/97). The essence of meaning, on Husserl's own analysis, is to be found in its autonomy from intuition, but Husserl turns right around and sacrifices this essence to the *telos* of knowledge. "To be radical, the difference that separates intention from intuition would nonetheless have to be *pro-visional* [*pro-visoire*]" (*SP*, 109/97). This sentence can be given two different readings. On the official Husserlian reading it would mean that the meaning-intention looks forward to, is oriented toward, its fulfillment in vision, that it effaces itself in the view of the object itself. It is merely provisional, where the prefix "pro-" means "before, in front of, on behalf of." Here "the genuine and true wanting-to-say is the will to say the truth [le vrai et authentique vouloir-dire est le vouloir dire-vrai]" (*SP*, 109/98, translation altered), and it is only for this reason, on the basis of this decision, that meaning is defined in terms of a relation to the object, that "sense in general" is "defined . . . on the basis of truth as objectivity" (*SP*, 111/99). This decision governs the entire project of a pure grammar and a pure logic.

Derrida claims that Husserl's "normality" is the result of his decision to accept truth as objectivity as the *telos* of sense: "This is what is meant by the concept of *normality* each time it occurs in Husserl's description" (*SP*, 109/98). As we have seen, in §26 of the First Investigation the concept of "normal sense" is oriented toward communication. Derrida would, I think, regard this difference as insignificant. Communication is rooted in the wanting-to-say of the speaker/ writer, and this wanting-to-say is, as we have just seen, a wanting-to-say-the-truth. But, as Derrida writes later, "intention is a priori (at once) *différante*: differing and deferring, in its inception" (Derrida 1988, 56).[9] On Derrida's reading, normality for Husserl is defined in terms of the pure self-presence of wanting-to-say, which Derrida claims to have deconstructed, and, correlatively, in terms of the decision to subject the sign to logic, to take knowledge and truth as the *telos* of sense. The two ultimately amount to the same thing.

This decision stands out as such when one realizes that since the rules of pure grammar are oriented toward possible cognition, all expressions that violate these rules must be declared to be "absolute nonsense," and this involves rejecting a great deal of poetic language as nonsensical:

> The efficiency and the form of signs that do not obey these rules, that is, that do not promise any knowledge, can be determined as nonsense (*Unsinn*) only if one has antecedently, and according to the most traditional philosophical move, defined sense in general on the basis of truth as objectivity. Otherwise we would have to relegate to absolute nonsense all poetic language that transgresses the laws of this grammar of cognition and is irreducible to it. (*SP*, 111/99)

Husserl's position turns out to be similar to the logical positivists' verifiability criterion of meaning, though Husserl's concept of intuition is much broader than theirs, as he insists in the *Ideas* when he writes, "If '*positivism*' is tantamount to an absolutely unprejudiced grounding of all sciences on the 'positive,' that is to say, on what can be seized upon originaliter, then *we* are the genuine positivists" (*Hua* III.1, 45/39). Husserl's concept of fulfillment, of evidence as the presence of the things themselves in contrast to an empty or merely symbolic intending of them, extends to values and practical action as well as the positive and eidetic sciences. But according to Derrida it still cannot make sense of linguistic expressions that are not aimed at cognition.

There is, as we have noted above, an alternative interpretation of the sense of Husserl's project here. In the *Logical Investigations* Husserl is interested, as he makes clear, in logic and the theory of objective knowledge. This leaves many aspects of linguistic use out of consideration, but that in itself does not prove that they must be rejected. Thus Robert Sokolowski has used Husserl's pure grammar precisely in order to study jokes, word-plays, and poetry:

> In poetry or in the lyrics of songs a still more primitive level begins to assert itself more strongly than in ordinary speech, the sensuous character of the expressions. To exploit the sensuous rhythms and color of a language, its grammatical form may be forced to suffer distortions, and the judgmental form may be so distended that we would be hard put to it to paraphrase or even mark out the sections, judgmental units, in what is being expressed. And yet, unless the exercise falls into sheer word-music, there must be a vestige of grammatical form and judgmental composition, whose very distortions may be part of the structure of the poem or lyrics. (Sokolowski 1974, 217–18)

Here a Husserlian position makes it possible to talk about texts that are not oriented toward "truth as objectivity" without reducing the orientation toward truth and objectivity to the play of *différance*. As Derrida's own text acknowledges, Husserl can and does recognize various "modes of sense," and this involves anything but "recognizing an initial limitation of sense to knowledge, of logos to objectivity, of language to reason" (*SP*, 111/99).

The Deferral of the Now

Having defined the living present in terms of absolute proximity and the instantaneous moment, Derrida easily concludes that while this living present is the fundamental, and fundamentally metaphysical, concept of phenomenology, it "is nevertheless *in fact*, really, effectively, etc., deferred *ad infinitum*. This *différance* is the difference between the ideal and the nonideal" (*SP*, 112/99). This conclusion is not only a consequence of Derrida's deconstruction of Husserl up to this point; it can also, Derrida thinks, be derived directly from the text of the First Investigation itself.

As Derrida lays it out, the argument for this is quite simple: (1) "Husserl shows that absolute ideality can only be on the side of objective expressions." (2) The fluctuation of meaning (*Schwanken der Bedeutungen*) in occasional expressions is a function of fluctuation in the act of meaning (*Schwanken des Bedeutens*) (see *LI* II.1, 91/I, 322). (3) "This allows [Husserl] to conclude, apparently against his former demonstration, that, in a subjective expression, the *content* may always be replaced by an objective and therefore ideal content: only the act then is lost for ideality." But (4), as Husserl admits, "we are infinitely removed from this ideal" (*LI* II.1, 91/I, 322), and the difficulty concerns an impossibility in principle of ever realizing the ideal (*LI* II.1, 90/I, 321). "As the ideal is always thought by Husserl in the form of an Idea in the Kantian sense, this substitution of ideality for nonidentity, of objectivity for nonobjectivity, is infinitely *deferred*" (*SP*, 112/100).

If we examine this argument in the light of the text of the First Investigation, a number of things become clear. Concerning (1), when Husserl contrasts essentially subjective and occasional expressions with objective expressions, the terms "subjective" and "objective" do not indicate that the latter is ideal and the former in some sense real. The point of the distinction is rather that in the one case our understanding of the intended meaning requires information concerning "the occasion, the speaker and the situation" (*LI* II.1, 81/I, 315), information not required in the case of objective meanings. This is important, for it suggests that when Derrida writes in (3) that the content of a subjective expression "may always be replaced by an objective and therefore ideal content," the last phrase distorts Husserl's position. *Both* contents are ideal, and Derrida himself quotes Husserl asserting just that: "The content meant by the subjective expression, with sense oriented to the occasion, is an ideal unit of meaning (*Bedeutung*) in precisely the same sense as the content of a fixed expression" (*LI* II.1, 90/I, 321, quoted at *SP*, 112/100). Indeed, this is what the replaceability is to demonstrate.

Now, it must be admitted that Husserl's statements concerning the replaceability of occasional expressions by objective expressions seems to conflict with his earlier recognition in §26 that replacing an occasional expression with words that express the universal semantic function of that expression would lead to a divergence in sense (*LI* II.1, 82/I, 315–16). But before we conclude that this is a straightforward contradiction, we should ask whether there is a reasonable interpretation on which there is no contradiction. I would suggest that there is such an interpretation. In §26 what is at issue is the identity of meaning, whereas what would seem to be important in §28 is the identity of the state of affairs that is asserted. As Husserl notes in §12, two sentences that have different meaning-contents can assert the same state of affairs (*Sachlage*). Thus "*a* is bigger than *b*" and "*b* is smaller than *a*" say different things, are different in meaning-content, but in both the same state of affairs is asserted, though in two different ways (*LI* II.1, 48/I, 288). When Husserl writes that "ideally speaking, each subjective expression is replaceable by an objective expression which will preserve the identity of each momentary meaning-intention" (*LI* II.1, 90/I, 321), what seems clearly to be at issue is the idea that the same state of affairs can be asserted in two different ways, once using occasional expressions and again using only objective expressions.

This leaves us with the question of the implications of the failure of the attempt to rid language of occasional expressions. This is a serious and complicated issue, and it cannot be discussed in any detail here. What must be recalled, once again, is that Husserl himself declared these passages a "tour de force," and part of what was at issue in that statement was the fact that empirical predications, which he declared essentially occasional, can still express truths in themselves once the concept of "truth in itself" is no longer one-sidedly oriented to truths of reason (cf. *LI* I, xii–xiv, 47–48). This is thus a problematic point at which to be drawing conclusions concerning the nature and limits of Husserl's project as a whole.

Derrida states his principle of continuity early in *Speech and Phenomena*, and although this leads to some readings one can quibble with, the general project of reading Husserl's early texts from the point of view of later developments is an interesting one. What is not acceptable, if one is interested in drawing conclusions concerning the nature of Hussserl's project in general, is reading early texts without taking into account later corrections: such a practice is unacceptable precisely given Derrida's own project. His question in the Introduction was the following:

> Do not phenomenological necessity, the rigor and subtlety of Husserl's analysis, the exigencies to which it responds and which we must first recognize, nonetheless conceal a metaphysical presupposition? Do they not harbor a dogmatic or speculative commitment which, to be sure, would not keep the phenomenological critique from being realized, would not be a residue of unperceived naïveté, but would *constitute* phenomenology from within, in its project of criticism and in the instructive value of its own premises? (*SP*, 2–3/4)

In this passage Derrida explicitly acknowledges that his interpretation will have to recognize the rigor possible within the framework of phenomenology, and this means paying careful attention to the corrections that are possible — not to mention the corrections that have been carried out — within that framework. As we have seen, at several points Derrida ignores such corrections — or what Husserl considered corrections — even though they are mentioned in the text he is reading.[10]

Conclusion

The final pages of *Speech and Phenomena* are concerned to draw, or rather redraw, the conclusions Derrida derives from his "deconstruction" of Husserl. The most general formulation of his conclusion is that since the *telos* of cognition, of truth as objectivity, is constitutive of the entire framework of Husserlian phenomenology; since that *telos* has been shown to rest on a decision that of necessity excludes forms of sense not oriented toward possible objects and truth; and since these modes of signification are more "primordial" (a word that can be used only with great care once the metaphysics of presence has been deconstructed), all of the distinctions whose legitimacy presupposes that framework — including all of Husserl's "essential distinctions" — are deconstructed along with it. As Derrida puts it, the possiblity of making these distinctions is "deferred *ad infin-*

itum" (*SP*, 113/101). These distinctions presuppose the metaphysical framework of presence, and the "discovery" of *différance* as that which "stands in for presence due to its radical self-deficiency" (*SP*, 98/88) has the result not so much that the distinctions cannot be made as that the aspects or elements distinguished *de jure* always turn out to inhabit one another *de facto*. *Différance* deconstructs the very distinction between the *de jure* and the *de facto*.

This is not really a denial of the phenomenon of presence — after all, Derrida himself announces in the Introduction that what is required is "to *see* [*voir*] the phenomenological critique of metaphysics betray itself" (*SP*, 3/5, emphasis added), and this presupposes the general distinction between empty and fulfilled intentions. Derrida attacks not so much this distinction itself as the metaphysical presuppositions that govern our understanding of it. It is not that presence, defined formally in terms of the contrast with absence, is impossible, but that it turns out to be impossible to give a clear characterization of what it would mean to say that fulfillment involves the presence of the object *itself*. Thus Derrida can assert that "*perception does not exist* or that what is called perception is not primordial, that somehow everything 'begins' with 're-presentation' " (*SP*, 50/45 n. 4), that "there never was any 'perception'; and 'presentation' is a representation of the representation that yearns for itself therein as for its own birth or its death" (*SP*, 116/103), and finally that "the thing itself always escapes" (*SP*, 117/104).

Looking back at *Speech and Phenomena* from our present perspective, it is difficult even to ask about the degree to which Derrida has actually established his conclusion. A reading that so distorts the text it is supposed to be interpreting cannot be said to establish anything at all concerning that text.

Part II
The Myth of Phonocentrism:
Of Grammatology

We have followed Derrida as he reads a privileged status of the voice into Husserl, and have seen his interpretation break down at almost every point. This raises the question whether this is an isolated breakdown in Derrida's general deconstruction of the philosophy of presence, logocentrism, and phonocentrism of the Western metaphysical tradition. Part II will extend the investigation of Derrida's identification of ''logocentrism'' as the primary characteristic of Western metaphysics. Derrida finds logocentrism determining the thought of a wide variety of thinkers, but in part I of *Of Grammatology* the two most important figures are Aristotle and Saussure. I shall argue that in both cases Derrida imports a ''logocentric'' metaphysics into the texts under consideration.

Chapter 9
Aristotle

In the Exergue to *Of Grammatology*, Derrida begins by calling the reader's attention to *logocentrism*, which he defines as "the metaphysics of phonetic writing" (*OG, 11/3*). The term "logocentrism" clearly bears a great burden in *Of Grammatology*. Derrida gives three dimensions of this burden: (1) The phonetization of writing, which has often enough been hailed as a great advance of civilization, "must dissimulate its own history as it is produced" (*OG*, 11/3), thus bearing the dark side of dissimulation as the condition of its own apparent worth. (2) Metaphysics finds the origin of truth in the *logos*, that is, in "the debasement of writing, and its repression outside 'full' speech" (*OG*, 12/3). *Logos* concerns speech and not the written word, not even the phonetic written word. The primacy of the phonetic in systems of writing is rooted in its submission to speech, a "debasement" that represses recognition of other forms of writing, forms that are not mere signs of signs and perhaps have their own productivity. (3) Scientificity is rooted in *logic*, which grants primacy to the *logos* or spoken word, and then (secondarily) to phonetic writing (see *OG*, 12/3–4).

Thus an entire philosophical program is presented in Derrida's account of logocentrism, and part I of *Of Grammatology*, entitled "Writing before the Letter," presents a sustained argument for this program.

Logocentrism is the "privilege of the *phōnē*," of the "system of 'hearing (understanding)-oneself-speak [*s'entendre-parler*]' through the phonic substance—which *presents itself* as the nonexterior, therefore nonempirical or noncontingent signifier" (*OG*, 17/7–8). It is centered on the idea of "a full speech that [is] fully *present* (present to itself, to its signified . . .)," an "originary speech itself shielded from interpretation" (*OG*, 17–18/8).

According to Derrida, this *logos* as the spoken word is the source of the entire Western tradition of metaphysics: "Within this logos, the original and essential link to the *phōnē* has never been broken," and "the essence of the *phōnē* would be immediate proximity to that which within 'thought' as logos relates to 'meaning,' produces it, receives it, speaks it, 'composes' it" (*OG*, 21/11). This is the Derridean thesis that is to be demonstrated in a variety of ways in this and other works. What is at issue is the ability of thought, in the voice, to be in command of meaning, and thus its ability to subject meaning to strictly logical and cognitive principles. Ultimately, it is the very sense and status of truth that is at stake.

The first step in the demonstration aims to show that Aristotle, as a representative of logocentrism in the sense defined, defends the required thesis concerning the essence of the *phōnē*. "If, for Aristotle, for example, 'spoken words (*ta en tē phōnē*) are the symbols of mental experience (*pathēmata tēs psychēs*) and written words are the symbols of spoken words' (*De interpretatione*, 1, 16a 3) it is because the voice, producer of *the first symbols*, has a relationship of essential and immediate proximity with the mind" (*OG* 21–22/11). Thus Aristotle's position is said to be logocentric because it groups the three phenomena of thought, speech, and writing into an essential duality:

{thought — speech} — writing

Thought and speech are not identified with each another, but their relationship is one of the "essential and immediate proximity" of the latter to the former.

> The feelings [*les affections*, for the Greek *pathēmata*; perhaps better translated as "the affections"] of the mind, expressing things naturally, constitute a sort of universal language which can then efface itself. It is the stage of transparence. . . . In every case, the voice is closest to the signified. . . . All signifiers, and first and foremost the written signifier, are derivative with regard to what would wed the voice indissolubly to the mind or to the thought of the signified sense, indeed to the thing itself. (*OG*, 22/11).

This passage is interesting for a number of reasons. In the first place, Derrida's suggestion that the affections of the mind (*pathēmata tēs psychēs*) constitute a kind of "universal language" must be recognized as a metaphor with rather strict limitations. There are resources for making use of this metaphor in Greek philosophy, most especially in Plato's depiction of thought as the "unuttered conversation of the soul with herself" (*Sophist* 263e3; see also *Theaetetus* 189e3–190a7; cf. Evans 1984, chap. 1.A), and Aristotle himself sometimes makes use of it. But even in Plato it is clear that it is a metaphor, an analogy, in some respects perhaps more closely related to the Platonic myths than to straightforward theory; and when Aristotle alludes to it he makes a clear distinction between the spoken word and "the discourse within the soul" (see *Posterior Analytics* 76b24; cf. Evans 1984, chap. 1.B). There is no suggestion that the discourse of the soul bears some intrinsic relation to the spoken word, and Aristotle never develops a theory of what medieval thought would call the mental word (*verba menti*; cf. Evans 1984, 7–11). In the second place, even if we work with the metaphor we must remember that the affections of the mind that are "the same for all" (*On Interpretation* 1, 16a), which express the nature of things because of formal causality, are not themselves true or false, for "truth and falsity imply combination and separation" (*On Interpretation* 1, 16a12). Thus, while Aristotle does claim that mental experiences as well as the things of which our experiences are "images" (on the concept of images in this context, see Evans 1984, chap. 1.B) are the same for all people, one should not import too much into what Derrida calls the "stage of transparence." Truth involves the activity of combination and division, and may be anything but immediately transparent to the knowing mind.

Third, there is a curious slippage in Derrida's own use of the term "signifier." He writes, "All signifiers, and first and foremost the written signifier, are derivative with regard to what would wed the voice indissolubly to the mind" (*OG*, 22/11). The expression "all signifiers" must, in the Aristotelian context, refer to spoken and written signifiers, but it is only (and not "first and foremost," whatever that might mean in the context of the "all") written signifiers that are derivative when contrasted with speech, with its more direct relation to mental experiences. This slippage is deliberate, as it is repeated in the sentences that follow: "The written signifier is always technical and representative. It has no constitutive meaning. This derivation is the very origin of the notion of the 'signifier' " (*OG*, 23/11). Thus, in Derrida's reading, the spoken symbol is first distinguished from the written symbol, but it then turns out that the essential characteristics of the written symbol are constitutive of the very notion of the symbol or signifier itself, and thus also characterize the spoken symbol. This will be a central thesis of the book, and it exemplifies what Derrida calls the general strategy of deconstruction, which involves a double strategy of overturning and displacing traditional oppositions (Derrida 1972, 41–42).

But is it Aristotle? In one sense it certainly is good Aristotle, for Aristotle recognizes that both spoken and written symbols are conventional. Both are "technical and representative"; neither has a "constitutive meaning": "Just as all men have not the same writing, so all men have not the same speech sounds" (*On Interpretation* 1, 16a). But given this, one wonders how Derrida can claim to find in Aristotle's treatment of the voice "a relationship of essential and immediate proximity with the mind." If "essential" and "immediate" are understood strictly in terms of the contrast with the mediacy of the written sign, we can make sense of the claim, but this is far from establishing that the voice is "wed indissolubly to the mind" (*OG*, 22/11).

Derrida offers no evidence that his original "because" clause, namely, "because the voice . . . has a relationship of essential and immediate proximity with the mind," presents an Aristotelian position. Aristotle is clearly committed to the primacy of speech over writing, but is this primacy to be attributed to a metaphysically privileged status of the voice, a status that would be explained by its essential and uniquely privileged "proximity with the mind"? Derrida himself offers reason to question this claim: "Between mind and logos [there would be] a relationship of conventional symbolization" (*OG*, 22/11). This would suggest the following very different grouping of the triad:

thought — {speech — writing}

where the latter two are both conventional. Thought is symbolized by spoken words, which are in turn symbolized by written words. Even if the relationship between thought and speech is "immediate" when contrasted with the mediacy of the written word, its conventionality is hardly consistent with the claim that the relationship is one of "essential and immediate proximity with the mind." And this latter claim is crucial if Derrida is to convict Aristotle of logocentrism in the sense specified, for only on that condition does it make sense to speak of an "absolute proximity of voice and being, of voice and the meaning of being, of voice and the ideality of meaning" (*OG*, 23/12).

Looking at our new schema of the Aristotelian position, we note that the placement of the brackets is determined by the conventionality of symbols in contrast to acts of thought. But what about the ordering within the brackets? Is there something essential to the voice that justifies its priority? Or should we look to writing for an explanation of the order? Derrida simply assumes that a positive answer to the first question puts us on the right track, in which case it would become plausible to speak of essential and immediate proximity, and of the voice being indissolubly wedded to the mind, even though nothing of the sort is found in Aristotle. But what about the second question: is there any natural reason for Aristotle to subordinate writing to speech even if we grant that neither exhibits an immediate proximity to, or is indissolubly wed to, the mind? Once the question is posed in these terms, there turns out to be a rather obvious answer: it is *phonetic* writing that very naturally appears to be a symbol of spoken words, and not writing in general. While it would be natural to call hieroglyphics (and the affections of the mind too, for there is an essential community of essence between things and thoughts in an Aristotelian metaphysics of form) symbols of things and rather implausible to think of them as symbols of spoken words, it is natural to think of phonetic writing as the symbol of spoken words, the latter in turn having a direct or indirect reference to things.

Derrida defines logocentrism as the metaphysics of phonetic writing, but the core of the logocentric position as he elaborates it concerns the privileged status of the *phōnē* itself, and not writing per se. The above analysis of Derrida's interpretation of Aristotle shows that he imports logocentrism in this sense into Aristotle rather than finding it there. The system "hearing (understanding)-oneself-speak [*s'entendre-parler*]" (*OG*, 23/12), with its intrinsic connection between speech/hearing and understanding, is not Aristotelian. It is not accidental that the deeply Aristotelian positions of medieval philosophy that do indeed speak of the "mental word" do not move in a Derridean direction (see Evans 1984, 7–9).

Chapter 10
Saussure

The deconstructive reading of Ferdinand de Saussure's *Cours de la linguistique générale* plays a crucial role in *Of Grammatology*, for in Saussure Derrida thinks that he can attack "the entire uncritical tradition which [Saussure] inherits" (*OG*, 67/46). If it can be shown that Saussure's work is governed by a "coherence of desire producing itself in a near-oneiric way . . . through a contradictory logic," this will "already give us the assured means of broaching the deconstruction of the *greatest totality*—the concept of the *epistēmē* and logocentric metaphysics—within which are produced, without ever posing the radical question of writing, all the Western methods of analysis, explication, reading, or interpretation" (*OG*, 67–68/46).

Reading Saussure

There are difficulties in the reader's approach to Saussure's *Course in General Linguistics*.[1] By this I do not mean the difficult and much discussed problems concerning the role and contribution of the original editors of the *Cours de la linguistique générale*, Charles Bally and Albert Sechehaye.[2] Even if we leave such questions aside, there remain serious problems, some of which were pointed out by Samuel Weber a decade ago: "What vitiates much discussion of Saussure is the tendency to reduce the *Cours* to a body of propositions concerning the nature and function of language while disregarding the context within which that thought defines itself" (Weber, 915). Weber reminded readers of Saussure that the distinctions drawn in the *Course* are not intended to be neutral reports on a preexisting natural reality, but are explicitly said to be the results of taking up a specific point of view, namely, that from which linguistics might be established as a science (Weber, 916). Thus there is a general context within which the *Course* must be read, and Derrida is quite attentive to this context, for it is precisely in this point of view itself that he will seek out a metaphysical presupposition that both constitutes and undermines the very scientificity of science (cf. *OG*, 12/3–4, 35/21, 43/27–28).

But this does not exhaust the way context and point of view are at work in the development of the *Course*. As the book unfolds, the questions initially posed are shifted and transformed; new perspectives are brought to bear that show earlier formulations to have been tentative, one-sided, and inadequate. For example, as Weber notes, when Saussure moves from asking what the sign is as an entity to asking how it works, the initial "representational-denominational conception of language is put into question" (Weber, 920). Robert Strozier has developed this point, emphasizing that "the context, indeed, has everything to do with Saussure's method: the method is the context." Strozier finds a repeated use of "positivistic" claims in the early phases of Saussure's discussion of a topic, where "positivistic" means "tak[ing] as discrete what will later be recognized as only abstractly separate" (Strozier, 50, 106 n. 1). This can easily lead to the discovery of apparent "contradictions" in Saussure's thought—discoveries that, however, are based on neglect of the context of the different claims:

> For example, the definition of the sign in Part I as composed of a
> signifier and a signified is a discrete explanation that is transcended in
> Part II, where in Chapter IV the sign is isolated abstractly. The prior
> definition leads to the latter as a necessary preliminary; yet how many
> repeat the initial discrete definition as Saussure's final word? Answer:
> the reference to that prior definition is literally *universal*. (Strozier,
> 106–7)[3]

As we shall see, Derrida falls prey to precisely this misunderstanding (cf. *OG*, 47/31).

There are problems in Strozier's analysis, however. He describes Saussure's method as being "an overdetermined one achieved by the *simultaneous* overlaying of a 'series' of abstract readings of the same data" (Strozier, vii). This emphasis on simultaneity leads Strozier to move much too quickly from the notion of context to a superficial acceptance of inconsistency and arbitrariness. He simply expects inconsistency rather than looking at the way context and perspectives structure fields and determine relevance: "Given Saussure's conception of the full subject [the investigative subject, whose point of view can be chosen at will— that point of view then determining what counts as 'natural' from that perspective], how could we expect *not* to find inconsistency and contradiction within the *Cours*? Inconsistency defines the method" (Strozier, 246; cf. 234).

Since inconsistency defines the method, and the method is the context, we cannot be surprised to learn that "there is no need to deconstruct Saussure's oppositions; the possibility of their deconstruction is implied at the very moment of their derivation" (Strozier, 244).

I would suggest, however, that once the shifting points of view are taken into account, what we are left with does not generally merit the title of contradictions.[4] There are at least three different dimensions according to which the various points of view that appear in the *Course* are ordered. The first one is the pedagogical, listener- (or reader-) oriented dimension in which later accounts supplant earlier ones:

> A commentary which did not respect this syntagmatic development [as "a consecutive text which unfolds 'syntagmatically' "] would be particularly inappropriate in the case of the *Cours*; for its expository method relies heavily on a technique of presenting successive reformulations of major points, examined in gradually increasing detail and from slightly different angles. (Some of the 'internal contradictions' in the work which critics have detected can be traced to the use of this technique.) (Harris, xvi)

The initial formulation may be oriented toward the presuppositions one's hearers will typically have, presuppositions that can best be broken down in a step-by-step process in which the final position is slowly developed (cf. Harris, 6, 11). Alternatively, the initial formulation may make use of formulations that make an immediate appeal to structures and distinctions that are familiar or easily understandable on the basis of prescientific experience and common sense, but that will have to be radically reformulated at a later stage. In neither case do the properly understood reformulations support the charge that the text is contradictory.

There is a second, particularly Saussurean dimension. Roy Harris notes that there are aspects of the *Course* in which "the exposition adopted . . . exemplifies admirably — and presumably not coincidentally — the Saussurean concept of 'value'. " Thus, rather than telling us what linguistics is, Saussure locates it in "an academic system of related but contrasting disciplines" (Harris, 11). Similarly, "the reader is never told exactly what *la langue* is at any point in the *Cours*: there is no definitive or final formulation. All we find are successive reformulations which bring out different contrasts between *la langue* and everything which *la langue* is not. The procedure is an object-lesson in Saussurean methodology, and in this sense the *Cours* itself is the great masterpiece of Saussurean linguistics" (Harris, 15). Clearly, given a traditional ideal of science, genuine contradictions (as opposed to differences) among such reformulations are not acceptable. But if this dimension is overlaid on the first or third dimension, the appearance of contradiction may well arise.

The third dimension in which the various formulations are ordered is method-ological: different formulations of varying degrees of theoretical adequacy may be appropriate at various stages of the concrete investigation of language. Thus when we cease simply speaking our language and make it the object of scientific investigation, it is quite natural and indeed necessary for us to mobilize our user's knowledge of the language (or our informants' knowledge of their language, if we are investigating a language unknown to us), making use of our working knowledge of meaning in order to identify the concrete entities of language, namely, those entities constituted by the association of signifier and signified: "To divide the [sound-]chain we must call in meanings. When we hear an unfamiliar language, we are at a loss to say how the succession of sounds should be analyzed, for analysis is impossible if only the phonic side of the linguistic phenomenon is considered" (*CGL*, 145/103). This phase works in what Strozier calls a "positivistic" manner, taking the units it identifies as naturally discrete. It is "positivistic" (if this word is appropriate in the first place) because it makes use of our competence as speakers as something given, taken for granted, seem-ingly entirely natural. But the naïveté in question is methodological and not philo-sophical. At a later stage we can subject the system of meanings in terms of which the linguistic signs were individuated to an analysis, in which case we dis-cover, according to Saussure, that the system is itself a system of differences, one developed along with of the system of signifiers.

Clearly, the same formulation can function in all three dimensions simulta-neously. The definition of the sign as the whole constituted by signifier and sig-nified belongs in the pedagogical dimension, since it appeals to the hearers' pre-scientific competence in their native language and sets the stage for the later introduction of the notion of linguistic value. But it also provides an operational definition of the sign that is appropriate to certain stages of investigation. Any reading of Saussure must be attentive to all three dimensions.

Logocentrism and Science

Derrida argues that the idea of science presupposes a certain relationship be-tween speech and writing: speech is original and writing is derivative. He writes of

> logocentrism: the metaphysics of phonetic writing . . . in the process of imposing itself upon the world, controlling in one and the same order:
>
> 1. the concept of writing . . .
> 2. the history of metaphysics . . .
> 3. the concept of science or the scientificity of science . . . (*OG*, 11–12/3).

He needs such strong formulations for his deconstructive strategy and rhetoric to work. It would not be sufficient to say that much philosophy of science, epistemology, and metaphysics has operated on the basis of a set of assumptions that are to be challenged by means of internal analyses and arguments. This would be a quite traditional philosophical strategy, one that would argue that many or all traditional theories are wrong and must be corrected or left behind. Derrida's strategy is different. His suggestion is that phonocentric metaphysics is the proper philosophy of the scientificity of science, and it follows that the deconstruction of metaphysics is the deconstruction of the scientificity of science. The deconstructive strategy aims at the very source of science itself, at the kind of question that gives rise to scientific investigation.

Saussure's question is: "What is both the integral and concrete object of linguistics?" (*CGL*, 23/7). The question is the question of essence, *ti esti*, the question "What is the sign?" (*OG*, 31/18). As in *Speech and Phenomena*, Derrida ties the original Socratic question "What is it?" with its allied distinction between the essential and the inessential to the metaphysics of presence. Here this has a double thrust. Within metaphysics, the essence of language will, according to Derrida, have to be found in an original presence that defines the essential—everything outside of that presence then being by definition external, extrinsic, at most merely representative of that original presence. It follows that "the 'formal essence' of the sign can only be determined in terms of presence" (*OG*, 31/18) and thus in terms of the presence of the spoken word to the signified. Derrida claims that it is possible to avoid this result only by challenging the question itself, by refusing to submit the sign to the logic or model of essence. This can be done only from within the thought of essence itself, for we have (as yet?) no other. Thus we cannot say "the sign has no essence, is not a thing," but only "the sign is that ill-named thing, the only one, that escapes the instituting question of philosophy: 'what is . . . ?' " (*OG*, 31/19). This writing "under erasure" (*sous rature*) uses a sign, which is necessary because there is no other, but it aims to set into relief and ward off the metaphysical commitments that sign brings with it.

Since the very idea of knowledge has its origin in "the system of 'hearing (understanding)-oneself-speak' through the phonic substance" (*OG*, 17/7), the field of the science of linguistics will be "the articulated unity of sound and sense within the phonie," and given this unity "writing would always be derivative, accidental, particular, exterior, doubling the signifier: phonetic. 'Sign of a sign,' said Aristotle, Rousseau, and Hegel" (*OG*, 45/29). Phonologism is an expression of *logocentrism*, for in one of its essential aspects the latter is "the metaphysics of phonetic writing" (*OG*, 11/3). Writing is derivative because it is representative, and in Derrida's reading this means that writing is not merely the "signifier of the first signifier," but also the "representation of the self-present voice, of the immediate, natural, and direct signification of the meaning" (*OG*, 46/30). Thus Derrida sees Saussure mobilizing an entire arsenal of oppositions rooted in metaphysics in his account of the relationship between (spoken) language and writing: "External/internal, image/reality, representation/presence, such is the old grid to which is given the task of outlining the domain of a science" (*OG*, 50/33). Derrida notes, however, that Saussure's entire account of writing is based on the exclusion of pictograms and ideograms, and once they are seen to be part of the spectrum of writing, "one realizes not only the unwiseness of the Saussurian limitation but the need for general linguistics to abandon an entire family of concepts inherited from metaphysics. . . . All this refers, beyond the nature/culture opposition, to a supervening opposition between *physis* and *nomos*, *physis* and *technē*" (*OG*, 49–50/33). Derrida also sees yet another prejudice at work in Saussure's treatment of language, a "massive limitation" (*OG*, 50/33) that restricts his discussion of writing to phonetic writing (cf. *CGL*, 46/ 26).

Derrida sees these two limitations as being anything but quirks on Saussure's part: they are essential for the delimitation of the field of linguistics as a closed field ruled by a closed structure of laws. On Derrida's reading, however, these limitations will turn out to be violent exclusions that both establish and threaten the scientificity of the science of linguistics: they establish linguistics by delimiting its field, and they undermine it because that which is left on the outside as being external, unreal, or unnatural (image, representation, and so on) resists the limitation, reasserting itself at the very center of the inside the limitation was to establish. The "hard and fast frontier" of the science of linguistics (*OG*, 50/33) has always already been breached, the closed field always already ruptured. The science established by Saussure's essential limitations is "a science that can no longer answer to the classical concept of the *epistēmē* because the originality of its field—an originality that it inaugurates—is that the opening of the 'image' within it appears as the condition of 'reality' " (*OG*, 50/33). This is the thesis Derrida will attempt to establish.

The "Natural Bond"

On Derrida's reading, Saussure answers the "What is it?" question in terms of the word as a unity of sense and sound, signifier and signified, in terms of "the indivisible units of the 'thought-sound' " (*OG*, 47/31). Given this answer, writing *as such* will have to be derivative and external, for graphic representation is external to the essence of the sign, is supplementary to it. It thus follows that the most rational form of writing is phonetic.

Strozier has questioned this reading:

Derrida is quite wrong about Saussure's use of the word as the unit in

linguistics and about his general conception of the sign. . . . Derrida
means here that if there exists a primary or natural thought-sound union,
then writing is excluded. But here he ventures for his quotations far
afield of the chapter on writing: the 'thought-sound' connection is in
Saussure based on the prior assumption that langue is entirely a
phenomenon of consciousness and the prior specification that 'sound' is
to be read as 'sound imagery'. (Strozier, 236 n. 2)

Strozier's remarks are apt as far as they go, but there are two issues here: In the
first place, Derrida is reading the *Course* as a single, timelessly present whole,
without paying attention to the shifting contexts as the text unfolds. We have
already pointed out that this can do real violence to the *Course*, and that is
Strozier's point. In the second place, however, Derrida claims to have solid
textual evidence for his reading, since he finds Saussure asserting a "natural
bond of sense to the senses" (*OG*, 53/35) that binds meaning (concept) to sound:
" 'The natural bond [*le lien naturel*],' Saussure says, 'the only true bond, the
bond of sound.' This natural bond of the signified (concept or sense) to the
phonic signifier would condition the natural relationship subordinating writing
(visible image) to speech" (*OG*, 53/35, quoting *CGL*, 46/25). This is Derrida's
favorite text in Saussure. He quotes it three times in *Of Grammatology* (*OG*,
53/35, 60/40, 65/44) and continues to refer to it in more recent texts.[5] This is no
accident, for it is the key to Derrida's reading of Saussure. Everything turns on
this one text: if Derrida's interpretation of it is correct, then his deconstruction of
Saussure's phonocentrism will succeed, regardless of how one might quibble
with specific details; but if that interpretation fails, Derrida's entire enterprise is
in danger of collapsing with it.

A look at the context of the quotation from Saussure seriously undermines the
plausibility of Derrida's reading. The passage from Saussure reads:

But how is the prestige of writing to be explained? First, the graphic
image of words strikes us as being something permanent and stable,
better suited than sound to constitute the unity of language through
time. Although that bond is superficial and creates a purely artificial
unity: it is much easier to grasp than the natural bond, the only true
one, that of sound. [Main comment s'explique ce prestige de l'écriture?
1. D'abord l'image graphique des mots nous frappe comme un objet
permanent et solide, plus propre que le son à travers le temps. Ce lien a
beau être superficiel et créer une unité purement factice: il est beaucoup
plus facile à saisir que le lien naturel, le seul véritable, celui du son.]
(*CGL*, 46/25, translation altered).[6]

The topic under discussion is "the unity of language throughout time" (*CGL*,
46/25, quoted at *OG*, 53/36). Saussure has been discussing primarily the relationship between (phonetic) writing and *pronunciation*, and what is at issue is

how changes in pronunciation are to be explained. He is interested in establishing that "language does have a definite and stable oral tradition that is independent of writing, but the influence of the written form prevents our seeing this" (*CGL*, 46/24), and his thesis is: "The pronunciation of a word is determined, not by its spelling, but by its history. . . . Precise laws govern its evolution. Each step is determined by the preceding step" (*CGL*, 53/31).

Thus nothing in the context indicates that "the true bond . . . of sound" refers to a "natural bond" between the privileged phonic signifier and its signified. The "bond" exists rather between the different stages of the history of the pronunciation of words. Saussure is arguing that we have here a relatively circumscribed region of objects governed by "precise laws." If these laws are to be discovered, the linguist must direct his or her attention precisely to this field, refusing to be distracted by other—from *this* point of view "external"—influences. This state of affairs is hardly surprising, as Saussure has already argued that "it is the viewpoint that creates the object" (*CGL*, 23/8), and what makes a specific viewpoint productive for Saussure is that it opens up a unified field—a "self-contained whole" (*CGL*, 25/9)—for scientific investigation.

Thus Derrida has not so much discovered a "natural bond" or connection between sense and sound at work in Saussure as imported such a bond into the text. Indeed, it would be surprising to find Saussure claiming a natural bond, for he explicitly questions the claim that "the function of language, as it manifests when we speak, is entirely natural" (*CGL*, 25/10, translation altered). He does reject the claim that "our choice happened to fall on the vocal organs," arguing that "the choice was more or less imposed by nature" (*CGL*, 26/10). But in the face of Derrida's insinuation of a metaphysical motif, the emphasis must be placed on the "more or less."[7] What is at issue is the relative convenience of an instrument, and this is an empirical matter, not a matter of essence. There is no reason why Saussure should have been surprised to learn that deaf people literally think in ASL: in this case we have a nonvocal sign that does not serve as a representative of a vocal sign. One might argue that what Saussure refers to as "the alphabet of deaf-mutes" (*CGL*, 33/16) is derivative from spoken language, but this would not hold of a full-blown sign language.

Saussure does speak of "thought-sound" (*pensée-son*) (*CGL*, 156/112, quoted at *OG*, 47/31 and 53/36), and this would seem to confirm Derrida when he sees the metaphysical "system of 'hearing (understanding)-oneself-speak' through the phonic substance" (*OG*, 17/7) at work in Saussure. But Saussure's point here is simply that a language does not consist of an articulated instrument—whether sounds or visible gestures—that is then related to an articulated system of thought. The two sides of the sign, signifier and signified, develop simultaneously. This does not affect the point that the selection of sound as the vehicle is at most "more or less imposed by nature."

Saussure is only following out the implications of his own principles when he argues that "the essential thing about a language [*la langue*] is . . . unrelated to the phonic character of the linguistic sign" (*CGL*, 21/7). The phonic side of the sign is not a thematic object of linguistics, but the science that Saussure chooses to call "phonology" is an important "auxiliary discipline." Similarly, it is clear that the linguist will have to be concerned with the system of writing of the language under study, but it is also clear that the linguist will be interested in phonetic writing for yet another reason, having to do with developing an effective set of instruments for scientific research: "The linguist needs above all else a means of transcribing articulated sounds that will rule out all ambiguity" (*CGL*, 56/33).

The Primacy of Speech in Saussure

Why, then, is Saussure so rabid in his efforts to remove writing from the proper object of linguistics?[8] This question is important, as Derrida quite properly insists that this rabid tone has to be accounted for, and for him this tone is a straightforward indication of Saussure's metaphysical commitments: "The tone counts; it is as if, at the moment when the modern science of the logos would come into its autonomy and its scientificity, it became necessary again to attack a heresy" (*OG*, 51/34). But the tone cannot be understood independently of what Saussure says in that tone. Once Derrida's reading of the content has been seen through, his account of the sense of the tone has to be revised.

The main reason for Saussure's rabid tone is, I think, to be found in his insistence that "language and writing are two distinct systems of signs" (*CGL*, 45/23), in which case each of them would provide a relatively circumscribed field for scientific study. That they might influence each other is never denied; indeed, Saussure insists on it. The point is that a science has to discover the principles governing each field as such before it goes on to study their interaction. The crucial thing to see is that all of Saussure's rather violent statements concerning the relationship between language and writing are made from the point of view of the linguist and directed to linguists. We have already seen that for Saussure, the object qua field for systematic scientific investigation is a function of the point of view selected, and the term "natural" is meaningful only as a function of such a standpoint. As a linguist, Saussure is focused on discovery of the principles and laws that govern a domain of objects, and anything that disrupts this is to be excluded from the purview of the science or from this phase of scientific investigation. The "prestige of writing" (*CGL*, 46/25, translation altered) that Saussure is so concerned to combat is above all the influence of writing on linguists as such: this is the context in which "writing obscures language" (*CGL*, 51–52/30). By disrupting (this term is itself perspectival; a more neutral term would be "influencing") the development of pronunciation, writing makes it more difficult for the linguist to discover the laws governing the evolution of pronunciation purely as such.

This situation allows for two different types of expression. Saussure can protest against the "false notions" (*CGL*, 52/30) of linguists, but these notions are not limited to linguists. They are rooted in a series of misconceptions that easily arise prior to explicit linguistic investigation, and the four explanations offered for the influence of writing are such misconceptions. This means that the way language in fact develops actually hides or disguises the principles and laws at work. For a scientist, this can seem deeply disturbing, and this circumstance leads to the second type of expression: influences that hide the principles at work seem from this perspective to be "tyranny," "pathological," a "monstrosity," and so on (*CGL*, 53–54/31–32).

It is telling in this context that although Saussure characterizes ideographic systems as those in which "each word is represented by a single sign that is unrelated to the sounds of the word itself" (*CGL*, 47/25), thus apparently maintaining the "representation of a representation" account of writing in general, he calls Chinese "a second language" (*CGL*, 48/26) whose expression of an idea need not be mediated by any representation of the spoken word.[9] In this case, "the substitution does not have the annoying consequences that it has in a phonetic system, for the substitution is absolute; the same graphic symbol can stand for words from different Chinese dialects" (*CGL*, 48/26, translation altered). Clearly, it is not writing as such that is a problem for Saussure, but only phonetic writing. There is no natural tendency for the Chinese character to affect pronunciation. Ironically, it is precisely the fact that phonetic writing "gives a fairly rational representation of the language" (*CGL*, 48/27, translation altered) that causes problems for the linguist.

There may be an additional reason for Saussure's insistence on the priority of the spoken form. I would suggest that it is not so much *writing* as the *written* that is the source of Saussure's irritation here. Saussure needs to posit a relationship between writing and speech because in the case of a dead language the language can be studied only by way of that which has been written. Thus he needs to find *some* adequate relationship between the written form and the primary object of linguistics. On the other hand, Saussure is interested in language not merely as an abstract system but as that which makes possible a *functioning* language: language is a medium of communication.[10] For Saussure, the association of concepts and sound-images is the psychological stage on which a language becomes effective. However, it is illuminating to ask whether, leaving aside the issue of the delimitation of a circumscribed field with its own principles and laws, and thus the question of the influence of phonetic writing on speech, Saussure would have any good reason to focus on speaking rather than the act of writing, on hearing/understanding rather than reading. What has been written can influence how we speak in ways that conceal the laws governing the evolution of speech.

But I see no Saussurean reason to say that the act of writing is intrinsically secondary to and derivative from speaking (*parole*).

For Derrida, Saussure's violent language is evidence of a logocentric bias gone wild, a metaphysical privileging of the voice as the transparent medium of thought. A more sober analysis shows that it is an expression of the passion of a scientist for a field of order he has discovered. This could have broader ramifications for Derrida, since he holds that logocentrism as the metaphysics of phonetic writing controls "*the concept of science* or the scientificity of science — what has always been determined as *logic*" (*OG*, 12/3). If, however, the voice is not necessarily given an absolute privilege in the articulation of a science of linguistics, we may wonder whether the claimed connection between the primacy of the voice and the primacy of logic can be defended: would the failure of the deconstruction of the primacy of the voice be the failure of the deconstruction of the logicality of logic?

Speaking Is Writing

We have seen that Saussure's little paragraph on the "natural bond" is crucial to Derrida's case against Saussure and that once Derrida's interpretation has been seen through, his broader case crumbles. With sharpened eyes, we can go back through Derrida's discussion of Saussure and analyze the rhetorical and argumentative structures at work (or should one say "at play"?) in it. I would like to demonstrate this by an analysis of one passage from the section entitled "The Outside Is the Inside":

> The thesis of the *arbitrariness* of the sign (so grossly misnamed, and not only for the reasons Saussure himself recognizes) must forbid a radical distinction between the linguistic and the graphic sign. No doubt this thesis concerns only the necessity of relationships between specific signifiers and signifieds *within* the allegedly natural relationship between the voice and sense in general, between the order of phonic signifiers and the content of the signifieds ("the natural bond, the only true one, that of sound"). Only these relationships between specific signifiers and signifieds would be regulated by arbitrariness. Within the "natural" relationship between phonic signifiers and their signifieds *in general*, the relationship between each determined signifier and its determined signified would be "arbitrary."
>
> Now from the moment that one considers the totality of determined signs, spoken, and a fortiori written, as unmotivated institutions, one must exclude any relationship of natural subordination, any natural hierarchy among signifiers or orders of signifiers. If "writing" signifies inscription and especially the durable institution of a sign (and that is the only irreducible kernel of the concept of writing), writing in general covers the entire field of linguistic signs. In that field a certain sort of

instituted signifiers may then appear, "graphic" in the narrow and
derivative sense of the word, ordered by a certain relationship with
other instituted—hence "written," even if they are "phonic"—
signifiers. The very idea of institution—hence of the arbitrariness of the
sign—is unthinkable before the possibility of writing itself, outside the
world as space of inscription, as the opening to the emission and to the
spatial *distribution* of signs, to the *regulated play* of their differences,
even if they are "phonic."

Let us now persist in using this opposition of nature and institution,
of *physis* and *nomos* (which also means, of course, a distribution and
division regulated in fact by *law*) which a meditation on writing should
disturb although it functions everywhere as self-evident, particularly in
the discourse of linguistics. We must then conclude that only the signs
called *natural*, those that Hegel and Saussure call "symbols," escape
semiology as grammatology. But they fall a fortiori outside the field of
linguistics as the region of general semiology. The thesis of the
arbitrariness of the sign thus indirectly but irrevocably contests
Saussure's declared proposition when he chases writing to the outer
darkness of language. This thesis successfully accounts for a
conventional relationship between the phoneme and the grapheme (in
phonetic writing, between the phoneme, signifier-signified, and the
grapheme, pure signifier), but by the same token it forbids that the latter
be an "image" of the former. Now it was indispensable to the exclusion
of writing as "external system," that it come to impose an "image," a
"representation," or a "figuration," an exterior reflection of the reality
of language.

It matters little, here at least, that there is in fact an ideographic
filiation of the alphabet. This important question is much debated by
historians of writing. What matters here is that in the synchronic
structure and systematic principle of alphabetic writing—and phonetic
writing in general—no relationship of "natural" representation, none of
resemblance or participation, no "symbolic" relationship in the
Hegelian-Saussurean sense, no "iconographic" relationship in the
Peircian sense, be implied.

One must therefore challenge, in the very name of the arbitrariness
of the sign, the Saussurian definition of writing as "image"—hence as
natural symbol—of language. (*OG*, 65–66/44–45, translation of
Saussure altered)

This argument needs to be taken apart.

In the first place, Derrida again misuses Saussure's reference to a "natural
bond." As we have seen, what Derrida refers to as the "allegedly natural relationship between the voice and sense in general" is at most a relatively natural
relationship, the recognition of which does not involve the metaphysical commitments Derrida takes such pains to insinuate into Saussure.

The next move in the argument hinges on the terms "inscription" and "the durable institution of a sign" as the sense of "writing."[11] Derrida initially concentrates on "institution": *all* signs are instituted. All signs are what they are only in terms of their differences from other signs. This is simply the Saussurean idea of differentiality or linguistic value: "In a language there are only differences *without positive terms*" (*CGL*, 166/120, translation altered). This idea can be mobilized against Saussure only if one presupposes a non-Saussurean "natural" (in the sense of *physis*) relationship of presence between "the order of phonic signifiers and the content of the signifieds." Furthermore, it feeds into Derrida's thesis that "phonic" signifiers are "written" only because he has equated "durable institution," which is to say linguistic value, with "inscription," a term that appears without warning scare quotes.

The third stage of the argument consists in playing the natural off against the arbitrary, arguing that Saussure's claim that writing is the representation of speech gets caught in a pincers movement between these two terms, in a classical dilemma or double bind. On the one hand, as sign, all writing is arbitrary (institution, *nomos*), and the relationship between phoneme and grapheme in phonetic writing is arbitrary. On the other hand, writing is to be an *image* of the spoken word. Saussure speaks of "the graphic image of words [*l'image graphique des mots*]" (*CGL*, 46/25, translation altered), which Derrida takes to be a "relationship of 'natural' representation, . . . of resemblance or participation." But Derrida makes no attempt to show that Saussure is committed to such a relationship of "natural" representation. Indeed, there is good reason to think that Saussure is not committed to any such thing, as he could write, "Linguistic signs are so to speak tangible; writing can fix them in *conventional images* [*images conventionnelles*]" (*CGL*, 32/15, translation altered, emphasis added). With this, the entire argument crumbles.

Conclusion

Derrida's strategy in the early pages of *Of Grammatology* is to characterize logocentrism in terms of the primacy of the "system 'hearing (understanding)-oneself-speak' " and thus in terms of the image of writing implied by it: w_t or traditional writing, writing that is purely representative of speech. He then generalizes certain aspects of w_t, namely, "the exteriority of the signifier," to "the exteriority of writing in general" (*OG*, 26/14) or grammatological writing, w_g. It then turns out that speech falls under w_g, since speech is just as much a differential system as writing is. The structure of the "overarching universal" that we found at work in *Speech and Phenomena* is clearly recognizable here: writing (w_g) is the genus of speech and writing (w_t). The problem with this strategy is that Derrida has to distort Saussure in order to "find" the metaphysical "system" in Saussure's text to begin with. Derrida has to focus exclusively on

Saussure's account of the sign in terms of the signifier/signified structure—indeed he has to distort that account—in order to construct a metaphysically phonocentric Saussure. Once one sees that w_g is nothing but the idea of linguistic value dressed up in a fashionable rhetoric, one sees that the entire "deconstruction" of Saussure has been performed with mirrors.

Conclusion
The Rigor and Ethics of Reading

They who make antitheses by forcing words are like those who make false windows for the sake of symmetry; their rule is not to speak accurately, but to make accurate figures.

—Pascal, *Pensées*

The Problem of Assessment

We have seen in the Introduction that Derrida's deconstructive approach to philosophical texts presents the critical reader with what appears to be a dilemma: a critical reading might seem to be committed to the very ideals of truth, rigor, and epistemic accountability deconstructed by the texts that are to be subjected to a critical reading. But this dilemma is simply a reflection of the task that deconstruction sets for itself, namely, that of subjecting itself to what Derrida calls the "classical norms" (*OG*, 8/lxxxix) even as it deconstructs the metaphysical underpinning of those very norms. Derrida thus insists "that within interpretive contexts . . . that are relatively stable . . . it should be possible to invoke rules of competence, criteria of discussion and of consensus, good faith, lucidity, rigor, criticism, and pedagogy" (Derrida 1988, 146). The present book responds to Derrida's own call for a "strong" reading of his texts.

The results of this critical reading are discouraging: the texts we have examined overwhelmingly fail to live up to their own standards. To be sure, Derrida writes that "the reconstitution of a context can never be perfect and irreproachable even though it is a regulative ideal in the ethics of reading, of interpretation,

167

or of discussion,'' and that therefore "the determination, or even the redetermination, the simple recalling of a context is never a gesture that is neutral, innocent, transparent, disinterested'' (Derrida 1988, 131). This is surely true, and I do not doubt that my reading of Derrida, Husserl, Aristotle, and Saussure can and will be challenged on specific points. This is as it should be. But I think that the general conclusion that these Derridean texts radically fail to make their case stands. As noted in the Introduction, I set out to avoid what Bernet calls the "unfruitful business'' of trying to "nail Derrida [by means of] supposed errors of interpretation in his reading of Husserl'' (Bernet 1986, 52). Derrida's texts made it impossible to redeem this promise: on a careful reading Derrida's texts "nail'' themselves.

One possible response to this conclusion might be that the entire enterprise of giving a critical reading of Derrida's texts is flawed from the start, *in spite of* Derrida's insistence on traditional rigor. One may well wonder whether my focus on the rigor of Derrida's reading is not a red herring that blocks even the attempt at a truly productive reading of Derrida. After all, philosophers have always "misread'' one another, and while we might note such misreadings carefully, we do not let them get in the way of our appreciation of the originality and power of the text we are reading. Aristotle may at times have set up a caricature of Plato, but we don't write off Aristotelian metaphysics just for that reason. Heidegger may well "misread'' Kant, but one can be of this opinion and still read *Kant and the Problem of Metaphysics* as an important Heideggerian text, one that develops and sheds light on what may be very powerful aspects of Heidegger's thought. One could read the book primarily to learn about Heidegger, not Kant, but this might in turn influence one's critical position vis-à-vis Kant. Thus, while the concept of rigor I have used is, I think, found in the Derridean texts themselves, there may be another form of rigor (or simply some other norm) that is more appropriate to reading these texts. Derrida himself has insisted on the necessity of "protocols of reading'' (Derrida 1981a, 63), but perhaps we are using the wrong protocol.

This question requires discussion from several points of view. (A) Paul de Man has suggested that Derrida's reading of Rousseau in *Of Grammatology* might best be considered a parody or fiction, but I shall show that questions of rigor and accuracy turn out to play an important role in de Man's reading of Derrida—with results that sometimes fly in the face of de Man's avowed intent (B) But the de Man/Scanlon suggestion that specific texts by Derrida might be most properly read as deliberate parody has to be taken seriously, and while I do not find that thesis compelling, nothing in my reading of *Speech and Phenomena* can be taken to disprove it. I shall argue, however, that reading that text as a satire robs it of any deconstructive force. (C) There is a Derridean alternative to reading *Speech and Phenomena* as a satire: it might be an example of what Derrida calls "dual writing.'' I shall argue that if he is there practicing dual writing, it fails to achieve its stated goal. (D) I shall argue that any attempt to separate the question of the significance of the Derridean enterprise as it is presented in these texts from the question of the rigor of Derrida's readings of Husserl and Saussure is condemned to failure.

The inescapable conclusion is that Derrida's texts must be measured in terms of their own standards of rigor, and that they fail to live up to those standards. But as I pointed out in the Introduction, these texts have exerted a broad influence and have been widely praised precisely for their rigor. In the final section of this chapter, I shall briefly discuss the questions this raises concerning the standards of reading and argumentation in contemporary intellectual debates.

Blindness and Insight: **Paul de Man's Reading of Derrida**

In "The Rhetoric of Blindness: Jacques Derrida's Reading of Rousseau," Paul de Man, who was one of the leading representatives of deconstruction in America, suggests that it might be inappropriate even to ask whether Derrida's story about Rousseau's involvement with language is at a certain point "accurate," since "it may well be offered as parody or fiction, without pretending to be anything else." De Man notes that "unlike epistemological statements,[1] stories do not cancel each other out, and we should not let Derrida's version replace Rousseau's own story of his involvement with language"(de Man, 119)

Later in the same essay de Man writes that "it would seem to matter very little whether Derrida is right or wrong about Rousseau," since "Derrida's own Nietzschean theory of language as 'play' warns us not to take him literally." To read such a text literally would be to miss the very thrust of the strategy it employs, namely, "the use of a philosophical terminology with the avowed purpose of discrediting this very terminology" (de Man, 137).

Finally, de Man ends his essay by posing a very specific alternative: "There are two possible explanations for Derrida's blindness with regard to Rousseau: either he *actually misreads Rousseau* . . . or he *deliberately misreads Rousseau* for the sake of his own exposition and rhetoric" (de Man, 139, emphasis added). But it turns out that this is not a real alternative in this case. In the course of a discussion of the first alternative, de Man concludes that "instead of having Rousseau deconstruct his critics, we have Derrida deconstructing a pseudo-Rousseau by means of insights that could have been gained from the 'real' Rousseau. The pattern is too interesting not to be deliberate" (de Man, 139–40).

Now, it is clear that de Man's distinction between Derrida's story about Rousseau and language, on the one hand, and Rousseau's own story about language, on the other hand, does not require or even allow one to dispense with all standards of rigor or accuracy in evaluating Derrida's reading of Rousseau. When de Man brings in certain passages that Derrida does not draw on, he says that Derrida's failure to include them was "within perfect right, within the logic of his own argument, which would consider these passages as redundant or dealt with elsewhere in the commentary.'' De Man can acknowledge Derrida's "right" to omit passages that, on de Man's reading, are contrary to Derrida's claims about Rousseau precisely because de Man claims that the price of every insight is a certain blindness, and de Man admits that his own reading will contain its omissions (de Man, 127n.). Here reading, it would seem, does not cancel out reading.

And yet, on de Man's reading the virtue of Derrida's reading of Rousseau is precisely that "the critical reading of Derrida's critical reading of Rousseau shows blindness to be the necessary correlative of the rhetorical nature of literary language" (de Man, 141). De Man's reading can claim to "show" this only because, at certain specific junctures, it claims to offer what can only be called a *better* reading, namely, one that does not exhibit the specific blindness of Derrida's reading. This enables de Man, in specific criticism of Derrida, to assert that "Derrida *misconstrues* as blindness what is instead a transposition from the literal to the figural level of discourse" (de Man, 139, emphasis added). De Man thereby shows, against his explicit intent, that Derrida's blindness/omission/ misconstrual is not structurally necessary for his insights. It turns out that de Man cannot avoid the question of the accuracy of Derrida's reading of Rousseau (though it is clear that this is not a matter of all or nothing). He must return to the question of the rigor of Derrida's reading. And once this is done, story can indeed cancel out story.

Deconstruction as Parody

We still have to consider, however, de Man's suggestion that we should not even *ask* (or care) whether Derrida's story about Rousseau (or, in the cases considered here, about Husserl and Saussure) is accurate or not, since it might be a parody or fiction. This is John Scanlon's suggestion: *Speech and Phenomena* should be read as a parody. In the first place (and this is itself a significant result), the reading of *Speech and Phenomena* I have offered provides no conclusive evidence against the de Man/Scanlon thesis. But perhaps it is possible to say more.

De Man wonders whether Derrida's reading of Rousseau even pretends to be anything but parody or fiction, and this question must be raised concerning the texts examined here as well. Is there indeed any reason to think that Derrida should or even wants[2] to be taken seriously when he writes, "It goes without saying that around that axis [of a reading that 'should free itself, at least in its axis, from the classical categories of history'] I have had to respect classical norms, or at least I have attempted to respect them" (*OG*, 8/lxxxix)? If the praise of philosophical rigor in Derrida's early work is unjustified, must we then follow Scanlon and regard that work (and perhaps praise it) as satire on philosophical rigor? A look back at the foregoing study of *Speech and Phenomena* offers what might seem to be a great deal of support for such a conclusion. Every chapter might be read as offering the reader hints that point in this direction. The following is an incomplete list:

(1) In the Introduction to *Speech and Phenomena*, Derrida asserts that Husserl's project of a pure logical grammar excludes aspects of the a priori of language. Yet what Derrida sees as excluded is precisely what Husserl wants to study in his pure grammar, and when Derrida returns to this topic in chapters 6 and 7, he explicitly recognizes this. Are we really to assume that Derrida does not notice that his reading of an important text has changed in the course of his writing? Perhaps this should rather be read as a wink at the reader not to take too seriously what seems to be happening on the surface of what is in reality a playful parody.

(2) In chapter 1 of *Speech and Phenomena*, Derrida claims that for Husserl meaning "is always a linguistic sense" (*SP*, 18/18), but fails to note that in the Introduction to the second volume of the *Logical Investigations*, Husserl is careful not to take any position on "the connection of thought with speech" (*LI* II.1, 3–4/I, 250). Again, in chapter 1 Derrida gives an accurate translation of Husserl's term *verflochten* as *entrelacé* ("interwoven") when he quotes Husserl, but uses the phrase *s'entrelacer, s'enchevetrer* ("interwoven or entangled") when discussing the passage in question, the latter term giving the discussion a new and unjustified direction. He then shifts to using the term *pris dans* ("caught up in"), which would be a fair translation of *verflochten*, and concludes that "Pris, c'est-à-dire contaminé [Caught up is the same as contaminated]"'(*SP*, 21/21). He thus slides from "interwoven" and "caught up in," first to "entangled" and then to the even more dramatically threatening "contaminated." Derrida's competence as a translator cannot be questioned here: he improves the official French translation, which translates Husserl's "allzeit . . . verflochten" by *toujours engagé*, to read *toujours entrelacé*; and by carefully including the German word in his French text Derrida provides an additional clue for any reader who might begin to suspect that the discussion has step by step cut any ties to the text ostensibly under discussion.

(3) In the course of his discussion of Husserl's concept of indication in chapter 2, Derrida silently reverses the order of Husserl's text, which enables him to read the generality of Husserl's account of motivation into his account of indication. The resulting distortion of Husserl's argument would be transparent to any reader who accompanied the reading of Derrida's text with a reading of the text under analysis—a normal procedure for scholars and one that Derrida surely would expect from a competent reader.

(4) In chapter 3, Derrida quotes Husserl's expression "as signs, namely as indications of one's own lived experiences," first interpreting it in a manner that clearly violates the sense of the text and then magnanimously deciding to treat it as a mere slip of the tongue, to be replaced by a reading that turns out to be a

straightforwardly proper reading of the text. No reader who bothers to read Husserl's sentence in its context will be misled. In the same chapter, Derrida presents some basic Husserlian distinctions, commenting, "unless one lends a constant and vigilant attention to differences such as these, one can understand nothing of phenomenology" (*SP*, 44/48). This leads to a discussion that culminates in statements so bizarre that they almost have to be deliberate distortions of Husserl.

(5) In chapter 4, Derrida uses a number of German terms, especially the word *Vorstellung*, but makes no attempt to specify which sense of the term is relevant. These passages can be read as a satire on "scholarly" writing by authors who think that a text is more profound the more foreign terms it includes. The fact that Husserl devoted considerable effort to distinguishing no less that thirteen different senses of *Vorstellung*, along with Derrida's failure even to mention this fact, makes the satirical force even stronger.

(6) In chapter 5, Derrida quotes a phrase out of context and then treats it as if it dealt with perception, when a glance at the context shows that it deals with representation (*Vergegenwärtigung, Re-Präsentation*) and not perception at all. This would be clear to anyone who looked at the Husserlian texts that Derrida is discussing with such an outward appearance of care. In the context, what one would normally take as the kind of slip anyone can make (the note card with the quotation gets in the wrong stack) produces a comic effect that might well be intended.

(7) In chapter 6, Derrida suggests that speech itself involves a suspension of the natural attitude. But in Derrida's own *Edmund Husserl's 'Origin of Geometry': An Introduction*, he had argued against Muralt's assertion of that very thesis. This flip-flopping of position without any attempt to give a reason for the change might be a clue that this piece of writing is not to be taken seriously in any straightforward sense.

(8) Finally, in chapter 7 Derrida argues that Husserl's own principles should have led him to an account of the essentially occasional expression "I" diametrically opposed to the account he in fact gives (*SP*, 107/96). The apparent plausibility of this claim depends crucially on the fact that Derrida has not presented the relevant details of Husserl's account of essentially occasional expressions. Once the details of Husserl's text are taken into account, Derrida's claim becomes nonsensical. This looks very much like a deliberate demonstration of the ease with which a position can be disguised by the use of selective quotation.

Should we therefore conclude that *Speech and Phenomena* is meant as satire, as Scanlon argues? Perhaps, but there are still some considerations that provide evidence to the contrary. Normally, the pleasure in reading a satire comes precisely from reading it *as* a satire. If readers were to take seriously Swift's proposal that surplus Irish children should be eaten as long as a fair market price is paid for them, we would point out the ways in which it satirizes texts that are intended to be taken seriously in a straightforward manner. They could then read the text with genuine pleasure. *Speech and Phenomena* is not a text of this sort. Once one assumes that it is a satire—if that is what it is—it ceases to be of much interest unless one takes pleasure in an Easter egg hunt, the object of which is to find more eggs in the form of misreadings or invalid arguments than any other reader. One might enjoy it as a private joke, as Richard Rorty suggests, but it remains just that—a *private* joke. In brief, if *Speech and Phenomena* is a satire, it does not fit into the traditional genre very comfortably—but then Derrida is anything but a great respecter of traditional laws of genre (cf. Derrida 1980).

Dual Writing

One might argue that the readings of *Speech and Phenomena* and *Of Grammatology* offered in this book are inadequate because they fail to take the rhetorical complexity of those texts into consideration. It might be argued that Derrida is doing *more* than offering a rigorous deconstructive reading, that he is practicing what he has called "dual writing." Any interpretation that failed to take both levels of such writing into account would necessarily be inadequate, so this possibility has to be investigated.

Looking back at his response to John Searle in "Limited Inc a b c . . . ," Derrida describes dual writing in the following manner:

"Limited Inc . . . " makes uncomfortable reading because its text is written in at least two registers at once, for it answers to at least two imperatives. On the one hand, I try to submit myself to the most demanding norms of classical philosophical discussion. I try in fact to respond point by point, in the most honest and rational way possible, to Searle's arguments, the text of which is cited almost in its entirety. On the other hand, in so doing I multiply statements, discursive gestures, forms of writing, the structure of which reinforces my demonstration in something like a practical manner: that is, by providing instances of "speech acts" which by themselves render impracticable and theoretically insufficient the conceptual oppositions upon which speech act theory in general . . . relies (serious/nonserious; literal/metaphorical or ironic; normal forms/parasitical forms; use/mention; intentional/ nonintentional; etc.). This *dual writing* seemed to me to be consistent with the propositions I wanted simultaneously to demonstrate on the theoretical level and to exemplify in the *practice* of speech acts. . . . Moreover, it was as though I was telling Searle, *in addition*: Try to interpret this text too with your categories—and to you, as well as the reader, I say: enjoy! (Derrida 1988, 114)

Enjoyment is a notoriously subjective thing, and I am certainly willing to acknowledge that there are many who have apparently read *Speech and Phenomena* with pleasure. My only question is whether or not that pleasure is based on a false assumption in the cases discussed here.

"Dual writing" as Derrida describes it is crucially dependent on the rigor of the first register: submission to "the most demanding norms of classical philosophical discussion." But even if this register fails to achieve its proclaimed goal, the second register might still succeed: it might indeed exemplify something that Derrida tried but failed (and perhaps failed for essential reasons) to demonstrate in the first register. In the case of "Limited Inc a b c . . . " one might argue that while in his attack on speech act theory Derrida might be guilty of serious misunderstandings and distortions, it might indeed be the case that the performance involved cannot be subjected to the confines of speech act theory. Failure on the first level need not, it would seem, condemn the text to failure on the second.

If *Speech and Phenomena* and the sections of *Of Grammatology* I have discussed are cases of dual writing, the first register clearly fails in their case. Is there then anything left to count as the second register? With the collapse of Derrida's readings of Husserl, Aristotle, and Saussure, what was to be a telling practical demonstration turns into a cute and self-indulgent game—a *mere* game that has lost contact with its opponent, the metaphysics it was supposed to deconstruct.[3]

Deconstruction and Rigor

In general, any attempt to cut the reading of Derrida's texts off from questions of the rigor and accuracy of his own reading turns those texts into little more than curiosities. In this respect, these texts cannot be compared to those of Aristotle or Heidegger, and there are specific reasons for this.

One might, for example, regard it as irrelevant that Derrida's discussion of Husserl involves serious distortions. Andrew Parker has taken this general approach, arguing that "phrases such as 'If Derrida is anywhere near the truth on Husserl' . . . simply have no bearing on the practice of deconstruction, for Derrida is interested not in being 'true' to Husserl but in reinscribing the notion of 'truth' as it *deconstructs* the Husserlian text" (Parker, 67).[4] But if one is to claim that Derrida's enterprise has a productive side that tells an interesting and even important story independent of being "anywhere near the truth" about Husserl or Saussure, one will have to find independent reasons to think that Derrida has actually shown, for example, that expression is a form of indication, or that *Beweis* is a form of *Hinweis* (cf. chap. 3 above). In other words, Derrida's story must be independently plausible, and it is hard to see how this can be established, even if one chooses never to refer back to Husserl's texts. The reason for this is that in *Speech and Phenomena* Derrida is careful not to offer any independent arguments for his conclusions. The entire deconstructive strategy of the book is to allow the argument to develop strictly and only from the reading of Husserl. One may well leave aside the question of the adequacy of the reading of Husserl, but if "Derrida's Husserl" is not independently plausible, the overall argument lacks plausibility. I would venture to suggest that a Husserl who argued like Derrida's Husserl would never have been taken seriously.

To take a specific example, we saw in chapter 6 that Derrida's attempt to show that Husserl is committed to the instantaneousness of the present fails to respect the demands of rigor in reading. One might argue that Husserl's and Derrida's stories are, up to a point, the same story. The difference might be thought to be that Derrida draws the radical conclusions required by that story, while Husserl tries to contain the story within the confines of a metaphysics of presence. If one looks at the text of *Speech and Phenomena*, however, the key source of the persuasiveness of Derrida's introduction of *différance* is the manner in which it is set off against the claims that Husserl is committed to the moment or *Augenblick* as a punctual instant and that this is crucial to his theory of meaning. In other words, the introduction of *différance* is no more plausible than the story of those metaphysical commitments, since one of the jobs of *différance* is precisely to account for the illusion of the phonocentric account. But the plausibility of this story is crucially dependent on Derrida's repeated claims that *Husserl's* analyses are rigorous and subtle (see *SP*, 2–3/4–5, 13–14/13–14, 40/37, 42/39, 61/55, 71/64, 91/81, 100/98).[5] The import of a deconstructive reading is parasitic on the rigor of the text being deconstructed. Since this is the crucial premise, the plausibility of the deconstructive story is in its turn also crucially dependent on the rigor of its reading of the rigorous Husserlian texts. We are thus brought back to Derrida's own demand for rigor. (It is surely no accident that de Man refers to Derrida's use of "Heidegger's and Nietzsche's fiction of metaphysics as a *period* in Western thought in order to dramatize, to give tension and suspense to the argument" [de Man, 137], and not to the metaphysics of presence itself as a fiction. The force of Derrida's story requires that the latter be more than a fiction.)

An alternative would be to emphasize the treatment of writing as the key to the introduction of *différance*. But when Derrida writes that "the possibility of writing dwelt within speech" (*SP*, 92/82), this requires that he begin with a certain concept of speech, namely, the "phonocentric" concept of the immediate self-presence of the voice that he attributes to Husserl and Saussure. Derrida tries to make this conception compelling in its own terms as a sort of transcendental illusion, but when the readings of Husserl and Saussure break down, the intrinsic plausibility of the phonocentric thesis becomes less compelling. Without this plausibility of the foil, the demonstration itself loses its force. Once again, it is hard to separate the plausibility of the story from the rigor of the reading.

It is clear that one can still use *Speech and Phenomena* as a source when trying to figure out or explain what Derrida means by "trace," "supplement," or *différance*. A number of authors have done so, and this may well help shed an initial light on those terms. But there is, I think, a limit to what one can learn from a text like *Speech and Phenomena*, given its radical lack of rigor. Similarly, the interview in which Derrida lays out four aspects of *différance* (Derrida 1981a, 8f.) is indispensable for getting a grasp on what Derrida means, but it does not pretend to offer a rigorous rationale. Both of these texts refer us back to other texts, and I shall consider only one, the essay *"Différance."*

"Différance" presents the move from Saussure's account of the differential nature of the sign to *différance* as something resembling an inference from effect to cause: "These differences are themselves effects," and "what we note as *différance* will thus be the movement of play that 'produces' . . . these differences, these effects of difference" (Derrida 1973b, 140–41). Thus at first glance we seem to have another in a series of very traditional metaphysical moves including Plato's move from the world of change to the unchanging world of the Forms, Leibniz's move from spatial and temporal movement to the realm of monads, Kant's move from phenomena to noumena, and so on. Of course, Derrida's move is not at all a traditional metaphysical move (not even in the purely negative Kantian sense), since the very concept of the "origin" can be used only under erasure, and *différance* does not refer to "intelligibility" (Derrida 1973b, 133, 141).

Derrida compares this "move" from difference to *différance* to the problem Saussure posed concerning the relations between *langue* and *parole*: "Language is necessary if speaking is to be intelligible and produce all its effects; but speaking is necessary for the establishment of language, and historically its actuality always comes first" (*CGL*, 37/18). Derrida rejects the metaphysics of such a solution:

> Since language . . . has not fallen from the sky, it is clear that the
> differences have been produced; they are the effects produced, but
> effects that do not have as their cause a subject or substance, a thing in
> general, or a being that is somewhere present and itself escapes the play
> of difference. . . . I have tried to indicate a way out of the closure
> imposed by this system, namely, by means of the "trace." (Derrida
> 1973b, 141)

This trace is, of course, *différance* (*OG*, 92/62).

Here one can see the systematic role Derrida's critical reading of Saussure's rejection of writing and his supposed assertion of a "natural bond" of sound and sense is to play. By insinuating a phonocentric insistence on the self-presence of the voice, Saussure, on Derrida's reading, prepares the way for the historical primacy of speech, which would appeal to a being that is present to itself. Thus when Derrida proposes to retain "at least the schema, if not the content, of the demand formulated by Saussure," *différance* comes to light as "the movement by which language . . . becomes 'historically' constituted as a fabric of differences'' (Derrida 1973b, 141). But this move depends for its plausibility on the background of the claimed ''natural bond'' and the phonocentric commitment to the voice, and once again, this presupposes the rigor of the interpretation of the ''natural bond.'' The same thing holds for the argument in *Of Grammatology*.

This result can be generalized as follows. The genealogy of *différance* is complicated, but the names Nietzsche and Saussure play a major role here. Without trying to untangle the different senses of the word ''play'' that are or could be at work in the following formulations, we might say the following:

> *Différance* is the condition of possibility of play(ing).
> *Différance* is the play(ing) that makes play(ing) possible.
> *Différance* is the play(ing) that ''produces'' the play(ing) in any play(ing).

It may be, as Rorty has suggested, a simple mistake to try to give a theoretical account of *différance*, a persuasive demonstration of the necessity of postulating *différance*. The only relevant — indeed the only possible — ''demonstration'' might be the playful reading of texts in which the play(ing) in the text becomes manifest. The proof (and that is surely not the ''right'' word) is in the doing. But, and this is my main point, such doing has a claim to our interest, as opposed to our amusement, only if, as Derrida recognizes, it submits itself to the ''classical norms'' of rigor. Setting up straw men and blowing them down — even in the name of parody and fiction — simply will not do the job.

Those who would argue that my entire approach simply misses the point of Derrida's work would be making a double commitment. They would first (like Rorty) have to reject Derrida's own claims concerning the role of the norms of classical discussion in these texts. They would then have to claim that what has shown itself, on my reading, to be a rhetoric that often serves to mask the lack of serious interpretation and argumentation, is really something completely different. It is hard to see whence such a suggestion could derive its plausibility. (It should be noted that Rorty's position is in fact stronger: he thinks that these early texts of Derrida are simply mistakes, that Derrida should not be pursuing rigorous argument in the first place. See Rorty 1989a, 207–09.)

Such an understanding of the practice of deconstruction not only is not Derrida's, it locks deconstruction into a private and ultimately solipsistic sphere. It will not do to hide behind the sometime slogan of deconstruction: ''All readings are misreadings!'' Understood in light of Derrida's inversion of Hegel (see chap. 3 above), this means that the distinction between reading and misreading, far from being rejected in principle, is to be reinscribed in terms of the overarching universal of misreading, and this reinscription itself must be the result of reading (however reinscribed), not misreading. This is why Derrida can write that ''the value of truth (and all those values associated with it) is never contested or destroyed in my writings, but only reinscribed in more powerful, larger, more stratified contexts'' (Derrida 1988, 146). In the present case, the attempted re-inscription fails in its own terms.

Scholes has recently described Derrida's practice as a "nihilistic herme-neutics" (Scholes 1989, 56–57). It is nihilistic because it recognizes "the idea of truth only as an indispensable fetish rather than an extratextual guarantee." Yet it remains a hermeneutics because "rigor is what Derrida uses to oppose the notion of truth as presence, truth as revelation; so that rigor, in this perspective, is the dark shadow of truth that haunts nihilistic hermeneutics" (Scholes 1989, 85). Scholes offers a detailed list of the appearances of the words "rigor," "rigor-ous," and "rigorously" in *Speech and Phenomena*, *Of Grammatology*, and *Po-sitions*, noting that these words also appear more than twenty times in the After-word to *Limited Inc* (Scholes 1989, 83–85). Rigor is, Scholes suggests, one of the "protocols of reading" that Derrida has demanded (Derrida 1981a, 63; Scholes 1989, 86). Such a protocol of course requires specification, and Derrida states that "I have not found any [protocols of reading] that satisfy me" (Derrida 1981a, 63). Such a specification would presumably be essentially incomplete and essentially negative, since the function of such protocols is essentially to serve as a "guardrail" (*OG*, 227/158) that ensures that "this transformation [of any read-ing] cannot be executed however one wishes" (Derrida 1981a, 63). A list of the types of errors Derrida commits in *Speech and Phenomena* might constitute the beginning of a specification of a protocol of rigor.

We are thus brought back to the demand for rigor, and we must therefore again confront the radical lack of such rigor in the texts analyzed in this book. The real question, the question posed by these texts themselves, is whether Derrida's read-ing of Husserl and Saussure succeeds *as a reading* (again: not *the* reading, but *a* reading). Here the answer is clear: it does not. These texts cannot be taken seri-ously as a "deconstruction" of texts by Husserl and Saussure—not, at least, if we orient our understanding of deconstruction toward Derrida's own criteria for it.

I certainly grant that every reading is a performance[6] or transformation (a "writing," if you will), but not every performance succeeds in being a reading. What one is left with in *Speech and Phenomena* and in the sections of *Of Gram-matology* I have discussed is a performance that, instead of reading the texts os-tensibly under discussion, enframes them as raw material for a writing that, for whatever reasons, ultimately exhibits no interest in those texts themselves.

The Reception of Derrida

Derrida has recently devoted attention to the state of reading and critical discus-sion in contemporary public discourse, and his diagnosis of some of his critics is damning. He finds some "who no longer respect the elementary rules of philol-ogy and interpretation, confounding science and chatter as though they had not the slightest taste for communication" (Derrida 1988, 157 n. 9). It is hard not to respond to this statement with a simple *tu quoque*, though the fact that I have not been able to disprove the de Man/Scanlon hypothesis that Derrida's texts might properly be read as parody indicates that one should be cautious here. But regardless of Derrida's intent, the reception of his early works is of considerable interest in this context. And here certain questions have to be raised.

In the Introduction, I quoted a number of influential philosophers from both the analytic and the continental traditions (Newton Garver and Rorty from the former, although Rorty increasingly escapes classification; David Wood and Hans-Georg Gadamer from the latter) each of whom praises the rigor of Derrida's deconstructive reading of Husserl in *Speech and Phenomena*. (The list of those who have either accepted Derrida's readings or at least taken them seriously would be much longer.) Wood notes that "Husserl scholars have not reacted too favorably to it, but it has had an enormous impact on the wider perception of the limits and indeed the very possibility of phenomenology" (Wood 1989, 111). There can be no doubt about the impact of Derrida's work on many contemporary attitudes toward Husserlian phenomenology. Writing from the point of view of literary criticism, Frank Lentricchia says that "sometime in the early 1970s we awoke from the dogmatic slumber of our phenomenological sleep to find that a new presence had taken absolute hold over our avant-garde critical imagination: Jacques Derrida" (Lentricchia, 159). The reference to "phenomenological slumber" makes it clear that *Speech and Phenomena* played a crucial role in this awakening. But given the results of my attempt to evaluate Derrida's reading of Husserl, one has to wonder just what it was that seemed so convincing and, moreover, so arresting. The growing body of critical response by Husserl scholars seems to have had little effect. White reports giving copies of his critical essay to three acquaintances sympathetic to Derrida. Each felt that White's treatment of Derrida was unfair—two of them "quite emotionally"—but none of them felt any need to go back to Husserl's *Logical Investigations* (White, 62 n. 14).

It should be clear that my goal in writing this book is not to defend Husserl, any more than I defend Aristotle or Saussure. I merely defend their texts against a reading that distorts them, often beyond recognition, while offering little as a replacement. But given the result of my investigation, one has to ask what counts as serious reading for those who praise the rigor of Derrida's texts. Are there protocols governing their reading—even such an obvious protocol as the demand that when reading a critical discussion of a text one should also read the text being criticized? Rorty and Gadamer content themselves with praising Derrida's "job" on Husserl (as Rorty puts it) without going into details. Only Wood has gone on to give, in a later text, a detailed reading of some of Derrida's texts, and at several points he notes that Derrida's argument is "defective," that "his argument is surely wanting," and that "the argument is tendentious in the extreme'' (Wood 1989, 115, 124–25). As I noted earlier, Rorty claims that a ''serious'' reading simply misses the true point of Derridean writing. But when he turns around to claim that in traditional terms ''Derrida does a first-class, highly professional, job on Husserl,'' Rorty fails to live up to those traditional terms themselves.

Given Derrida's enormous success and the frequency with which writers concerned to demonstrate his respectability in traditional terms appeal to the ''rigor'' of his early work, it must be asked what accounts for this success and for the role of these particular texts in that success. Michèle Lamont has given a sociological analysis of the ''intellectual market'' targeted with such success by Derrida. Lamont's analysis, which is quite fascinating, may or may not be adequate. It is clear, however, that to the extent that the texts I have discussed played and play a role in this dramatic success story, the success of Derrida's work has been based on a failure to subject those texts to the kind of critical reading that is supposed to be the norm in intellectual discussions.

There are of course other texts, other pathways to deconstruction. Indeed, Derrida himself insists that ''deconstruction is always 'something else,' '' and that ''deconstruction does not exist somewhere, pure, proper, self-identical'' (Derrida 1988, 141). Thus each text will have to be considered in its own terms. These early texts can at most, however, be considered a private pleasure, and even that status may well rest on a misunderstanding. Whether this conclusion holds for our understanding, appreciation, and perhaps enjoyment of Derrida's later writing is a topic for further investigation.

Signature

Derrida has an undeniable talent for putting — or at least seeming to put — his pen on important and difficult issues, and for doing so in ways that, at least on first reading, seem to be both enlightening and troubling. In addition, there can be no doubt that Derrida can be a penetrating reader: his work on the poetry of Paul Celan in "Shibboleth" (Derrida 1986a) and on Francis Ponge in *Signéponge* (Derrida 1984c) are ample proof of this. While both of these, and especially the latter, are quite clearly performances in their own right, one rarely has the sense that the performance occurs at the expense of the text with which Derrida is dealing.

This stands in stark contrast to the texts I have discussed in this book. That is, I think, a shame, and ultimately our loss, for one would love to see the results if Derrida were to put his undoubted abilities to work in a serious confrontation with the work of Husserl.

As a result of this state of affairs, this is a very different book from the one I originally planned to write. When I began this project, I knew that *Speech and Phenomena* contained some curious readings and misreadings of Husserl, but I also thought it contained the outline of an interesting critique of Husserlian phenomenology, one that would bear enough similarity to some aspects of Sellars's theory of judgment to make a dialogue between Sellars and Derrida possible. Some years ago, it was Sellars, whose theory of judgment can be described as a Kantianism after the linguistic turn, who awoke me from what came to seem like a dogmatic slumber concerning the Husserlian theory of judgment (cf. Evans 1983; Evans 1984, chap. 5 and the appendix; Evans 1989), and I hoped that

Derrida would be of some help in working out the implications of a broadly "Sellarsian" phenomenology for the philosophy of the human sciences. As I proceeded with work on the book, however, this project proved to be impossible in that form. The misreadings of Husserl, the simple ignoring of relevant texts, and the arguments that began to fall apart as soon as they were distilled from the obscure prose—all of this made a philosophical dialogue with Derrida, at least in terms of these texts, impossible.

In addition, I was completely unprepared for the way Derrida's reading of Saussure's exclusion of writing from the object of linguistics fell apart when confronted with the text of the *Course in General Linguistics* itself. (Note that Derrida's attack on the "self" of any "itself" cannot affect this claim: there is a relative "itself" of the *Course* in contrast to Derrida's arbitrary misreading, and this self would remain unaffected even if it were possible to give concrete content to Derrida's "deconstruction of the self." I do not think Derrida has ever intended to challenge this kind of point.) It was at this stage that my original project broke down completely, for it was precisely Saussure, with his claim that "in language there are only differences" (*CGL*, 166/120), who seemed to offer the best point of contact between Sellars and Derrida.

Sellars too conceived of language as a differential or functional structure (see Sellars 1974b), and it was Sellars more than any other philosopher I know who rigorously pursued the question of the consequences of such a conception of language for epistemology, metaphysics, and the philosophy of science. His attack on the "myth of the given" in his classic essay "Empiricism and the Philosophy of Mind," in which the concept of the given is framed so broadly that it covers not only the sense-data of classical empiricism but also the self-evident first principles of rationalism and even, Sellars thought, Hegel, seemed to offer an interesting counterpart to Derrida's attack on the metaphysics of presence. When Sellars writes:

> The real test of a theory of language lies not in its account of what has been called (by H. H. Price) 'thinking in absence,' but in its account of 'thinking in presence'—that is to say, its account of those occasions on which the fundamental connection of language with non-linguistic fact is exhibited. And many theories which look like psychological nominalism [the theory that all intentional phenomena involve the use of verbal symbols] when one views their account of thinking in absence, turn out to be quite 'Augustinian' when the scalpel is turned to their account of thinking in presence. (Sellars 1963, 162)

one could easily rewrite these sentences, whose context is the analytic philosophy of the 1950s, to express Derridean concerns in the poststructuralist context of the 1960s.

Rather than announcing that his rejection of the given yields a deconstruction of the very notion of truth (compare *OG*, 21/10), Sellars worked out a subtle account of the various dimensions of the concept of truth (cf. Evans 1978, 192–98) within a broadly Peircean framework. But in his elaboration and extension of Sellars's approach, Jay Rosenberg shows that the critical comparison and evaluation of competing and incommensurable theories, which would allow us to order them in terms of their adequacy as predecessor and successor theories (a *conditio sine qua non* for Sellars's scientific realism), presupposes theories that essentially involve *measurement* (Rosenberg, 368). This indicates that this dimension of truth cannot be found in the nonquantitative sciences of man, the *Geisteswissenschaften*.

Here one might well wonder whether Derrida should not begin to come into his own. This was my question. Unfortunately, the tremendous gap between Sellars's careful and patient working through of issues and Derrida's retooling of texts to fit his preconceived ideas of what they must be saying makes a dialogue impossible, at least in terms of the texts considered here.[1] This is doubly unfortunate, for a Sellarsian philosophy of the human sciences would be an important contribution.

This result is disappointing from yet another perspective. The confrontation between speech and writing that Derrida sets out to stage certainly seems to touch on important philosophical issues. Consider, for example, the following contrast: On the one hand we have the Platonic Socrates of the early dialogues, the Socrates who never writes a word of philosophy, whose philosophical activity is concentrated in raising the same questions again and again in living dialogue with whomever he chances to meet. The philosophical life that Socrates represents seems to be essentially a life devoted to a certain kind of speech. From this point of view, the later attack on writing in the *Phaedrus* (274c–275b) makes good Socratic sense.[2] But one should note that Socrates' entire life, on his own account, is played out against the background of and made possible by something that Derrida would call a kind of writing or inscription—namely, the laws of the city of Athens (*Crito* 50a–51c). Speech, which is the medium of philosophy and of the life worth living, and which must be generated ever anew (cf. Evans n.d.), presupposes a certain form of "writing." Contrast the emphasis on speech in Socratic wisdom with the emphasis on writing in the Talmudic tradition. Here the emphasis is on that which is inscribed, the written, the text. As Leon Wieseltier writes, the sight of a page of the Talmud "is the sight of tradition itself." Where for the Socrates of the *Phaedrus* writing is the cause of forgetfulness, of reliance on what is external rather than on one's own inner resources, the page of the Talmud (quite a different page indeed) is "a slap in the face of slovenliness and superficiality" (Wieseltier, 3) a slap in some ways parallel to Socrates' "gadfly" function in Athens (*Apology* 30e). This contrast, not between speech and writing, but between a certain kind of speech and a certain kind of writing, might be thought to raise serious and pressing issues in a time that in so many ways has lost its living tie with both tradition and the power of critical thought that for Kant, as for Socrates, was the very essence of enlightenment.

While I am not in a position to assert that Derrida never has anything of substance to offer in this respect (for example, in his reading of Rousseau; "Plato's Pharmacy" seems rather disappointing in this respect), it is clear that the discussions ostensibly devoted to speech and writing in *Speech and Phenomena* and in the sections of *Of Grammatology* I have discussed cannot be taken as contributions to any ongoing discussion. They offer the carefully constructed *appearance* of such a contribution, but we have seen that it is a mere appearance. And if I am charged with using a metaphysical vocabulary here, I can only reply that it is rooted in the experience of reading Derrida's own texts.

Notes

Introduction

1. Cf. Mohanty 238–40. Mohanty first says that "Derrida's otherwise fine and perceptive study suffers from one grave oversight" (240), but he goes on to question a whole series of Derrida's claims.

2. Cf. Searle 1983a for his most sustained general critique. Derrida has responded in Derrida 1988, 111–54.

3. Bernasconi puts the distinction in the title of his review of Rodolphe Gasché's book *The Taine of the Mirror*: "Deconstruction and Scholarship" (Bernasconi 1988). As is so often the case with "X and Y" titles, the "and" tends to become a "versus."

4. For Derrida's own recent reflections on this passage, see Derrida 1988, 147–48.

5. This is the traditional interpretation of the Socrates of the early Platonic dialogues, but there are alternatives. Cf. Evans 1990d.

6. Heidegger 1927, §6. Heidegger also used the much more violent word *Zerstörung* in his famous Davos disputation with Ernst Cassirer (cf. Heidegger 1973, 245; also Gasché, 133, and Rapaport, 3–9). It has recently been suggested that "de-structuring" is the best translation for Heidegger's *Destruktion* (cf. Bernasconi 1989, 231, and Michelfelder and Palmer, 7).

7. Heidegger took over the term *Abbau* (literally: "deconstruction" or "unbuilding") from Husserl. For a discussion of Husserl's method of *Abbau* that corrects some misconceptions found in the work of David Carr and Gasché, see Evans 1990a.

8. Bernasconi points out that Derrida originally used *détruire*, changing it to *déconstruire* a year later (Bernasconi 1989, 235; see also Derrida 1987, 267).

9. Cf. Ellis's discussion of the "explanations" of the term by Derrida, Derrideans, and commentators on Derrida in Ellis, 31f.

10. Cf. Liddell and Scott; Pape.

11. For an excellent general discussion of the relevant issues in Heidegger, see Marx, pt. III, chaps. 3–5.

12. Heidegger refers to *De interpretatione*, chaps. 1–6. See Stassen, §6, and Gethmann, 107ff., for discussions of this text from a Heideggerian perspective.

13. Heidegger was Husserl's assistant in the 1920s, and it is hard not to read this passage as a critique of Husserl's *Logical Investigations*, which was the Husserl text Heidegger preferred to teach during that period. The First Investigation is entitled "Expression and Meaning [*Ausdruck und Bedeutung*]," and Derrida devotes a large portion of *Speech and Phenomena* to the opening paragraphs of that investigation.

14. Given the publication dates of *Being and Time* and *Formal and Transcendental Logic*, it would be interesting to speculate on Heidegger's influence, one way or the other, on this paragraph.

Chapter 1. *Speech and Phenomena*: The Introduction

1. In "Signature Event Context" Derrida characterizes pure logical grammar as the theory of "the universal conditions of possibility for a morphology of significations *in their cognitive relation to a possible object*" (Derrida 1988, 12, emphasis added). This misses the point of pure grammar, as Husserl's reference to "a field of laws indifferent to all objectivity" shows. For this reason, the claim that the laws of Husserl's pure grammar hold only "in a context determined by a will to know" (Derrida 1988, 12) is unconvincing.

2. Bachelard has noted that the Fourth Investigation is misleading because its examples have not been fully formalized, which Bachelard explains as a consequence of the introductory character of the *Investigations*. But in *Formal and Transcendental Logic* the examples are usually formalized. See Bachelard 6–7. On the entire issue of pure grammar, see also Edie 1987, 37–59 and 128–30 n. 4.

3. This has also been pointed out by White (White 55f.). As Derrida is clear and insistent about the distinctions later in the book, one wonders whether he had read the Fourth Investigation very carefully when the Introduction to *Speech and Phenomena* was being written. His rendition of the sense of pure logical grammar there has all the earmarks of a hasty search for evidence to support a predetermined thesis.

4. The English translation is missing the words "and transcendental life." The German terms mean "aliveness or vitality," "life," "mental process" or "lived experience," "living present," and "spirituality." The root word *Leben* or "life" appears in all but the last word.

5. The following discussion is based primarily on the "Amsterdam Lectures" (*Hua* IX, 302–49), as this is the text Derrida refers to. Other principal texts are the *Encyclopedia Britannica* article (*Hua* IX, 278–301), *Formal and Transcendental Logic* (*Hua* XVII, §99), and the *Crisis* (*Hua* VI, §§53–54, §§69–72).

6. I have argued elsewhere that there is a tension between these two attributes of God in Descartes (see Evans 1984, 23–24). If God is all-powerful in the radical sense Descartes uses, God's supposed goodness cannot be used to prove that God is not a deceiver. Descartes' attempt to get around this difficulty is ingenious (see the beginning of the Fourth Meditation), but ultimately the argument is circular.

7. See also *Ideas*, vol. I, where Husserl speaks of the "absolute being of the immanent" (*Hua* III.1, §44).

8. It originally appeared in English as the Introduction to the English edition of the Boyce-Gibson translation.

9. This distinction was not always clear in some early forms of Neo-Kantianism. "Because nothing can be thought independently of thinking, [early forms of Neo-Kantianism] thought that they had to conclude that nothing can be thought *as* independent of thinking" (Brelage, 93).

10. The English translation reads "illustration" instead of "illusion" (*illusion*) (*SP*, 15/15).

11. Words in parentheses are not found in Derrida's Introduction, but their presence is implied.

Chapter 2. "Sign and Signs"

1. It is, I think, one of the few systematic weaknesses of David Allison's English translation of *Speech and Phenomena* that it notes Derrida's translation, but then simply uses "meaning" to translate *bedeuten*. This not only fails to convey the flavor of Derrida's text, it also makes it hard to tell whether the German term would be *bedeuten* or *Bedeutung*.

2. This ambiguity in the term goes back to the use of the Latin *intentio* to translate the Arabic *ma'na*. In the Dominican and Franciscan schools, *intentio* was synonymous with *ratio*, which was in turn the Latin translation of *logos* (*Historisches Wörterbuch der Philosophie*, vol. 4, 470). Cf. Spiegelberg.

3. Derrida 1973a. The title is usually translated "Form and Meaning . . . " Manfred Frank takes over Derrida's reading in lecture 14 of *What Is Neostructuralism?*

4. Derrida offers his own translation of Husserl here, one that is an improvement on the published French translation.

5. This kind of move is not unique in Derrida's writing. Cf. "Declarations of Independence," where he moves from the claim that in a declaration of independence constation and performance are "indissociably mixed" to the claim that this is an "indispensable *confusion*" (Derrida 1986a, 11; cf. Evans 1990c).

6. The English translation reads "intention" rather than "intentional right."

7. Cf. *LI* II.1, 23–24/I, 269, quoted by Derrida at *SP*, 22/21. Both the English and the French translations of this passage have a questionable aspect. Husserl writes: "Beschränken wir uns zunächst, wie wir es bei der Rede von Ausdrücken unwillkürlich zu tun pflegen, auf Ausdrücke, die in lebendigen Wechselgespräch fungieren . . . " (*LI* II.1, 24/I, 269). Findlay's English translation reads: "If, as one *unwillingly* does, one limits oneself to expressions employed in living discourse . . . " Derrida's French translation, which deviates from the Élie, Kelkel, and Schérer translation, reads: "Si nous nous limitons d'abord, comme nous avons coutume de le faire involontairement . . . " Both translations are misleading. The term *unwillkürlich* in this context means neither "unwillingly" nor "involuntarily." It rather indicates what we naturally or nonarbitrarily do. Thus the passage might be translated: "If we limit ourselves, as we naturally do when speaking of expressions, to expressions employed in living discourse . . . " The official French translation, which is better than Derrida's, reads: " . . . comme nous avons coutume de le fair spontanément quand nous parlons d'expressions . . . " (vol. 2, 29).

8. See Schutz 1966; Ricoeur, chap. 5.

9. This is not the only way of reading the early Socratic dialogues. Cf. Evans 1990d.

10. This is a very Nietzschean approach: "The question 'what is that?' is a positing of meaning from the viewpoint of something else. The 'essence,' the 'essential nature,' is something perspectival and already presupposes a multiplicity. At the bottom of it there always lies 'what is that for *me*?' (for us, for everything that lives, etc.)" (Nietzsche, 140). It goes without saying that the same thing would apply to the "me."

Chapter 3. "The Reduction of Indication"

1. Findlay translates *Bezeichnen* as "standing for." This is a bit clumsy, since it is hard to speak of "standing for" with respect to "the action which produces the marking (the branding or chalking etc.)," as Husserl does (*LI* II.1, 24/I,270). "Designation" is smoother. (*Désignation* is the term used in the French translation.)

2. Hegel, whom Derrida often calls upon as one of the purest representatives of phonocentrism, states that spoken language is more original that written language, and that within written language alphabetical writing is "more intelligent" than hieroglyphics. (And it is only alphabetic writing that is a "sign of a sign.") But Hegel also notes that when one becomes practiced in reading alphabetic

script, the written signs cease functioning as signs of signs, since "in using them we no longer need to have the mediation of the sounds before us in consciousness," thus "transforming the alphabetic writing into hieroglyphics" (Hegel 1969, §459). Hegel's remarks confirm the *functional* nature of the distinction between indication and expression.

3. Findlay translates both *Beweisen* and *Hinweisen* as "demonstration." I have followed Cairns's suggestion of "pointing," though Derrida's suggestion of *allusion indicative* ("indicative allusion") is elegant.

4. In order to make this clear, Derrida offers his own translation of Husserl's definition of the indicative sign, since the French translation of the *Investigations* translates *Bestand* as *réalité*, and this has led to some rather confusing moments in translations of *La voix et le phénomène*. Allison's English translation has Derrida saying that "Husserl intentionally uses very general concepts (*Sein*, *Bestand*), which may cover being or subsistence" (*SP*, English translation, 28). "Subsistence" in this passage translates Derrida's *consistance*, which is Derrida's translation of *Bestand*. But when, just a few lines later, Derrida offers his own French translation of Husserl's definition, using *consistance* to translate *Bestand*, Allison uses Findlay's translation, which has "reality" for *Bestand*, although Derrida has just pointed out (in an implicit criticism of the French translation that applies equally to Findlay's translation) that in Husserl's text *Bestand* is to be carefully distinguished from *Realität*. The German translation of Derrida's text produces similar confusion, translating Derrida's own phrase as "*das Sein oder die Konsistenz*," and then following that by Husserl's original text, with *Bestand*.

5. It should perhaps be noted that Husserl is not merely giving a conventional definition of a word. He is attempting to determine the essential structure of the phenomenon of indication. Derrida clearly recognizes this.

6. In his discussion White chooses to follow Findlay in translating *Hinweis* as "demonstration."

7. König shows that this is the logical form of Leibniz's fundamental metaphysical categories of "force," "thought", and "monad."

8. An example would be the following text: "The relation of 'mis' (mis-understanding, misinterpreting, for example) to that which is not 'mis-,' is not at all that of a general law to cases, but that of a *general possibility inscribed in* the structure of positivity, of normality, of the 'standard.' All that I recall is that this *structural possibility* must be taken into account when describing so-called ideal normality, or so-called just comprehension or interpretation, and that this possibility can be neither *excluded nor opposed*. An entirely different logic is called for" (Derrida 1988, 157).

Chapter 4. "Wanting-to-Say as Soliloquy"

1. Derrida writes that following Husserl's transcendental turn, the "solitary mental life" of the *Investigations* will be described "as the noetic-noematic sphere of consciousness" (*SP*, 35/33). This is at least imprecise: Husserl would describe it *in terms of* the noetic-noematic correlation, but not *as* that correlation.

2. This marks an important advance in Husserl's phenomenology of time-consciousness. For a study of the issues involved here, see Evans 1990b.

3. White argues that when Derrida writes, "as long as we identify *Sinn* and *Bedeutung*, nothing that resists the *Deutung* can have sense or be language in the strict sense" (*SP*, 38/36), "the subtext is that a locution expresses only *Sinn* or *Bedeutung*, and that Husserl's lack of distinction between the two reveals that he takes the locution to express only a meaning, not an object" (White, 52). White is reading Derrida in terms of Frege's distinction between *Sinn* and *Bedeutung*, while Derrida is alluding to Husserl's distinction in the *Ideas*. One might argue that in the language of the *Ideas*, facial gesture would have a *sense* (*Sinn*), a nonthematic, horizonal, latent sense, but not a meaning (*Bedeutung*).

4. Around 1920 Husserl describes something like this reduction to ownness as a "deconstruction" (*Abbau*) (cf. *Hua* XIV, 483–84; Evans, 1990a).

5. It is worth noting here that according to Husserl's account, the reduction to ownness works only on the *noematic* correlate of consciousness, leaving the *noetic* side untouched: "*What is specifically peculiar to me as ego, my concrete being as a monad,* . . . includes [my] every intentionality and therefore, in particular, the intentionality directed to what is other; but, for reasons of method, the synthetic effect of such intentionality (the actuality for me of what is other) shall at first remain excluded from the theme" (*Hua* I, 125/94; cf. 124/93). In lectures delivered at the New School for Social Research in the early 1960s, Dorion Cairns argued that this is an "essential impossibility," as it violates one of the most fundamental principles of phenomenology, the correlation between noesis and noema. It is also clear that this account of the reduction to ownness is inadequate for Husserl's own purpose, which is that of describing the genetic constitution of the sense "alter ego." The concept of an "analogizing transfer" of sense in a "primal instituting" (*Hua* I, 141/111) requires an *Abbau* that is both noematic and noetic. Thus in addition to misusing the reduction to ownness, Derrida fails to take a critical look at the reduction itself. I am familiar with Cairns's critique through notes taken by Fred Kersten.

6. The Sixth Investigation contains an appendix entitled, "Outer and Inner Perception: Physical and Psychic Phenomena."

7. This phrase is noteworthy: it is a cardinal tenet of phenomenology that consciousness is always already consciousness of the world.

8. The Findlay translation quoted at *SP*, 44/41, contains the phrase "in uncommunicated, interior mental life," but the word "interior" translates nothing in the German, which reads "in dem sich im Verkehr nicht mitteilenden Seelenleben" (*LI* II.1, 35/I, 278).

9. The Findlay translation has "however" for *doch*, which fails to capture the sense of the sentence. Derrida's French translation reads *Toutefois* (*SP*, 52 of the original), which makes the same error. The published French translation reads *Car*, which is much better.

Chapter 5. "Wanting-to-Say and Representation"

1. It should be noted that the other twelve meanings are by no means all species of this general meaning.

2. Husserl later abandoned this account of the ideality of the sign as a species (cf. *Hua* XXVI, 142; Parpan, 118f.).

3. The English translation should read "an image is not 'positional' [*positionelle*]" instead of "an image is not 'propositional' " (*SP*, 61/65).

4. Both the passage as quoted in *Speech and Phenomena* and the Kersten translation misinterpret the word *dasselbe*, taking it to refer to "essence" rather than to *Erlebnis*.

Chapter 6. "Signs and the Blink of an Eye"

1. Husserl calls this "the adequate perception of the temporal object" (*Hua* X, 38), but it should be noted that this is not "adequate" in Husserl's technical sense (cf. *LI*, II.1, 34/I, 278; II.2, 120f./II, 764f.; *Hua* III.1, §138).

2. It will become clear that this is how *Derrida* is reading this passage.

3. This has been noted independently by Wood 1989, 124.

4. He does mention "absolute subjectivity," quoting a long passage in which Husserl uses the term, in a later footnote (*SP*, 94/84 n.9), but without clarifying the context.

5. For an exposition and critique of Husserl's theory of absolute time-constituting consciousness, see Evans 1990b.

6. It should be noted that it is only immanent temporal objects such as acts and sensations that are in question here. Transcendent perception is never certain for Husserl.

7. For a general discussion of the trace in Derrida, see Gasché, 186–94.

8. The Kersten translation of the *Ideas* translates *originär* by both "original" and "originary."
9. See Seebohm, chap. 7, "The Critique of Critique," for a discussion of these issues.
10. See *Hua* VIII and Landgrebe.

Chapter 7. "The Voice That Keeps Silence"

1. Derrida notes that according to Heidegger, the infinitive form is based on the third-person present indicative (cf. Heidegger 1953, 70/77). Tugendhat, discussing Charles Kahn's *The Verb 'Be' in Ancient Greek*, writes, "For someone today simply to start out from talk of 'Being' ('*das Sein*') as Heidegger has done is unsurpassably naive" (Tugendhat 1976, 89n./413n.; cf. Tugendhat 1977–78).
2. Compare *OG*, 17/7: "The system of 'hearing (understanding)-oneself-speak [*s'entendre-parler*]' through the phonic substance . . . " See the discussion in chapter 10 below.
3. Derrida identifies the phenomenological voice with Saussure's acoustical images (*SP*, 85/76), but as the "phenomenological voice" is an imagined voice, the two can hardly be equated.
4. Derrida writes in this context of a "spontaneous neutralization of the factual existence of the speaking subject, of words, and of the thing designated" (Derrida 1978a, 67), but it is not clear whether this involves more than the eidetic reduction, and Husserl makes it quite clear that there are eidetic sciences that move within the horizon of the world.
5. The final sentence is quoted in the English translation, but not in the French original.
6. For a general discussion of supplementarity, see Gasché, 205–12.

Chapter 8. "The Supplement of Origin"

1. Descombes writes: "In his commentary on the *First Logical Investigation*, Derrida notes that the Husserlian requirement for the signified object to be present in order to fulfill the signifying intention is unjustifiable, simply with regard to an analysis of signification. We certainly have no need to see the show in order to understand the comments of someone who has" (Descombes, 73–74/63). This manages to get both Husserl and Derrida wrong.
2. The Allison translation reads "like indication." Since Derrida's *comme indice* translates Husserl's *als Anzeichen* (*LI* II.1, 33/I, 277; Derrida never quotes this sentence), the *comme* must be read to mean "as." Allison's "like" seems to make more sense in Derrida's context, but this merely indicates a problem in the context.
3. The same thing seems to be at work when Derrida later writes that "The 'symbol' always points to 'truth'; it is itself constituted as a lack of 'truth' " (*SP*, 109/97).
4. The passage Derrida quotes from §26 of the First Investigation begins: "An essentially indicating character . . . " (*LI* II.1, 85/I, 318, quoted at *SP*, 105/94, in the Findlay translation, which Allison uses). It should read: "The essentially occasional character . . ."
5. I suspect that a similar confusion occurs when Derrida reads Searle's statement that "sentences are precisely the realizations of the intentions" (Searle 1977, 202). Derrida notes that the word "realization" "implies of course achievement or 'fulfillment' " (Derrida 1988, 121), but it is not clear that Searle's use of the term should be given the Husserlian overtones Derrida suggests. In his book *Intentionality*, Searle writes that "the performance of the speech act is necessarily an *expression* of the corresponding Intentional state" (Searle 1983b, 9). (It goes without saying that replacing "realization" with "expression" would not constitute much of an improvement in Derrida's eyes.)
6. Derrida expresses amazement at Husserl's appeal to an "individual concept." This is a Leibnizian influence at work.
7. Scholes has perceptively noted that Derrida "claims that what [Bertrand] Russell called the 'trivial' sense of the word is the only sense that counts" (Scholes 1988, 290).
8. This line of analysis is extended by Gurwitsch in Gurwitsch 1985, 66f.

9. See Scholes 1988, 286f., for a discussion of this move and its implications for a theory of communication.

10. The texts in question are contained in the French translation of the *Logical Investigations* to which Derrida refers.

Chapter 10. Saussure

1. I have chosen to use the Wade Baskin translation of the *Course* rather than the recent Roy Harris translation. While the Harris translation is in many ways an improvement, at crucial points it imports an interpretation at odds with the original text.

2. In *Of Grammatology* Derrida quite properly chose to ignore Saussure's notes, which were being edited for publication, as his concern was with the text that had played an important role in the development of linguistics and philosophy since its publication in 1916. The same decision has governed Harris's new translation of the *Course* as well as his commentary.

3. This is clearly an exaggeration, as Saussure's notions of a "system of differences" and "value" had a profound influence on structuralism and poststructuralism.

4. I am not claiming that the text of the *Course* is absolutely consistent. I am suggesting that neglect of the developing perspectives and contexts leads to an inflation of apparent contradictions.

5. In "My Chances/*Mes Chances*," Derrida writes, "No natural bond, to use Saussurian terminology, between the signified and the signifier" (Derrida 1984b, 15).

6. Harris's translation of the final sentence reads: "Although the connexion between word and written form is superficial and establishes a purely artificial unity, it is none the less much easier to grasp than the natural and only authentic connexion, which links word and sound" (*CGL*, Harris translation, 26). Harris violates the limits of translation by reading into the text an interpretation that requires altering the text itself, an interpretation hardly supported by the text and its context. Since he thinks that Saussure is contrasting the connection between word and written form with the connection between word and sound, he substitutes "the connection between word and written form" for *Ce lien*. Similarly, he translates *unité de la langue* as "linguistic unit" rather than "unity of language," and he has to substitute "the natural and only authentic connexion, which links word and sound" for "le lien naturel, le seul véritable, celui du son."

7. In a 1968 interview, Derrida does take note of Saussure's assertion that "it is not spoken language that is natural to man, but the faculty of constituting a language, that is, a system of distinct signs" (*CGL*, 26/10, quoted at Derrida 1981a, 21), but still insists that this stands in "contradiction" with the privilege of the voice in the *Cours*.

8. Harris argues that since Saussure includes writing among the systems of "signs that express ideas" (*CGL*, 33/16), "from this it is already clear that from a Saussurean point of view written signs are signs in their own right, and do not owe this status to their connexion with speech" (Harris, 41).

9. Harris argues that in the phrase "a second language," "the word *seconde* implies a relationship of semiological dependence between two separate systems" (Harris, 19). This seems to be a case of overreading. Saussure has been arguing that the object of linguistics is "the spoken forms alone" (*CGL*, 45/24); thus the admission of an ideogrammatic system to the status of a genuine *langue* means its elevation to the status of the normal object of linguistics: it is a second *langue* (in addition to the one we find associated with phonetic writing).

10. Cf. Reid, 32–33; Harris, 24–25.

11. The quotation marks around the term "writing" seem to perform two functions. Here Derrida seems to be simply referring to the word. But when it reappears in the phrase "instituted—hence 'written,' " the quotation marks would seem rather to indicate that the word is being used in a nonnormal sense.

Conclusion: The Rigor and Ethics of Reading

1. I assume that this simply refers to truth claims.

2. Scholes notes that in "Limited Inc a b c . . . ," "[Derrida] speaks on behalf of author's intention, though he tries to employ a syntactic form that will allow him to do this by a ventriloquial process: 'when *it* uses or mentions . . . *it* is also to signify.' Surely intention is at stake in this utterance. Derrida would have it that *Sec*—that is, the text, the writing—is the agent in this case. . . . But can anyone doubt that it is Derrida's own authorial *amour propre* that animates his defense of the intention . . . of the text that bears his signature?" (Scholes 1989, 67–68).

3. This would also be the result if one were to argue that *Speech and Phenomena* must be read in terms of the double strategy Derrida suggests in "The Ends of Man," namely, "deconstruction without changing terrain . . . , by using against the edifice the instruments or stones available in the house," and deconstruction by the decision "to change terrain, in a discontinuous and irruptive fashion, by brutally placing oneself outside" (Derrida 1972, 162/135). If it should be argued that both strategies are at work in this text, I would reply that surely a distortion of the terrain a priori renders impotent any attempt to place oneself outside *that terrain*, regardless of the brutality of the attempt.

4. Parker is discussing Frank Lentricchia, *After the New Criticism*.

5. It is noteworthy that in Scholes's catalogue of Derrida's uses of the word "rigor" and its derivatives in *Speech and Phenomena*, the vast majority are descriptions of Husserl's text, not of Derrida's own reading (Scholes 1989, 83).

6. Derrida has of course emphasized the performance aspect of his texts (cf. Derrida 1988, 43).

Signature

1. This is not to say that all such dialogues are impossible. Wheeler's comparisons of Derrida with Quine and Davidson might be an example (Wheeler 1986a and 1986b).

2. Foucault claimed that the writing in question is writing of a very specific kind, that of the *hypomnemata* or copybook that came into fashion in Plato's time (Foucault, 363f.). Compare Rosen's critical discussion of Derrida's "Plato's Pharmacy" in "Platonic Reconstruction," where he argues that in the *Phaedrus* "speech and writing are the same as imitations of the divine *logos*, but they differ in their political function" (Rosen, 60).

Bibliography

Note: Quotations of foreign-language works are from published translations unless otherwise indicated.

Aristotle. *The Basic Works of Aristotle*. Edited by Richard McKeon. New York: Random House, 1941.

Bachelard, Suzanne 1968. *A Study of Husserl's Formal and Transcendental Logic*. Translated by Lester E. Embree. Evanston: Northwestern University Press.

Bergmann, Gustav 1964. "The Ontology of Edmund Husserl." *Logic and Reality*. Madison: University of Wisconsin Press, 193–224.

Bernasconi, Robert 1988. "Deconstruction and Scholarship." *Man and World* 21:223–30.

_____ 1989. "Seeing Double: *Destruktion* and Deconstruction." *Dialogue and Deconstruction*. Edited by Diane P. Michelfelder and Richard E. Palmer. Albany: State University of New York Press, 233–50.

Bernet, Rudolf 1985. Introduction to Edmund Husserl, *Texte zur Phänomenologie des inneren Zeitbewusstseins (1893–1917)*. Edited by Rudolf Bernet. Hamburg: Felix Meiner.

_____ 1986. "Differenz und Anwesenheit: Derridas und Husserls Phänomenologie der Sprache, der Zeit, der Geschichte, der wissenschaftlichen Rationalität." *Phänomenologische Forschungen* 18:51–112.

Brelage, Manfred 1965. *Studien zur Transzendentalphilosophie*. Berlin: Walter de Gruyter.

Bruns, Gerald L. 1989. *Heidegger's Estrangements: Language, Truth, and Poetry in the Later Writings*. New Haven: Yale University Press.

Cairns, Dorion 1973. *Guide for Translating Husserl*. The Hague: Martinus Nijhoff.

_____ 1976. *Conversations with Husserl and Fink*. The Hague: Martinus Nijhoff.

Caputo, John 1987. *Radical Hermeneutics*. Bloomington: Indiana University Press.

Culler, Jonathan 1982. *On Deconstruction*. Ithaca: Cornell University Press.

de Man, Paul 1983. "The Rhetoric of Blindness: Jacques Derrida's Reading of Rousseau."

Blindness and Insight: Essays in the Rhetoric of Contemporary Criticism. Minneapolis: University of Minnesota Press. 2d ed., 102–41.

Depp, Dane 1987. "A Husserlian Response to Derrida's Early Criticisms of Phenomenology." *Journal of the British Society for Phenomenology* 18:226–44.

Derrida, Jacques *SP. La voix et le phénomène.* Paris: Presses Universitaires de France, 1967. English translation by David Allison: *Speech and Phenomena.* Bloomington: Indiana University Press, 1973.

———— *OG. De la grammatologie.* Paris: Les Editions de Minuit, 1967. English translation by Gayatri Chakravorty Spivak: *Of Grammatology.* Baltimore: Johns Hopkins University Press, 1976.

———— 1972. "Les fins de l'homme." *Marges de la Philosophie.* Paris: Les Editions de Minuit, 129–64. English translation by Alan Bass: "The Ends of Man." *Margins of Philosophy.* Chicago: The University of Chicago Press, 1982, 109–36.

———— 1973a. "Form and Meaning: A Note on the Phenomenology of Language." In *SP,* 107–28.

———— 1973b. *"Différance."* Translated by David Allison. In *SP,* 129–60.

———— 1978a. *Edmund Husserl's 'Origin of Geometry': An Introduction.* Translated by John P. Leavey. Stony Brook, N.Y.: Nicolas Hays.

———— 1978b. *Writing and Difference.* Translated by Alan Bass. Chicago: University of Chicago Press.

———— 1979c. *Spurs: Nietzsche's Styles.* Translated by Barbara Harlow. Chicago: University of Chicago Press.

———— 1980. "Le loi du genre." *Glyph* 7:176–201. English ranslation by Avital Ronnell: "The Law of Genre." *Glyph* 7:202–32.

———— 1981a. *Positions.* Translated by Alan Bass. Chicago: University of Chicago Press.

———— 1981b. "Plato's Pharmacy." *Dissemination.* Translated by Barbara Johnson. Chicago: University of Chicago Press, 61–171.

———— 1983. "The Time of a Thesis: Punctuations." *Philosophy in France Today.* Edited by Alan Montefiore. Translated by Kathleen McLaughlin. Cambridge: Cambridge University Press, 34–50.

———— 1984a. "Deconstruction and the Other [An Interview]." Richard Kearney. *Dialogues with Contemporary Continental Thinkers.* Manchester: Manchester University Press, 107–26.

———— 1984b. "My Chances/*Mes chances*: A Rendezvous with Some Epicurean Stereophonies." Translated by Irene Harvey and Avital Ronell. *Taking Chances.* Edited by Joseph H. Smith and William Kerrigan. Baltimore: Johns Hopkins University Press.

———— 1984c. *Signéponge/Signsponge.* Translated by Richard Rand. New York: Columbia University Press.

———— 1986a. "Declarations of Independence." Translated by T. Keenan and T. Pepper. *New Political Science* 15:7–15.

———— 1986b. "Shibboleth." *Midrash and Literature.* Edited by Geoffrey Hartman and Sanford Budick. New Haven: Yale University Press, 307–47.

———— 1987. *The Post Card: From Socrates to Freud and Beyond.* Translated by Alan Bass. Chicago: University of Chicago Press.

———— 1988. *Limited Inc.* Evanston: Northwestern University Press.

———— 1989a. "Three Questions to H. G. Gadamer." *Dialogue and Deconstruction.* Edited and translated by Diane P. Michelfelder and Richard E. Palmer. Albany: State University of New York Press, 52–54.

———— 1989b. "Interpreting Signatures (Nietzsche/Heidegger): Two Questions." *Dialogue and Deconstruction.* Edited and translated by Diane P. Michelfelder and Richard E. Palmer. Albany: State University of New York Press, 58–71.

Descombes, V. 1983 *Grammaires d'objets en tous genres*. Paris: Les Editions de Minuit. English translation by Lorna Scott-Fox and Jeremy Harding: *Objects of All Sorts: A Philosophical Grammar*. Baltimore: Johns Hopkins University Press, 1986.

Edie, James 1987. *Edmund Husserl's Phenomenology: A Critical Commentary*. Bloomington: Indiana University Press.

———— 1988. "Husserl vs. Derrida." Paper presented at the annual meeting of SPEP, Northwestern University.

Ellis, John, 1989. *Against Deconstruction*. Princeton: Princeton University Press.

Evans, J. Claude 1978. "Pure Pragmatics and the New Way of Words." *Philosophische Rundschau* 25:176–99.

———— 1983. "Das Problem der prädikativen Kompossibilität." *Sozialität und Intersubjektivität*. Edited by R. Grathoff and B. Waldenfels. Munich: Fink, 51–67.

———— 1984. *The Metaphysics of Transcendental Subjectivity*. Amsterdam: Gruener.

———— 1989. "Predicative Compossibility and Transcendental Logic." *Proceedings of the Sixth International Kant Congress*. Edited by Gerhard Funke. Pittsburgh: Center for Advanced Research in Phenomenology and University Press of America, 209–18.

———— 1990a. "Phenomenological Deconstruction: Husserl's Method of *Abbau*." *Journal of the British Society for Phenomenology* 21:14–25.

———— 1990b. "The Myth of Absolute Consciousness." *Crises in Continental Philosophy*. Edited by Arleene Dallery and Charles Scott. Albany: State University of New York Press.

———— 1990c. "Deconstructing the Declaration." *Man and World* 23:175–89.

———— 1990d. "Socratic Ignorance–Socratic Wisdom." *Modern Schoolman* 47:91–109.

Foucault, Michel 1984. "On the Genealogy of Ethics: An Overview of Work in Progress [An Interview]." *The Foucault Reader*. Edited by Paul Rabinow. New York: Pantheon 340–72.

Frank, Manfred 1983. *Was ist Neostrukturalismus*? Frankfurt: Suhrkamp. English translation by Sabine Wilke and Richard Gray: *What Is Neostructuralism*? Minneapolis: University of Minnesota Press, 1989.

Gadamer, Hans-Georg 1989a. "*Destruktion* and Deconstruction." *Dialogue and Deconstruction*. Edited by Diane P. Michelfelder and Richard E. Palmer. Translated by Geoff Waite and Richard Palmer. Albany: State University of New York Press, 102–13.

———— 1989b. "Hermeneutics and Logocentrism." *Dialogue and Deconstruction*. Edited by Diane P. Michelfelder and Richard E. Palmer. Translated by Richard Palmer and Diane Michelfelder. Albany: State University of New York Press, 114–25.

———— 1989c. "Letter to Dallmayr." *Dialogue and Deconstruction*. Edited by Diane P. Michelfelder and Richard Palmer. Translated by Geoff Waite and Richard Palmer. Albany: State of University of New York Press, 93–101.

Garver, Newton 1973. Preface to *SP* (English translation).

Gasché, Rodolphe 1986. *The Taine of the Mirror*. Cambridge: Harvard University Press.

Gethmann, Carl Friedrich 1974. *Verstehen und Auslegung: Das Methodenproblem in der Philosophie Martin Heideggers*. Bonn: Bouvier.

Gurwitsch, Aron 1964. *The Field of Consciousness*. Pittsburgh: Duquesne University Press.

———— 1966. *Studies in Phenomenology and Psychology*. Evanston: Northwestern University Press.

———— 1974. *Phenomenology and the Theory of Science*. Edited by Lester Embree. Evanston: Northwestern University Press.

———— 1985. "Outlines of a Theory of 'Essentially Occasional Expressions.' " *Marginal Consciousness*. Edited by Lester Embree. Athens: Ohio University Press, 65–79.

Harris, Roy 1987. *Reading Saussure*. La Salle: Open Court.

Harvey, Irene 1986. *Derrida and the Economy of Différance*. Bloomington: Indiana University Press.

Hegel, G.W.F. 1969. *Wissenschaft der Logik. Werke*, volume 6. Frankfurt: Suhrkamp. English translation by A. V. Miller: *Hegel's Science of Logic*. New York: Humanities Press, 1969.

———— 1970. *Enzyklopädie der philosophischen Wissenschaften. Werke*, volume 10. Frankfurt: Suhrkamp.

Heidegger, Martin 1927. *Sein und Zeit*. Tübingen: Max Niemeyer. English translation by John Macquarrie and Edward Robinson: *Being and Time*. New York: Harper and Row, 1962. English translation of the Introduction by Joan Stambaugh in collaboration with J. Glenn Gray and David Farrell Krell. *Martin Heidegger: Basic Writings*. Edited by David Farrell Krell. New York: Harper and Row, 1977, 37–90.

———— 1950. "Der Ursprung des Kunstwerkes." *Holzwege*. Frankfurt: Vittorio Klostermann, 7–68. English translation by Albert Hofstadter: "The Origin of the Work of Art." Martin Heidegger, *Poetry, Language, Thought*. New York: Harper and Row, 1971, 15–88.

———— 1953. *Einführung in die Metaphysik*. Tübingen: Max Niemeyer. English translation by Ralph Mannheim: *An Introduction to Metaphysics*. Garden City: Anchor Books, 1961.

———— 1954a. "Logos (Heraklit, Fragment 50)." *Vorträge und Aufsätze*. Pfullingen: Gunther Neske, 223–48. English translation by David Farrell Krell: "Logos (Heraclitus, Fragment B 50)." Martin Heidegger, *Early Greek Thinking*. San Francisco: Harper and Row, 1984, 59–78.

———— 1954b. "Die Frage nach der Technik." *Vorträge und Aufsätze*. Pfullingen: Gunther Neske, 9–40. English translation by William Lovitt: "The Question concerning Technology." Martin Heidegger, *The Question concerning Technology and Other Essays*. New York: Harper and Row, 1977, 3–35.

———— 1973. *Kant und das Problem der Metaphysik*. Frankfurt: Vittorio Klostermann. 4th ed.

———— 1975. *Die Grundprobleme der Phänomenologie*. Edited by Friedrich-Wilhelm von Herrmann. Frankfurt: Vittorio Klostermann. English translation by Albert Hofstadter: *The Basic Problems of Phenomenology*. Bloomington: Indiana University Press, 1982.

———— 1978. "Zur Seinsfrage." *Wegmarken*. Frankfurt: Vittorio Klostermann. 2nd ed., 379–420. English translation by William Kluback and Jean T. Wilde: *The Question of Being*. New Haven: College and University Press, 1959.

———— 1979. *Heraklit*. Frankfurt: Vittorio Klostermann.

Held, Klaus 1962. *Lebendige Gegenwart*. The Hague: Martinus Nijhoff.

Historisches Wörterbuch der Philosophie. Edited by Joachim Ritter and Karlfried Gründer. Darmstadt: Wissenschaftliche Buchgesellschaft, 1971–.

Hopkins, Burt C. 1985. "Derrida's Reading of Husserl in *Speech and Phenomena*: Ontologism and the Metaphysics of Presence." *Husserl Studies* 2:193–214.

Husserl, Edmund *LI. Logische Untersuchungen*. Tübingen: Max Niemeyer, 1901, 2d ed. 1921. 4th ed. 1968. English translation by John Findlay: *Logical Investigations*. London: Routledge and Kegan Paul, 1970. French translation by Hubert Elie in collaboration with Lothar Kelkel and René Schérer: *Recherches logiques*. Paris: Presses Universitaires de France, 1961.

———— 1938. *Erfahrung und Urteil*. Edited by Ludwig Landgrebe. Hamburg: Classen. English translation by James Churchill and Karl Ameriks: *Experience and Judgment*. Evanston: Northwestern University Press, 1973.

———— 1939. "Entwurf einer 'Vorrede' zu den 'Logischen Untersuchungen' (1913)." *Tijdschrift voor Philosophie* 1:106–33, 319–39. English translation by P. J. Bossert: *Outline of a 'Preface' to the Logical Investigations*. The Hague: Martinus Nijhoff, 1975.

———— 1968. *Briefe an Roman Ingarden*. Edited by Roman Ingarden. The Hague: Martinus Nijhoff.

Husserliana

Hua I: *Cartesianische Meditationen und Pariser Vorträge*. Edited by S. Strasser. The Hague:

Martinus Nijhoff, 1963. 2d ed. English translation by Dorion Cairns: *Cartesian Meditations*. The Hague: Martinus Nijhoff, 1960.

Hua II: *Die Idee der Phänomenologie*. Edited by Walter Biemel. The Hague: Martinus Nijhoff, 1958. English translation by William P. Alston and George Nakhnikian: *The Idea of Phenomenology*. The Hague: Martinus Nijhoff, 1964.

Hua III.1: *Ideen zu einer reinen Phänomenologie und phänomenologischen Philosophie: Erstes Buch*. Edited by Karl Schuhmann. The Hague: Martinus Nijhoff, 1976. English translation by F. Kersten: *Ideas Pertaining to a Pure Phenomenology and to a Phenomenological Philosophy*. The Hague: Martinus Nijhoff, 1982.

Hua III.2: *Ideen zu einer reinen Phänomenologie und phänomenologischen Philosophie: Ergnzende Texte (1912–1929)*. Edited by Karl Schuhmann. The Hague: Martinus Nijhoff, 1976.

Hua V: *Ideen zu einer reinen Phänomenologie und phänomenologische Philosophie: Drittes Buch*. Edited by Marly Biemel. The Hague: Martinus Nijhoff, 1971.

Hua VI: *Die Krisis der Europäischen Wissenschaften und die transzendentale Phänomenologie*. The Hague: Martinus Nijhoff, 1962. English translation by David Carr: *The Crisis of European Sciences and Transcendental Phenomenology*. Evanston: Northwestern University Press, 1970.

Hua IX: *Phänomenologische Psychologie*. Edited by Walter Biemel. The Hague: Martinus Nijhoff, 1968.

Hua X: *Zur Phänomenologie des inneren Zeitbewusstseins (1893–1917)*. Edited by Rudolf Boehm. The Hague: Martinus Nijhoff, 1966.

Hua XI: *Analysen zur passiven Synthesis*. Edited by Margot Fleischer. The Hague: Martinus Nijhoff, 1966.

Hua XII: *Philosophie der Arithmetik*. Edited by Lothar Eley. The Hague: Martinus Nijhoff, 1970.

Hua XIV: *Zur Phänomenologie der Intersubjektivität*. Part II. Edited by Iso Kern. The Hague: Martinus Nijhoff, 1973.

Hua XV: *Zur Phänomenologie der Intersubjektivität*. Part III. Edited by Iso Kern. The Hague: Martinus Nijhoff, 1973.

Hua XVII: *Formale und Transzendentale Logik*. Edited by Paul Janssen. The Hague: Martinus Nijhoff, 1974.

Hua XXVI: *Vorlesungen über Bedeutungslehre: Sommersemester 1908*. Edited by Ursula Panzer. The Hague: Martinus Nijhoff, 1987.

James, William 1950. *The Principles of Psychology*. New York: Dover.

Kearney, Richard 1986. *Modern Movements in European Philosophy*. Manchester: Manchester University Press.

Kimmerle, Heinz 1988. *Derrida zur Einführung*. Hamburg: Edition SOAK.

Knüfer, Carl 1975. *Grundzüge der Geschichte des Begriffs 'Vorstellung' von Wolff bis Kant*. Hildesheim: Georg Olms. (Reprint of a 1911 dissertation.)

König, Josef 1978. "Das System von Leibniz." *Vorträge und Aufsätze*. Edited by Günther Patzig. Freiburg: Karl Alber.

Lamont, Michèle 1987. "How to Become a Dominant French Philosopher: The Case of Jacques Derrida." *American Journal of Sociology* 93:584–622.

Landgrebe, Ludwig 1962. "Husserls Abschied von Cartesianismus." *Philosophische Rundschau* 9:133–77. English translation by R. O. Elveton. *The Phenomenology of Edmund Husserl*. Edited by Donn Welton. Ithaca: Cornell University Press, 1981, 66–121.

Leavey, John, and David B. Allison 1978. "A Derrida Bibliography." *Research in Phenomenology* 8:145–60.

Lentricchia, Frank 1980. *After the New Criticism*. Chicago: University of Chicago Press.

Liddell, Henri George, and Robert Scott. *A Greek-English Lexicon*. Oxford: Clarendon Press, 1940.

Llewelyn, John 1986. *Derrida on the Threshold of Sense*. New York: St. Martin's Press.

Marx, Werner 1961. *Heidegger und die Tradition*. Stuttgart: Kohlhammer. English translation by Theodore Kisiel and Murray Greene: *Heidegger and the Tradition*. Evanston: Northwestern University Press, 1971.

Michelfelder, Diane P., and Richard E. Palmer 1989. Introduction to *Dialogue and Deconstruction*. Edited by Diane P. Michelfelder and Richard E. Palmer. Albany: State University of New York Press, 1–20.

Mohanty, J. N. 1974. "On Husserl's Theory of Meaning." *Southwestern Journal of Philosophy* 5:229–44.

Muralt, André de 1974. *The Idea of Phenomenology: Husserlian Exemplarism*. Translated by Garry L. Breckon. Evanston: Northwestern University Press.

Nietzsche, Friedrich 1980. *Sämtliche Werke*. (Kritische Studienausgabe in 15 Bänden.) Volume 12. Edited by Giorgio Colli and Mazzino Montinari. Berlin: Walter de Gruyter.

Norris, Christopher 1987. *Derrida*. Cambridge: Harvard University Press.

Nuchelmans, Gabriel 1973. *Theories of the Proposition*. Amsterdam: North-Holland.

Pape, W. 1954. *Griechisch-Deutsches Handwoerterbuch*. Graz: Akademische Druck- u. Verlagsanstalt.

Parker, Andrew 1981. "*'Taking Sides' (On History: Derrida Re-Marx)*." *Diacritics* 11:57–73.

Parpan, Reto 1985. "Zeichen und Bedeutung: Eine Untersuchung zu Edmund Husserls Theorie des Sprachzeichens." Dissertation: Ruprecht-Karl-Universität Heidelberg.

Pinkard, Terry 1988. *Hegel's Dialectic*. Philadelphia: Temple University Press.

Plato. *Apology* and *Crito*. *Plato: Five Dialogues*. Translated by G.M.A. Grube. Indianapolis: Hackett, 1981.

_____ *Phaedrus*. Translated by R. Hackforth. *Plato: The Collected Dialogues*. Edited by Edith Hamilton and Huntington Cairns. New York: Pantheon, 1963.

Rapaport, Herman 1989. *Heidegger and Derrida*. Lincoln: University of Nebraska Press.

Reid, Wallace 1974. "The Saussurian Sign as a Control in Linguistic Analysis." *Semiotext(e)* 1:31–53.

Ricoeur, Paul 1967. *Husserl: An Analysis of His Philosophy*. Translated by Edward G. Ballard and Lester E. Embree. Evanston: Northwestern University Press.

Rorty, Richard 1982. "Philosophy as a Kind of Writing: An Essay on Derrida." *Consequences of Pragmatism*. Minneapolis: University of Minnesota Press, 90–109.

_____ 1984. "Deconstruction and Circumvention." *Critical Inquiry* 11:1–21.

_____ 1989a. "Is Derrida a Transcendental Philosopher?" *Yale Journal of Criticism* 2:207–17.

_____ 1989b. "Two Meanings of 'Logocentrism.' " *Redrawing the Lines*. Edited by Reed Way Dasenbrock. Minneapolis: University of Minnesota Press, 204–16.

Rosen, Stanley 1987. *Hermeneutics as Politics*. New York: Oxford University Press.

Rosenberg, Jay 1980. "Coupling, Retheoretization, and the Correspondence Principle." *Synthese* 45:351–85.

Saussure, Ferdinand de *CGL. Cours de la linguistique générale*. Edited by Charles Bally and Albert Sechehaye. Paris: Payot, 1955. 5th ed. English translation by Wade Baskin: *Course in General Linguistics*. New York: McGraw-Hill, 1966.

Scanlon, John 1991. "Pure Presence: A Modest Proposal." Forthcoming in *Derrida and Deconstruction*. Edited by Lester Embree and William McKenna. Athens: Ohio University Press.

Scholes, Robert 1988. "Deconstruction and Communication." *Critical Inquiry* 14:278–95.

_____ 1989. *Protocols of Reading*. New Haven: Yale University Press.

Schuhmann, Karl 1985. "An Early Interpretation of Husserl's Phenomenology: Johannes Daubert and the *Logical Investigations*." *Husserl Studies* 2:267–90.
———— 1987. "Questions: An Essay in Daubertian Phenomenology." *Philosophy and Phenomenological Research* 47:353–84.
———— 1988. "Die Entwicklung der Sprechakttheorie in der Münchner Phänomenologie." *Phänomenologische Forschungen* 21:133–66.
Schutz, Alfred 1966. "The Problem of Transcendental Intersubjectivity in Husserl." *Collected Papers III*. Edited by Ilse Schutz. The Hague: Martinus Nijhoff, 51–83.
Schwab, Martin 1986. "The Rejection of Origin: Derrida's Interpretation of Husserl." *Topoi* 5:163–75.
Searle, John 1977. "Reiterating the Differences: A Reply to Derrida." *Glyph* 1:198–208.
———— 1983a. "The World Turned Upside Down." *New York Review of Books* 30/16:74–79.
———— 1983b. *Intentionality: An Essay in the Philosophy of Mind*. Cambridge: Cambridge University Press.
———— 1984. "Reply to Louis H. Mackey." *New York Review of Books* 31/1:48.
Seebohm, Thomas 1962. *Die Bedingungen der Möglichkeit der Transzendentalphilosophie*. Bonn: Bouvier.
Sellars, Wilfrid 1963. *Science, Perception, and Reality*. London: Routledge and Kegan Paul.
———— 1974a. *Essays in Philosophy and Its History*. Dordrecht: Reidel.
———— 1974b. "Meaning as Functional Classification." *Synthese* 27:417–37.
Sokolowski, Robert 1974. *Husserlian Meditations*. Evanston: Northwestern University Press.
Spiegelberg, Herbert 1981. " 'Intention' and 'Intentionality' in the Scholastics, Brentano and Husserl." *The Context of the Phenomenological Movement*. The Hague: Martinus Nijhoff, 3–26.
Spivak, Gayatri Chakravorty 1976. Introduction to *OG* (English Translation).
Stassen, Manfred 1973. *Heideggers Philosophie der Sprache in 'Sein und Zeit.'* Bonn: Bouvier.
Strozier, Robert M. 1988. *Saussure, Derrida, and the Metaphysics of Subjectivity*. Berlin: Mouton de Gruyter.
Tugendhat, Ernst 1967. *Der Wahrheitsbegriff bei Husserl und Heidegger*. Berlin: Walter de Gruyter.
———— 1976. *Vorlesungen zur Einfuehrung in die sprachanalytische Philosophie*. Frankfurt: Suhrkamp. English translation by P. A. Gorner: *Traditional and Analytical Philosophy*. Cambridge: Cambridge University Press, 1982.
———— 1977–78. "Die Seinsfrage und ihre sprachliche Grundlage." *Philosophische Rundschau* 24/25:161–76.
Ulmer, Gregory L. 1985. *Applied Grammatology*. Baltimore: Johns Hopkins University Press.
Weber, Samuel 1979. "Saussure and the Apparition of Language: The Critical Perspective." *Modern Language Newsletter* 91:913–38.
Wheeler, Samuel C. 1986a. "Indeterminacy of French Interpretation: Derrida and Davidson." *Truth and Interpretation: Perspectives on the Philosophy of Donald Davidson*. Edited by Ernest LePore. Oxford: Blackwell, 477–94.
———— 1986b. "The Extension of Deconstruction." *The Monist* 69/1:3–21.
White, Alan 1987. "Reconstructing Husserl: A Critical Response to Derrida's *Speech and Phenomena*." *Husserl Studies* 4:45–62.
Wieseltier, Leon 1989. Review of *The Talmud. The Steinsaltz Edition. New York Times Book Review*, 17 December, p. 3.
Wood, David 1987. "Beyond Deconstruction?" *Contemporary French Philosophy*. Edited by A. Phillips Griffiths. Cambridge: Cambridge University Press, 175–93.
———— 1989. *The Deconstruction of Time*. Atlantic Highlands: Humanities Press.

Zaner, Richard 1971–72. ''Discussion of Jacques Derrida, 'The Ends of Man.' '' *Philosophy and Phenomenological Research* 32:384–89.

Index

Compiled by Hassan Melehy

J. Claude Evans is associate professor of philosophy at Washington University in St. Louis. He is the author of *The Metaphysics of Transcendental Subjectivity: Descartes, Kant and Wilfrid Sellars* (1984) and of articles on Plato, Kant, Husserl, Habermas, and Derrida. He is also the translator of *Phenomenology and Marxism* (1984) and *Philosophers in Exile: The Correspondence of Alfred Schutz and Aron Gurwitsch, 1939-1959* (1989).